HIDDEN HISTORY OF THE GRAIL QUEENS

HIDDEN HISTORY OF THE
GRAIL QUEENS

DOUGLAS GABRIEL

Our Spirit, LLC
2019

2019
OUR SPIRIT, LLC

P. O. Box 355
Northville, MI 48167

www.eternalcurriculum.com
www.ourspirit.com
www.gospelofsophia.com
www.neoanthroposophy.com

2019 Copyright © by Our Spirit, LLC

All rights reserved. No part of this publication may
Be reproduced, stored in a retrieval system, or transmitted,
in any form or by any means, electronic, mechanical,
recording, photocopying, or otherwise, without prior written
permission of the publisher.

Library of Congress Control Number: 2019908404

ISBN: 978-0-578-53400-8 (paperback)
ISBN: 978-0-578-53399-5 (eBook)

Contents

Chapter 1: Are You on the Quest for the Grail?. 1

Chapter 2: Grail Queens of the Blood Relics 21

Chapter 3: Holy Crusades and Pilgrimages 37

Chapter 4: Grail Queen Lineage. 45

Chapter 5: Sophia and the Holy Grail 75

Chapter 6: Origin and Meaning of the Grail 83

Chapter 7: Many Forms of the Holy Grail 95

Chapter 8: Fiery Spear from Heaven. 109

Chapter 9: Guardians of the Grail:
　　　　　 The Michaelic Knights 139

Chapter 10: Holy Blood Mysteries 159

Chapter 11: The Search for the True Holy Lance 183

Chapter 12: Rudolf Steiner's Grail Quest. 229

Chapter 13: Conclusion: The Holy Grail is Your Higher
　　　　　　Spirit—Seek It! 237

Bibliography *245*

Quest

Chapter 1

Are You on the Quest for the Grail?

Every aspiring soul seeks union with nourishment that only the spirit can provide, a sort of quest for the holy grail to transcend the physical and re-enter a paradisiacal state of consciousness. You may call it enlightenment, the golden moment of illumination, or the quest for the holy grail of your personal yearnings, among many other names. This seemingly insatiable desire arises like a flaming sword that cuts through the barriers separating the soul and its spiritual longing to find the garden of paradise again and gain the fruit of the Tree of Life. Like a powerfully hurled spear of fire, the awakened consciousness that is gleaned from wielding a flaming sword of wisdom falls like a meteor piercing the heart and opens a wound that blossoms into a brilliant vessel of love. This vessel of consciousness and compassion overflows with the descending rain of love coming from the fiery thoughts of wisdom that rush in to the pierced, humble heart-grail of the spiritual aspirant.

This process of awaking consciousness is the physical signature of the cosmic descent of the human spirit into the heart and soul. It is an ongoing process and must be sought after like the quest of the grail knights or "The Way" of the early Christians.

It takes an open, seeking soul that has purified itself beforehand to witness and participate in this wondrous process of human spiritual evolution called the "search for the holy grail."

Throughout history, humanity has described this process in many different myths, legends, stories, and religious beliefs. The holy grail mysteries of the blood have been little understood as a process of spiritual evolution. Often, in Christian religious beliefs, the stories of human spiritual evolution are directly linked to the life, passion, death, and resurrection of Jesus of Nazareth. Jesus becomes the archetypal human being, the "Second Adam," who redeems the Fall from Paradise and opens the way back to the Garden of Eden. Thus, to the Christian, the blood of Jesus Christ becomes the redemption of the fall of humanity into this earthly world. Truly the blood of God, through his only begotten Son, became the vehicle of redemption as it was spilled into the earth through the Passion and Crucifixion of Jesus.

The "blood of the gods," which the Greeks called "ichor," was occasionally shared with humanity by Zeus having children with female humans. These half-human, half-god heroes and heroines often had to conquer great evil on the earth to attain immortality in the stars, just as Hercules and Psyche did to gain eternal life. The divine ichor in the blood veins of Hercules from his father Zeus made it possible for him to become immortal. Ichor was shared with Hercules as a sort of gift from Zeus, the gift of divine blood that causes immortality and pseudo-divinity in a human being.

Whether we examine the stories of the Greek heroes, the Hindu god Krishna, or the Norse god Odin, we find that divine beings who sustain our world often sacrifice themselves for the good of humanity. There are numerous pre-Christian "solar heroes" that prefigure the deeds of Jesus Christ. These pagan Mysteries were melded into the stories, myths, and legends that surround Jesus. The Roman Catholic Church, much like the Romans before them, often amalgamated the deities and beliefs of those who they conquered into their own pantheon of gods and goddesses. Jesus Christ, for the Romans, became the ultimate solar hero who fulfilled all prophecies and had the same characteristics of prior divine solar heroes.

Jesus is the archetypal representative of humanity and each seeking soul can identify with the suffering of what is called, the "Twelve Stages of the Cross." These stages seem to replicate the steps of suffering that awakened consciousness in many gods and heroes. The Christian path of the holy grail, "The Way," is one of longsuffering love, deep compassion, and ageless wisdom that arises from devotion to the holy blood Mysteries of the Passion of Jesus Christ.

Right up until the time of Abraham, human and animal blood sacrifices were the propitiating offerings that communicated with the divine beings who live outside of the seen world. Blood sacrifices were a central focus of many ancient religions and cultures. Blood, offered up to the gods, was the primary substance that humans believed the gods were interested in. Burnt offerings were also part of many devotional rituals, including burning the body after death as a means to cross over the threshold into the spiritual world. Throughout all these spiritual practices, blood was the key to religious and spiritual experience and was believed to be the vessel of consciousness.

When Jesus, the Son of God, offered his blood and body as a sacrifice of redemption for the prior "original sin" of humanity incurred in paradise, the scales of human evolution tipped in favor of the spirit. Pre-Christian beliefs predicted the archetypal blood sacrifice of Jesus Christ, whose blood and body were given to the earth as spiritual seeds to alleviate the continuing fall of humanity into cold, dark matter. Jesus Christ's spiritual deed enkindled the fire of spirit that descends from heaven to warm our hearts with the same love God expressed in offering His only Son as the "final blood sacrifice." Through this blood sacrifice, Jesus donates to each person a "living drop" of spiritual blood, like divine ichor, straight to their heart. This living blood ("The Life") can receive the descent of the Pentecostal tongues of flames ("The Truth") and the fiery love and compassion of Jesus Christ ("The Way") to regain its divine nature. Finding and understanding this "living blood" is the spiritual inheritance needed to ascend back to the Garden of Paradise with the Holy Grail—the transformed human heart.

When we use the flaming Sword of Wisdom (Sophia) to cut the ties of attachment to this world and seek the heavenly kingdom that Jesus came from, our thoughts become spiritual fire that pierces fear, doubt, and hatred and burns away earthly dross. Wielding the Sword of Wisdom begins the process of ascending back to paradise. The blood of Christ is everlasting and was seeded into the earth and the hearts of every person, whether they believe in Christianity, Buddhism, Judaism, or any other belief. All religions, mythologies, and effective spiritual paths point to the reality that the lower self can rise into a higher self through virtuous thoughts, feelings, and actions. The goal is always the same—it is the attainment of the Holy Grail that feeds us the exact spiritual nourishment that we need to take the next step in our personal spiritual evolution. This holy grail is connected directly to "living blood" that is necessary to ascend to spiritual worlds through the higher self. It is not the grail that we actually seek; it is the spiritual blood inside the grail that nourishes the soul and connects with the spirit.

It is incumbent upon the aspirant of the spirit to master the same twelve stages (Herculean labors) that Jesus of Nazareth conquered through His passion, death, and resurrection. Each knight or lady of the grail must pass tests to be allowed to find the Holy Grail and learn to use it to turn their blood into a vehicle of spiritual consciousness that transcends the physical world. In the grail traditions, the knights who attain the grail must then become faithful guardians of the grail and protect it from unworthy eyes. Thus, the chivalrous knight must conquer his own inner demons and dragons before he comes to the Grail Castle to witness the procession of the Keepers of the Grail, the Grail Maidens, as they display the bleeding spear and the vessel that catches the blood. And even then, after beholding the grail procession, the worthy grail knight might not have developed enough higher consciousness to understand what he has seen and then ask the appropriate question, "Whom does the grail serve?"

Might and valor serve the grail knight only in the beginning stages of the quest. Seeking the grail ultimately brings you to your own personal "Dark Knight" that you must conquer with faithfulness, devotion, and love—not war, fighting, and killing. These first stages are appropriate for grail seekers to tame the dragon, conquer the ills of the outside world, and turn from the physical sword and spear to the spiritual flaming Sword of Wisdom and the Spear of Love and Mercy. The tools of war must become spiritual tools that conquer the knight's lower self.

It is the unending desire to seek and find the higher self in the outer world that embodies the quest in the first stages. The dutiful knight of the divine fights to control lower desires of selfishness and vice. When virtue wins the battle with vice, the Holy Grail is recognized as a worthy cause for the sacrifices made throughout the quest. It is a slow and often difficult pilgrimage path ("The Way") back to paradise.

The archetypal nature of Jesus Christ's blood-sacrifice starts with the divine Trinity deciding to send the only Son of God to earth to mitigate the effects of evil upon the human body, soul, and spirit. Christ, the second being in the solar logos, makes the ultimate sacrifice and descends into a human body with its many limitations and still unredeemed evil. This was the greatest pain and humiliation that a divine being could endure. To move so far back in spiritual evolution and unite with humanity's slow spiritual growth was the ultimate sacrifice of all times: the death of a God. Christ offered His blood and body as the gifts that keep growing, like a grail overflowing with love and mercy feeding all who approach. Each person who takes up this Christ (higher self) impulse and fans the flame of love for all beings in their heart (grail) becomes a living image of what Christ has accomplished so perfectly. We simply follow the path ("The Way, The Truth, and The Life") that we have been shown by Jesus Christ's perfect example. We need only follow "The Way" of Christ to fulfill the mission of attaining the blood Mysteries of the Holy Grail in our own Christ-filled heart.

Heavenly Grail

The Christian story of the Holy Grail starts in heaven with the sin of Lucifer, whose pride made him refuse to bow down to Adam and Eve after God the Father had created them. Lucifer believed he could create a better man and woman. He sat on the throne of God and claimed to be as great as God the Father. Lucifer was one of the brightest of angels and his light was great, but it still paled next to the light of the throne of God. Lucifer was so jealous and prideful that his hubris drove him away from the presence of God and into the darkest corners of heaven, where he fashioned great stones of light for his crown and a mighty sword to strike down his enemies.

When Lucifer came before the throne of God again, the Archangel Michael was on the right side of God with a flaming sword of power and a spear of might. The Archangel Gabriel stood on the left side of God and in front of the newly created human beings who were hiding behind the throne. In his hand, Gabriel held the Lily of Heaven, a pure grail-vessel of beauty and grace. Lucifer had become a dragon of darkness, and his hatred filled him until he directly attacked the throne of God. The Archangel Michael struck the crown of Lucifer from his prideful head and the central green stone of the crown was dislodged and fell like a meteor from the presence of God. Michael then used his spear to cut a huge gash into the outer wall of heaven to let the stone and Lucifer fall from heaven into the outer darkness. As he fell, the Father of Lies swept one third of the human souls up with his tail and pulled them down into the darkness with him. The dragon fell like a meteor to the earth pulling humans, like falling stars, behind him.

The stone of Lucifer's crown fell into the deepest part of the earth, Palestine. It was found and brought to the King of Tyre, who polished it into a bowl that looked like a heavenly emerald. This bowl was given to King Solomon by the King of Tyre to place in the holy of holies of Solomon's Temple. Joseph of Arimathea used this bowl to gather the blood of Jesus of Nazareth during and after the crucifixion. When the blood of the Son of God touched the stone of Lucifer's crown (Solomon's Bowl), the redemption of Lucifer and humanity began. The blood of the gods (divine consciousness-ichor) had spread to all humans and merged with their blood (spiritual-consciousness) transforming the human being into a potentially immortal, divine being. And Lucifer, having Jesus Christ's human/divine blood pour into his "jewel of the crown" emerald bowl, finally bowed before a human (Jesus of Nazareth) and recognized his sin of pride which caused his fall from paradise. This began the redemption of evil.

When the blood of Christ united with the earth, humanity was given the blood of the gods (ichor) that can transform the kingdom of Lucifer (earth) into a sacred Grail Castle. These secrets are referred to as the Mysteries of the Holy Blood Relics and the Quest for the Holy Grail. If a seeking aspirant (grail knight) understands the living imagination of the Crucifixion and Resurrection of Jesus, he has entered the Grail Castle where the Grail Maidens (the Three Marys) display their devotion to the grail and ask the important question: Whom does the grail serve? Each seeker can quest for the grail and use "The Way" to find the entrance to the Grail Castle so they might awaken and ask the "grail question," hopefully being morally developed enough to understand the answer.

Every element involved in the Fall from Paradise and the Crucifixion of Jesus are important tools for the questing knight and lady of the grail. In the first stage of seeking, we are all soldiers of the divine trying to right the wrong and conquer the dragons and wild animals that exist in humans below the virtue of the heart. We need the sword of Michael to strike pride from our haughty heads and let the jewel of the crown become a humble, simple stone that falls into the flowing compassion and love of the heart. We also need the fiery spear of heaven that can hold the demons and dragons at bay without killing them. We need to use the spear to keep the distance between our higher Michaelic/angelic forces and the lower forces derived from the seven deadly sins of vice and immorality led by Lucifer and his hosts. The spear also cuts open the prideful wall of the mind so that consciousness can find its home in the heart instead of cold, earth-bound thinking centered in the head. We must not separate the Sword of Wisdom and the Spear of Love but use them together as spiritual weapons to conquer the dragon of selfishness that rules the lower nature of human vices.

We can also be seen as the Archangel Gabriel in this heavenly grail imagination. Gabriel is the archangel of the moon, as Michael is the archangel of the sun. Gabriel rules procreation, birth, and the blood forces of the female body that are embodied in the image of Gabriel holding a pure white lily: a six-sided chalice that represents the female womb. Gabriel appears to Mary as the messenger of God who brings the blessings of the Holy Spirit and delivers the Son of God to her pure soul. At the time of the Fall of Lucifer, Gabriel held back two thirds of humanity while Lucifer was pulling one third down into darkness with him as he fell from heaven. Gabriel also held back and protected two very special souls who would later become the vehicles for Mary and Jesus when they incarnated on the earth—the one and only time they would incarnate in a physical human body. These bodies would become the "new Adam and Eve" under the cross, which became the "new Tree of Life" granting immortality.

One of the reasons Lucifer could not accept God's creation of the human being was because Lucifer knew that one day, every human being could complete the quest and become "like a god." Humans not only could be redeemed and become capable of returning to paradise at will, but also would one day become the masters of Lucifer and his minions who still worship the dark forces. When the Holy Grail is attained, humans will outstrip Lucifer's attempts to return to heaven. Lucifer's pride made him turn away from fully witnessing the Crucifixion and Resurrection of Jesus Christ. Lucifer still denies that Christ has redeemed his fallen "jewel of the crown," as well as the entire earth and all of humanity. Lucifer can no longer find the grail himself because of his pride, jealousy, and hatred. He can only see that some humans have attained the grail and have ascended back to heaven.

Someday, the legends say, Lucifer will be completely redeemed by the wisdom of Sophia and the love of the Holy Spirit.

Upon close examination, we see that the same spiritual "tools" were present at the Crucifixion and the Fall from Heaven and Paradise. Archangel Michael's sword of wisdom was present in the wisdom of Mary who mustered the strength to endure witnessing the passion, pain, and death of Jesus knowing that he was the Son of God. This wisdom could only be fully held in the heart of the Mother of Jesus. It took both the wisdom and strength of Michael and Gabriel combined to "hold all these things in her heart." Mary was so transformed by her experience that she ascended (Assumption of the Blessed Virgin Mary) bodily into paradise after her Dormition (three days of sleep). Wisdom became love through Mary and the Holy Grail was attained as she ascended into heaven before the followers of Christ to join Her son next to the Throne of God.

Mary, the mother of Jesus, also used her body as a holy grail to birth the "holy blood" of Jesus, a pure spirit who had never incarnated in a human body before (or after). Mary transformed into a living grail whose blood became the vehicle for the divine blood to incarnate. Mary birthed the spirit of the sun, the solar deity, for the redemption of all humanity through the most cruel and vile death of Jesus Christ that was transformed into a divine gift for human spiritual evolution. Mary was over-lighted by Gabriel to bring forth the most perfect human body possible. Thus, through this process she became a "virgin soul" who was the perfect example of a soul questing for the Holy Grail and finding it by reuniting with the divine—our paradisiacal home—our higher spiritual self.

The Archangel Michael was said to be the only angelic hierarchy who could bare to witness the Crucifixion and death of the Son of God. It was Michael who guided the hand of the Roman Centurion Longinus to pierce the heart of Jesus with his spear because Longinus was partly blind and would have needed guidance. Longinus pierced the heart to demonstrate that Jesus was already dead and did not need to have the Sanhedrin break his legs to expedite his death by suffocation. It was a merciful and loving deed that Longinus did to open the heart of Jesus to bleed for all humanity's redemption. Upon piercing the outer chamber of Christ's heart, blood and water (plasma) gushed forth and struck Longinus in the eyes, healing him of his blindness. Thereupon Longinus called out that "this surely must be the Son of God."

At the moment of piercing Christ's sacred heart, an eclipse occurred along with a great storm and an earthquake. The earthquake allowed the blood of Christ to enter deep into the earth. Longinus's spear broke in half and the spearhead separated from the staff and heated to red hot. It looked as if the broken spear had cut a gash into the earth so that the blood of Christ might enter. Longinus fell from his horse in amazement and then saw that the Spear of Phinehas, the Sanhedrin's banner of authority, had also broken and fallen to the ground. This was the same spear used to behead John the Baptist for Salome and Herod. Thus, the spear of the Roman centurion becomes the Lance of Love as the evil Spear of Phinehas is vanquished and, at the same time, it was reported that the veil that hides the Temple's Holy of Holies had been rent from top to bottom so that the Ark of the Covenant was no longer hidden from the eyes of the believers. This was confirmation that Christ's deed redeemed both Lucifer's War in Heaven and humanity's Fall from Paradise.

Earthly Grail

Legends tell us that Joseph of Arimathea brought Solomon's Bowl to the Last Supper that Jesus had with his disciples. Joseph then brought the bowl to the Crucifixion and used it to capture the blood and water that flowed from Christ's side. Joseph and Longinus also helped take down the body of Jesus from the cross to clean and prepare it for burial. Longinus and Joseph became very close and worked together later in their ministry to spread the truth of "The Way" of Christ's life, even to far away England.

Thus, Solomon's Bowl, the vials of water and blood, the spearhead of Longinus, the sponges used during the Crucifixion, pieces of the holy cross, the holy nails, the veil of Veronica, the burial linens, and numerous other "blood relics" were gathered by the seekers of "The Way" and given to Jesus's mother and Mary Magdalene. The alabaster vials that held the oils used on the feet of Jesus were also considered holy and were preserved. These "holy blood relics" (grails) were protected by the "Soldiers of God," like Longinus, while revered and worshiped by the women who became the first Grail Maidens and keepers of the holy blood relics.

Just as Gabriel holds the grail lily as a representation of the female blood mysteries of birth and the moon, so too, Mary Magdalene was seen by some as the wife of Jesus and the mother of his child(ren). There are numerous legends concerning these ideas and different stories say they had either three male children, two male children, or one female child. The male children are often confused with the children of both Joseph of Arimathea and Longinus, who were the founders of Arthurian grail lore in England where Joseph and Longinus established the first church in Christendom at Glastonbury.

In other versions, the female child of Jesus and Mary Magdalene was named Sarah, the wondrous child, who was the founder of the Merovingian line of monarchs in France. Much attention has been focused on this child in books and movies suggesting that the holy blood line of Jesus and Mary Magdalene continues to this day. There are a great deal of legends concerning the child(ren) of Jesus of Nazareth; we will examine them later in this presentation.

Even though legends and traditions exist concerning the children of Jesus and Mary, to carry the "blood Mysteries" into a bloodline is somewhat speculative. Many believe that it is a given that Jesus, "the Rabbi," had to have been married because it was a prerequisite to becoming a rabbi. Mary Magdalene, the one the Lord loved, is certainly the best candidate as his wife knowing that Jesus seemed closest with her and that she was truly the most faithful follower. It also seems common sense that the Mother of Jesus and Mary Magdalene would cherish and guard any blood relics of Jesus. To add a child to the blood Mysteries, opens the scope of why the women seemed most faithful and devoted to the instructions and teachings of Jesus. Surely, the first Christian community surrounding the Mother of Jesus would have held all the blood relics as sacred, especially if Jesus had offspring.

The Way of the Cross

Besides the Three Marys beneath the cross, there were three men also: Longinus, Joseph of Arimathea, and John the Beloved (Lazarus raised). Perhaps there was also a child in the womb of Mary Magdalene. The other followers were terrified and did not have the strength to witness the death of the Son of God. Mary, the Mother of Jesus, and the other witnesses stayed together after the Crucifixion and eventually ended up in Ephesus. Mary created the devotional practice, *The Way of the Cross* to worship the passion, death, and resurrection of Jesus Christ. Near her house in Ephesus, Mary created a religious practice of walking "The Way" through the "Stations of the Cross" that imitated the path of the *Via Dolorosa* in Jerusalem, the 'way of sorrow' that Jesus tread to Calvary. Mary called this devotional practice the *Via Crucis* or *Stations of the Cross*, which had twelve stations replicating the path of sorrow that Jesus walked. Each station added another sorrow to the blood Mysteries of the Stations of the Cross.

One of the most important elements of the devotional practices of Mary and her followers were the Stations of the Cross that became part of "The Way" of Christian devotion to Jesus Christ. Each station held a sacred blood relic that included the crown of thorns, Jesus's clothes, blood from the scourging, the holy cross, Veronica's veil, the nails of the cross, the Holy Lance of Longinus, the Last Supper cup, the vials that captured the blood and water, the sponges, the burial linen, and perhaps references to a child(ren) of Mary Magdalene. Each Station of the Cross, that relived in prayer the suffering of Jesus, was dedicated to an aspect of his suffering and the relic that was associated with that suffering. Mary and her followers started a devotional "Way" that imitated the Passion of Jesus Christ. She also stayed faithful to Jesus's request to re-enact the ritual of the Last Supper using Solomon's Bowl as the cup (blood of Christ) and the spearhead of Longinus to cut the bread (body of Christ) during the service. The spear, chalice, and blood became the symbols of the new Christian religion that celebrated the Blood Mysteries of Jesus Christ.

It is the "way of suffering," through the Stations of the Cross, that became the example that the disciples of Jesus followed in their devotional life. Many Christian followers were martyred only after great suffering that they endured without regret. Some Christian saints were tortured repeatedly, and yet they would not die until they were beheaded like John the Baptist. It is said that Longinus was tortured in twelve ways and would not die. Finally, when the king beheaded Longinus, the blood that burst forth landed in the king's eye and healed his blindness. This theme is common with the saints who converted to Christianity after being a soldier.

Longinus was the beginning of a long line of "Soldiers of God" who were depicted on a horse with a spear defeating a dragon. This is the archetype of the soldier of Christ taming the dragon within themselves and turning from war and death to "The Way," which is won through love, compassion, and kindness. This theme continued until it became a true grail path from soldier to saint—from chivalrous knight to the courts of love.

The Way of Suffering was exemplified quite clearly in a Longinus-type Orthodox saint named Phanourios, who turned from war to love and was tortured in twelve different ways and yet would not die. Phanourios was also said to have traveled back to Eden, getting past the angel with the flaming sword, to pick an apple from the Tree of Life. Phanourios' deed symbolizes the ultimate goal of immortality, which comes along with belief in Jesus of Nazareth, the Son of God, who conquered death for all humanity. Phanourios, like Longinus, is an example of a seeker of "The Way" who spiritually develops through his belief in "The

Way" of Christ, much like the grail knight who develops from "dullness to blessedness." This is the common path of the Soldier of God who devotedly dedicates his/her life to being a guardian and protector of the blood Mysteries of the grail stream.

Mary, the Mother of Jesus, was the keeper of the grail (Solomon's Bowl), the spear, the blood of Jesus, and the other relics that were used in devotional rituals that imitated and relived "The Way" of Jesus Christ. Each blood relic was a tool of suffering that needed to be transformed into a sacred tool using the healing forces of Christ that were also in the object. These physical items were a memory of the love of Christ and, therefore, transformed his suffering into the ultimate tool of healing and victory. The blood relics of the divine Son of God possessed great power for good, even though it seems like they originally were used for evil. Without the divine sacrifice of Jesus, which was accomplished in total freedom as a human being, the earth would have slowly died due to entropy. Christ added the levity and ectopy that bring life and goodness to the evils of His suffering. Thus, to relive his Passion with understanding and compassion is to transform suffering into wisdom and love.

Jesus Christ's Passion and Resurrection also gave new life to the blood of every human that will ever live on the earth. Christ's blood turned our planet into a newly budding sun and the human heart that receives the overflowing blessings of Christ's love and mercy will be enlivened and renewed by the forces of life burgeoning in the cosmos. Truly, the quest (The Way) for the Holy Grail is achieved through nourishment from the risen Christ (The Life): a never-ending wellspring of grace, mercy, and love (The Truth).

Stages of the Grail Quest

We have found that there are *soldiers of the grail, seekers of the grail*, and *the keepers of the grail* (grail maidens, queens, and kings) who work together to guard the Masteries of the blood relics of Jesus Christ. In the early days, the Christian community revolved around the Three Marys at Ephesus and the first official Christian church at Antioch, led by Peter and others. Antioch became the outer center of the faith while Ephesus became the spiritual heart of Christian practices. For eleven years, the Three Marys and John the Beloved deepened the devotional practices of the Stations of the Cross and revered the blood relics entrusted to their loving care. When the Mother of Jesus was bodily assumed into heaven before the eyes of the seventy-two disciples, the time had come to disperse to the four corners of the world to spread the Gospel of Jesus.

Joseph of Arimathea, Longinus, Mary Magdalene, Mary Cleops, Mary Magdalene's child Sarah, Maxium, Saint James (brother of Jesus), and numerous others sailed to France and encountered many Eastern religious beliefs. Mary Magdalene and the others spread the Gospel and debated every idea until they convinced the pagans that Christianity was the true and proper "Way" to find eternal life. Many Christian churches were founded as Mary Magdalene, Sarah, and James traveled from Eastern France to Western Spain. The path of their ministry created a pilgrim's path of the holy blood relics from Vezaley (France) to Compostela (Spain). Eventually, this pilgrim's path became the Camino (way) de Santiago. Other pilgrim paths of the evangelists stretched all the way to Scotland, where some say the descendants of Mary Magdalene and Jesus (through Sarah) still live to this day.

Joseph and Longinus traveled by sea from France to England, where Joseph had worked as the principal tin-trader for the Hebrews. Many years before, Joseph had brought Jesus to England on one of his merchant ships. Jesus was deeply impressed by Glastonbury Tor and built a simple altar of sticks there as an offering. Later, a small church was built around this altar, and it became the first officially recognized church in Christendom. When Joseph returned to Glastonbury with Longinus, he established this "first" Christian church and subsequently became the leader of the grail knights of King Arthur's Round Table. This first church was recognized, with the beginning of the first church councils, as the primary seat of the establishment of Christianity. In this instance, Glastonbury was particularly important because it was partially built by the hands of Jesus of Nazareth himself. The children of Joseph and Longinus (some say children of Jesus) became prominent in English history concerning the knights of King Arthur's Round Table. It is said that Joseph brought the Holy Grail (bowl and vials) while Longinus brought his Spear of Love and Mercy to Glastonbury where they were key relics in establishing Christianity and grail legends in England.

Tangible Holy Grail Relics

Throughout the Camino de Santiago, from France to Spain, we find the legends of numerous grails that have found their way into churches, monasteries, and holy places. The legends and stories that accompany these relics are varied and do not match up, especially seeing that there are over one hundred grails in European churches that claim to be the "authentic" cup used by Jesus at the Last Supper. Numerous spears associated with Longinus can also be found in Christian churches along with the blood of the foreskin of Jesus, numerous crowns of thorns, nails of the cross, and the pieces of the true cross, among other blood relics.

The habit of creating third-class relics by touching first- or second-class relics became very popular in the centuries after Jesus. It seemed that Christians needed something tangible from this world to help them believe in a person who lived long ago and now rules invisibly from another kingdom. Even the bones of saints became a touchstone for these early Christians needing proof of the spirit.

Pre-Christian stories of spiritual tools of the gods became mixed with Christian stories of Jesus and the saints. Celtic and Norse myths were mixed with Mithraic, Persian, Indian, and Egyptian beliefs to explain the blood Mysteries of Jesus Christ in tangible ideas that were familiar to those the Christians evangelized. In France and Spain, the pantheistic ideas of the Romans were prevalent and the Arabic influence in Spain sparked a revolution of ideas about chivalry, courtly love, and grail quests. Most of the grail romance stories came from France as offerings to the Queens of Aquitaine, Castile, Leon, Aragon, Toulouse, and throughout the entire Occitania. Arthurian legends were also written in France, and they begin with stories of Joseph of Arimathea (grail), Longinus (spear) and their miracles and the spiritual sustenance associated with these grail relics (blood Mysteries).

Courtly Love was a "Way" to turn the soldier (knight) of the grail into a seeker of the grail, who ultimately could become a guardian or protector of the holy blood/grail Mysteries. The chivalrous knight vows allegiance to the ladies of the grail, who are the Grail Maidens or Keepers of the Grail who were known originally as the Maidens of the Holy Wells, who gave travelers well-water in a golden bowl and wondrous food to nourish them.

The pre-Christian Celtic blood Mystery myths describe a Grail Maiden carrying a platter with a severed head upon it, while another Grail Maiden holds a spear above it as blood drips onto the platter (grail). This idea is found in Christian beliefs as the head of John the Baptist being brought before Salome and Herod on a silver platter. Thus, an ancient pagan belief pre-figured the reality of the "way of suffering" of Jesus and his followers. Ancient symbols and ideas were not simply adopted by Christians to get their point across to people who had already developed such beliefs. The ancient beliefs were developed by priests and priestesses who were naturally clairvoyant; accordingly, what they worshiped was the truth of what would one day manifest as the fulfillment of their direct clairvoyant experiences.

Ancient beliefs coincide with Christian beliefs because they are describing the same spiritual realities that eventually come to pass. For example, the Finnish *Kalevala* makes a clear prediction about Jesus of Nazareth at the end of the epic, long before Christian times. A clear foreknowledge of the spiritual realities that had yet to manifest were predicted in most ancient beliefs and can be found merged with Christian beliefs, legends, and tales.

It would be fair to say that Jesus of Nazareth fulfilled all true prophecy and the symbols and spiritual tools of the ancients became physical reality through the life, death, and resurrection of Jesus Christ. No *one* belief in the ancient world was comprehensive and all-encompassing enough until the one and only incarnation of Jesus Christ merged all prior beliefs into a direct experience of the Holy Grail through the nourishment of the Holy Spirit at Pentecost.

It is instructive to study the beliefs of the past and understand how the Crucifixion of Jesus becomes the most important moment in human spiritual evolution. The divine deed of the death of Jesus was the "turning point" of human history. From that time forward, the awakened consciousness of the human being became able to seek and find the Holy Grail through their own spiritual striving: "The Way." Through this individualized path of spiritual self-development, each of us can redeem the expulsion from paradise and attain the spiritual tools for ascending back to heaven and gaining our spiritual self.

The search for the Holy Grail is also the path of the prodigal son who leaves home to seek his fortune and eventually realizes that he must simply return home to accept his inheritance. In this process of redemption, the seeker must tame desire and birth the Holy Grail in their heart. This heart-grail is renewed and given eternal life through the Blood Mysteries of Jesus Christ.

Understanding the blood Mysteries of the Passion of Christ (The Way) create a pilgrimage path to the Holy grail which may appear quite differently for each person. Some people need a spiritual tool like a relic, a cup, a spear, a nail, or a piece of the cross upon which redemption was won to give them the faith to maintain the quest and follow "The Way" of Jesus's Passion. Others need only the idea of the grail as an analogy or a symbol to attain its nourishment though gaining living, imaginative thinking. While yet others need only their mind (flaming sword), their heart (holy grail), and their tamed dragon of desires (spear) to be refined into the wisdom, love, and mercy of Christ (the higher self). Whether physical tool, idea, or virtuous path, the quest for the grail can become the Christian way of suffering that leads to the higher self finding its divine nature.

Whom Does the Grail Serve?

The Holy Grail is often described as emitting brilliant light from something descending from above and overfilling a vessel with spiritual substance. The grail also feeds every true need of those who witness it, including nourishing the body, soul, and spirit. Each person experiences the grail differently, and it must be sought after and is seldom attained until great quests, purifications, and oblations have been made before the vision of the Holy Grail. Many seekers quest after the mysterious grail, but few find it and subsequently become protectors or stewards of the grail. After a lifetime of searching, some seeking knights have come to the Grail Castle and asked the question: "Whom does the grail serve?" This question begins the process of understanding the grail, which ultimately can end in inheriting the crown of the Grail King or Grail Queen. In the process, the seeker who has found the Grail Castle can become a Grail Maiden who devotedly serves the grail.

We are told that the kingdom of heaven was filled with light, wisdom, and love emanating from the throne of God. The throne was so brilliant that few could look upon its splendor and glory. All the hierarchies of the angels gathered around the throne to receive nourishment and bask in the magnificence of God. No angel, no matter how high, could rise to the full glory of God's throne and its glory. This "throne of God" was the original archetypal grail of heaven that all the angels emulated and wished to imitate. Serving this wondrous throne was the highest desire of all the angels until Lucifer's pride led him to believe that he could sit upon the throne of God. It was this desire to attain the throne (grail) before the requisite path had been followed and the appropriate "blessedness" had been attained that led to the sin of Lucifer. It was this jealousy of the throne of God (heavenly grail) that led to Lucifer's fall from heaven.

Much like the stories of heaven before the fall, the Garden of Eden was filled with light, love, and everything that Adam and Eve needed to live a beautiful life. The plants, the animals, and the garden itself were all there to nourish and provide for them. The Tree of Life, in the center of the garden, was a wondrous source of living waters that flowed in all directions and fed all living things with its burgeoning life. God spoke to Adam and Eve and tended their every need with love and care. The Tree of Life was a brilliant, living fountain of nourishment that was unending. The Garden of Eden and its Tree of Life are a paradisiacal imagination of a living and conscious Holy Grail. Adam and Eve were complete and satisfied with the nourishment provided to them in the Garden of Eden. It was their desire to "be like God" that led them to disobey and create the sin of jealousy, pride, and separateness that caused the expulsion from Paradise—much like the sin of Lucifer.

The Crucifixion of Jesus Christ was the turning point of time that sparked a divine flame that has grown into a brilliant light of love through his sacrifice. The Tree of Life was transformed into a throne of victory through the holy cross as Jesus Christ implanted his divine blood into the earth and began the process of the earth turning into a living sun. We are told that we are "gods in the becoming," perhaps like the earth transforming into a sun. Only a few faithful followers could look upon Christ's death on the cross where Lucifer's fall from Heaven and Adam and Eve's expulsion from the Garden of Eden were completely redeemed. The Old Dragon, who fell to Earth, was conquered by the power of Christ's divine, selfless deed that conquered the selfish deeds of Lucifer and Adam and Eve. The desire to quickly become "like the divine" is jealous self-gratification of one who is not yet ready to sit upon the throne of the divine. The quest for the grail is the slow and steady path to claim our inheritance to someday sit upon the divine throne rightfully as the Grail King or Grail Queen.

Chapter 2

Grail Queens of the Blood Relics

The women around Jesus Christ were the true "keepers of the grail," the blood relics of the Passion and Crucifixion. These holy blood relics were kept for devotional purposes by the Three Marys and were used in the Stations of the Cross, the early ritualistic reliving of "The Way of the Cross" that the Three Marys, John, Joseph, and Longinus had witnessed. The quest to understand Jesus Christ's ministry became a path of spiritual development called, "The Way." It was the example of Jesus's Passion that would bring many followers from the paths of evil, war, and death to "The Way" of truth and life. The holy blood relics became a touchpoint for the followers who devotedly walked the same path of Jesus's Passion that leads to spiritual redemption, love, and eternal life.

The European response to the grail family (early Christians) and the holy blood relics was profound and led monarchs to the Crusades, both in Spain and the Holy Land. Freeing the Holy Land for pilgrims who wished to go to the land where Jesus Christ had walked was a deep longing for monarchs who had essentially become soldiers of Christ. Gaining the Holy Land was also about finding holy relics that might help deepen the beliefs of Christians looking for any physical substance that might link them to their God.

Blood sacrifices were common in pre-Christian times, and therefore the divine blood sacrifice of Jesus Christ already had fertile ground in which to plant the seeds of Christian beliefs. Jesus Christ was the fulfillment of many prophecies and predictions from pre-Christian beliefs. Christianity did not steal their beliefs; they simply saw Jesus as the penultimate expression of all true moral beliefs before the time of the Crucifixion and Resurrection.

The blood Mysteries that already existed were well known by the wise women who surrounded Jesus Christ. It was the Mother of Jesus, Mary Magdalene, and Martha who tended Jesus and gave their entire life over to his ministry. Many say that Jesus was married to Mary, who was the sister of Lazarus, later called John the Beloved. With the help of Joseph and Longinus, the Three Marys and John protected and revered the blood relics of Jesus. These physical objects that had touched the holy blood of the savior were cared for with the greatest of devotion and love.

Down through time, whether it be the blood relics or a blood descendent of Jesus through Mary Magdalene, the blood of Jesus Christ turned everything it touched into a "grail" or holy object that brings mercy, compassion, and nourishment through simply witnessing it. Two people might see the grail, but only the pure soul would witness its power and grace. This was true also with the Crucifixion itself, when only a few people could muster the courage and strength to witness the death and resurrection of Jesus Christ. This ability to witness the grail and receive its gifts is a path to one's spiritual self that the early Christians called "The Way" and later Europeans called the Quest for the Holy Grail.

The chain of custody of the grail objects associated with the holy blood relics of Jesus went from the Mother of Jesus and Mary Magdalene to Joseph of Arimathea, Longinus and the others around the Three Marys. When the Mother of Jesus was assumed directly into heaven, Mary Magdalene, Joseph, and Longinus took some of the grails, including Mary's child(ren), to France and later to Glastonbury in England. The travels of these "grails" create an amazing history of grail legends that mix and match grail objects with Celtic and Irish myths and legends, as well as the written grail stories and the attempts to emulate those stories with the European Courts of Love, which revolved around the Women of the Grail.

European grail stories often tell of the marvelous Grail Castle that is the scene of the Grail Procession that is performed by Grail Maidens in front of the Grail King who has been wounded and is ineffectual. It is the Grail Maidens (Grail Queens) who possess and keep the grail safe and continue the grail ritual from generation to generation. Each king that protects and guards the grail also has a queen. The Queen's celebration of Courtly Love tempers the soul of the grail knights and the Grail King as they tame their lower passions and purify themselves to receive the gifts of the grail. It is only the Grail Maidens who exclusively handle the grail in the sacred procession that displays the grail cup and spear. The grail knight searches for the grail and the Grail Castle, but the Grail Maidens already live there and serve the grail devotedly. It seems that the Grail Maidens are like the Maidens of the Holy Wells who have always been the keepers of sacred springs since time began.

As we trace the "keepers of the grail," we find that often the men (kings, princes, and so on) are off fighting wars while the women maintain possession of the holy relics, including any form of grail that might be part of the kingdom or the church. There was a long tradition that queens would take a spiritual vow to hold the sacred relics and objects of legendary power during war in secure monasteries, churches, castles, and fortified cities. This special office of power brought many of the greatest and most revered holy blood relics into the hands of the queens of Europe down through the ages. From the Mother of Jesus to Constantine's mother Helena, to Urraca of Leon and Castile, the sacred grail objects have been handed down from one woman to another in a long line of grail families. This lineage is the holy order of Grail Queens who, not only have attained the grail but also protect and guard it. These Grail Queens also serve as Grail Maidens who are the true "keepers of the grail" and the devoted priestesses of the Holy Grail Blood Mysteries and the Procession of the Grail.

Maidens of the Wells—Maidens of the Grail

The Grail tradition first appears in literature written for the European Grail Queens, like Chretien de Troyes' *Perceval* at the end of the twelfth Century. Chretien never finished his poem, leaving an unresolved story and an incomplete picture of what the grail truly is. The unfinished poem was continued and finally completed by four other writers. Two other poets were drawn to create preludes (prologues) explaining the background to Chretien's story: *The Elucidation Prologue* and *Bliocadran Prologue*.

In the *Elucidation Prologue*, a great mystery of the Grail is revealed that is often overlooked that may well be the heart of Grail lore that has been ignored for hundreds of years.

The anonymous text known as, *The Elucidation* recounts the story of the "Maidens of the Wells" and attributes the creation of the Wasteland of the Grail myths to their violation by King Amangon. These Maidens of the Wells are representatives of the goddess of nature, the fertility of the land, and dwellers of both this world and the land of Faery. Not many people are aware that the Grail was needed to restore the Wasteland of the wounded king. That restoration depended on finding and bringing the Maidens of the Wells back to the restore the land. The healing of the Grail king is dependent upon the procession of the Grail Maidens which might help find the new Grail king who can heal the wounded Rich Fisher King.

The Elucidation explains that originally, throughout the land, there were many Maidens of the Wells. These enchanting, faery-like women were the site guardians of all the sacred springs and wells throughout most of Europe. Across the land, any traveler, pilgrim or knight, could visit the local Maiden of the Well and be refreshed with food and drink from the sacred spring of that location. All was idyllic until one dark day, a bad king, King Amangon, raped one of the Maidens of the Wells and encouraged his men to do likewise with all the other Maidens of the Wells. Because of this crime, the Maidens took away their golden cups from the wells and left the land—thus the land died and became the barren wasteland of the grail stories.

Many of the seemingly human maidens that King Arthur's knights encountered while seeking the Holy Grail, were the living descendants of the original Maidens of the Wells. Arthurian Knights rescuing and defending maidens has a deeper and more profound meaning than simply romantic chivalry and gallantry. The actual Quest for the Holy Grail was partly to restore the land, and the knights, by helping and protecting the maidens that they encountered, were actively calling the divine feminine fairies back to the land so that it could live and be fertile again. The Maidens of the Wells were a personification of the life-giving spirits of fresh clean drinking water and the life-sustaining bounty of the earth giving each person what they needed—"provided he ask reasonably." Some thinkers have considered the Maidens of the Wells to be water spirits like undines [1], nixies, sprites, and elementals who keep nature healthy and alive.

When King Amangon and his knights violated the Maidens of the Wells, Logres became dead and desolate, the trees ceased to bloom, the grasses and flowers withered, and the streams and springs dried up. The wounding of the land was the same as the wounding of the Rich Fisher King and the disappearance of his Grail Castle.

When Arthur's knights come across a band of maidens and knights in the forest, they initially fight, but Arthur's knights eventually learn that the maidens are the daughters of Maidens of the Wells. Realizing what had happened, Arthur's knights wandered the land, seeking the Grail Castle of the Rich Fisher King, which had vanished when the maidens were violated. The knights of King Arthur seek to avenge the Maidens of the Wells and restore the grail and access to the lost paradisiacal Faery world, remembered through ancestral clairvoyant memory. On their quest, Arthur's knights encountered evil knights who kept them occupied in long wars, yet their quest to restore the generous hospitality of the Maidens of the Wells and the Faery grail continued unabated.

Even in our modern times, we need to find a way to restore the holy wells and reinstate their faery guardians, the Maidens of the Wells, who are the midwives between the physical and spiritual worlds. The restoration of the Maidens of the Wells is a mission to save Mother Earth and the last connections we have to the living land of elemental beings where the sacred waters flow. *The Elucidation* is a forgotten story of the loss of the memory of the faery world and the role of the Maidens of the Wells in Grail lore.

The Maidens of the Wells and the Grail Maidens are one and the same and their well-being is directly connected to the restoration of the health of all nature—healing the wasteland. The Maidens represent not only the past matriarchal cultures, but also their natural clairvoyance, which gave them a sacred rapport with nature through living waters found at springs. The connection to the land of faery, the Arthurian Brocéliande, was the transcendental aspect of finding a Maiden of the Wells and drinking from her golden cup/grail. Strange encounters led knights and some royalty to fall in love with these Maidens of the Wells and even marry them, as in the story of Melusina [2], who was the mythical founder of numerous European dynasties.

We learn from this ancient pre-Christian tradition that as long as there was peace in the land and the Maidens of Wells were respected, the land was healthy and alive. But once the bridge between the faery world and the physical world was destroyed by violating the Maidens of the Wells, the connection between the two worlds ended. After that severing, only the pure of heart could find the Grail Castle and the Grail Maidens who would provide divine repast and heal the soul just as the Maidens of the Wells had done in the past.

The Elucidation has sometimes been dismissed as an afterthought to Grail lore, but this short poem actually contains the synthesis of the whole Grail tradition and explains many aspects of Grail lore that remain unexplained otherwise. The task of reconciling the human and faery worlds is similar to what priestesses did in ancient temples to bridge the physical world with the spiritual/faery world. Essentially, the Maidens of the Wells were a type of clairvoyant oracle, as well as a portal to the divine which provided transcendental nourishment and replenished the life of soul and spirit. The task of healing the breach between these worlds constitutes part of the search for the Holy Grail—finding the golden cup of the Maidens that quenched all hunger and thirst. The Arthurian knights questing for the grail tried to right the wrong of King Amangon and his knight's violation of the Maidens of the Wells and reconcile the torn fabric between worlds.

Devoutly accomplishing the quest for the Holy Grail, or finding the Maidens of the Wells, can restore the wasteland and bring back a sacred reverence for the natural world and the faery spirits who enliven it. This uniting with the spiritual/faery world is an analogy for spiritual self-development just as the quest for the Holy Grail is for the marriage of the soul to the spiritual self.

Below, we present selections from *The Elucidation*, written anonymously in France after the first stories of the Grail had been presented. The author is one of the few to link the Holy Grail lore with the already existing tradition of the Maidens of the Wells. These traditions can be found throughout the world in many forms. This poem is most illuminating because it indicates the original mythological and legendary aspects of the Grail Maidens (Maidens of the Wells) that have seldom been addressed in Grail literature.

The Elucidation

Yet how and why the powerful country of Logres was destroyed was noised and bruited widely; time was, it was much discussed.

The kingdom went to ruin; the land was so dead and desolate that it wasn't worth two bits; they lost the voices of the wells and the maidens who dwelled in them.

Indeed, the maidens served a very important purpose: no one who wandered the highways, whether at night or in the morning, ever needed to alter his route in order to find food or drink; he had only to go to one of the wells.

He could ask for nothing in the way of fine and pleasing food that he would not have forthwith, provided he asked reasonably.

At once a damsel would come forth from the well, as I understand: travelers could not have asked for one more beautiful!

In her hand, she'd be bearing a golden cup with bacon, meat pies, and bread.

Another maiden would come carrying a white towel and a gold and silver platter, in which was the food that had been requested by the man who'd come to be fed.

He was warmly received at the well; and if this food did not please him, she would bring a number of others, joyfully and generously, according to his desires.

One and all, the maidens happily and properly served all those who wandered the highways and came to the wells for food.

King Amangon was the first to violate their hospitality: he behaved wickedly and underhandedly; afterwards many others did likewise because of the example given by the king who should have protected the maidens and guarded and kept them safe.

He forced himself upon one of the maidens and deflowered her against her will and took the golden bowl from her and carried it off along with the girl, then had her serve him ever afterwards.

Ill luck was to come of it, for no maiden served again or came forth from that well to help any man who happened by and requested sustenance there; and all other travelers followed the king's example.

God! Why didn't the other vassals act according to their honor? When they saw that their lord was raping the maidens because of their beauty, they likewise raped them and carried off the golden bowls.

Never afterwards did any maiden serve or come forth from any of the wells; know that this is the truth.

My lords, in this way the land went into decline and the king who had so wronged them and those who'd followed his example all met a dreadful end.

The land was so wasted that no tree ever bloomed there again, the grasses and flowers withered, and the streams dried up.

Afterwards no one could locate the court of the Rich Fisher, which had made the land resplendent ...

In the kingdom of Logres were all the riches of the world; the peers of the Round Table came there in the time of King Arthur; none so good have been seen since then.

These were such good knights, so worthy and so strong and so bold, so sturdy and so brave, that as soon as they heard tell of the adventures they wished to restore the wells.

They all swore an oath together to protect by their arms the maidens who'd come forth and the bowls they'd be carrying, and to destroy the lineage of those who had so harmed them that they had stopped coming forth from the wells.

The knights gave alms and prayed to God that He might restore the wells to the state in which they had been originally; and for the honor they would thus pay them they intended to request their service.

But no matter how hard they searched they could never find them; they could never hear any voices and no maiden ever ventured forth.

Written anonymously.
Translated by William W. Kibler from the Camelot Project.

The Bliocadran Prologue

The *Bliocadran Prologue* was written as another prequel to Chrétien's *Perceval* by Lenora D. Wolfgang. It is an 800-verse prologue to the *Conte du Graal (Perceval)* of Chrétien de Troyes where Perceval's father, Bliocadran dies in a tournament three days before Perceval is born. Seven months later, the mother flees with her son to the waste forest.

Eleven brothers of Perceval's father had also died in tournaments, and so Perceval's mother wishes to hide her son from the consequences of chivalry. She chooses a site and has a manor built. The *Bliocadran Prologue* ends with Perceval going out to hunt in the forest, and his mother telling him to beware of men covered with iron. He returns that day having encountered neither beasts nor men.

Analogous to the continuations of Chrétien de Troyes writings that sought to conclude the unfinished *Perceval*, the *Bliocadran Prologue* is a prequel that seeks to give an explanation about who Perceval's father was—a descendant of Joseph of Arimathea who, according to the version in Robert de Boron's *Joseph*, preserved the cup from the Last Supper in which he received the blood of the crucified Christ.

Chrétien's sketch of *Bliocadran* reinforces the theme of the transition of chivalry from that of worldly and violent pursuits to one of a high and holy purpose in the pursuit of the Holy Grail. The condemnation of the tournament is acted out in the story of Bliocadran and his brothers, and after initial mistakes and blunders, the effect on Perceval will be his acceptance of the new chivalry to which he leads the way in the *Conte du Graal*.

Notes

1. Undines or ondines are a category of elemental beings associated with water, first named in the alchemical writings of Paracelsus. Similar creatures are found in classical literature—particularly Ovid's Metamorphoses. Later writers developed the undine into a water nymph. Undines are almost invariably depicted as being female, and are usually found in wells, springs, rivers, and waterfalls. The undine group contains many species, including nereides, limnads, naiades, potamides, and mermaids. Although they resemble humans in form, they lack a human soul. To achieve immortality, they must acquire one by marrying a human. Such a union is not without risk for the man, because if he is unfaithful, then he is fated to die. Paracelsus

described these elementals as the "invisible, spiritual counterparts of visible Nature, many resembling human beings in shape, and inhabiting worlds of their own, unknown to man because his undeveloped senses were incapable of functioning beyond the limitations of the grosser elements."

2. Melusine (or Melusina) is a figure of European folklore and Celtic mythology who was a female spirit of fresh water in a sacred spring. She is usually depicted as a woman who is a serpent or fish from the waist down (much like a mermaid). She is also sometimes illustrated with wings, two tails, or both. Her legends are especially connected with the northern and western areas of France, Luxembourg, and the Low Countries. The House of Luxembourg (which ruled the Holy Roman Empire), the Counts of Anjou and their descendants the House of Plantagenet (kings of England) and the French House of Lusignan (kings of Cyprus) are said in folk tales and medieval literature to be descended from Melusine.

Courtly Love and Grail Lore

The Holy Grail tradition was intimately connected to Courtly Love. Courtly Love was born in the lyrics of court poets and singers, first appearing with Provencal poets in the eleventh century, including itinerant and courtly minstrels such as the French troubadours and trouveres, as well as the writers of lays. Texts about Courtly Love, including lays, were often set to music by troubadours and minstrels to praise the grace and beauty of "fair maidens."

Courtly Love was a medieval European literary conception of love that emphasized nobility and chivalry, just as with the

King Arthur's knights. In the high Middle Ages, a "game of love" developed around these ideas as a set of social practices. "Loving nobly" was considered an enriching and improving practice, even spiritual. The lover (idolizer) accepts the independence of his mistress and tries to make himself worthy of her by acting bravely and honorably (nobly) and by doing whatever deeds she might desire, subjecting himself to a series of tests (ordeals) to prove to her his ardor and commitment.

The practice of courtly love was developed in the castle life of four regions: Aquitaine, Provence, Champagne, and Burgundy from around the time of the Eleanor of Aquitaine brought ideals of courtly love from Aquitaine first to the court of France, then to England, where she was queen to two kings. Her daughter Marie, Countess of Champagne brought courtly behavior to the Count of Champagne's court. Courtly Love found its expression in the lyric poems written by troubadours, such as William IX, Duke of Aquitaine (1071–1126), one of the first troubadour poets.

Poets adopted the terminology of feudalism, declaring themselves the vassal of the lady and addressing her as midons (my lord), which had the dual benefits of both allowing the poet to use a code name (so as to avoid having to reveal the lady's name) and at the same time be flattering by addressing her as his lord. The troubadour's model of the ideal lady was the wife of his employer or lord, a lady of higher status—usually the rich and powerful female head of the castle. When her husband was away on Crusade or other business, she dominated the household and cultural affairs; sometimes this was the case even when the husband was at home. The lady was rich and powerful, and the poet gave voice to the aspirations of the courtier class, for only those who were noble could engage in courtly love. This new kind of love saw nobility not based on wealth and family history, but on character and morality.

Hispano-Arabic literature from Spain, as well as Arabic influence on Sicily, provided a further source, in parallel with the Greek Ovid, for the early troubadours of Provence. Like the troubadours, the Sufi Arabic poets and poetry of Muslim Spain express similar views of love as both beneficial and distressing.

Given that practices like courtly love were already prevalent in Al-Andalus and elsewhere in the Islamic world, it is very likely that Islamic practices influenced the Christian Europeans. William IX, Duke of Aquitaine, for example, was involved in the ongoing Reconquista in Spain, so that he would have encountered Muslim culture a great deal. In eleventh century Spain, a group of wandering poets appeared who would go from court to court, and sometimes travel to Christian courts in southern France, a situation closely mirroring what would happen in southern France about a century later. Contacts between these Spanish poets and the French troubadours were frequent. The metrical forms used by the Spanish poets were also like those later used by the troubadours.

Courtly Love is cherished for its exaltation of femininity as an ennobling, spiritual, and moral force, in contrast to the ironclad chauvinism of the clergy and monarchy. The condemnation of Courtly Love in the beginning of the thirteenth century was seen by the church as heretical and tries to take the focus away from the feminine. However, other scholars note that Courtly Love was certainly tied to the Church's effort to civilize the crude Germanic feudal codes in the late eleventh century. In the Germanic cultural world, a special form of Courtly Love can be found, namely Minne.

As the etiquette of Courtly Love became more complicated, the knight might wear the colors of his lady: where blue or black were sometimes the colors of faithfulness, green could be a sign of unfaithfulness. Salvation, previously found in the hands of the priesthood, now came from the hands of one's lady. Devotion and dedication to one's lady was a type of restoration of the Maidens of the Wells, which seems to be one of the obvious sources for the Courts of Love.

Protector Queens of the Grail

The selection below from Rose Walker shows that the historical underpinnings of the tradition of "Female Grail Keepers" is quite clear in Spain and Occitania. The Spanish "infantado tradition" is the main reason grail relics in Spain and southern France did not automatically become the possessions of the Pope in Rome, who usually claimed the lands and wealth of many crusaders but also the first-rights on all relics found in the Holy Land. In Spain, this tradition was not as clearly followed as it was throughout the Roman Catholic Church's control in other places in Europe. Even the relics of the First Crusade, led by Raymond IV, returned to France through his wife, Queen Elvira of Castile. Elvira became the Queen of Castile and Leon and thus inherited many French and Spanish holy blood relics. She also would have had the "missing" Spear of Antioch that her husband used in the battles to win Jerusalem in the First Crusade.

A selection from: *Sancha, Urraca and Elvira: the virtues and vices of Spanish royal women "dedicated to God"* by Rose Walker, Courtauld Institute of Art:

> The chronicle, *Historia Silense*, probably completed in the early twelfth century, speaks of Alfonso VI's father, King Fernando (and Queen Sancha), giving the monasteries of his kingdom (that is broadly speaking Leon and Castile) on his death in 1065 to his daughters Urraca and Elvira. It says: "He entrusted to his daughters all the monasteries of his whole kingdom in which they might live until the end of this life without being tied to a husband."
>
> Urraca and her sister, Elvira, were both in charge of all the monasteries of Leon and Castile during the period of the Liturgical Change. Although there is very little, or no attention paid to Urraca and Elvira's position in the works of mainstream historians of medieval Spain, there are some works which help us to fill in the background, notably a study of another Sancha, sister to Alfonso VII.
>
> In the mid-tenth century Rarniro II, king of Leon, built a monastery for his only daughter—also called Elvira. It was part

of, or attached to, the palatine complex in Leon and was called San Salvador de Palaz de Rey. The arrangement required Elvira to be *deovora*, that is literally "vowed to God."

In the tenth century, precisely in 978, Count Garda Fernandez of Castile and his wife gave a gift to the Lord Jesus Christ and his saints: "their daughter Urraca." They gave her the monastery of Saints Cosmas and Damien at Covarrubias together with many estates and other monasteries "to have, hold, protect and defend." From this and other sources we understand that an *infantado* could only be held by an unmarried woman, that it was usually given to her by her father, that it reverted to the male line after her marriage or death and that it gave her considerable wealth and power in that she controlled vast monastic estates and exercised judicial and economic authority in just the same way as the count or king himself would have done if he had not entrusted it to her.

Urraca appears to have acted as the abbess of the palatine abbey, by her time a double monastery and re-dedicated to Saint Isidore. Her mother, Sancha, had also held the infantado before her marriage to Fernando I and was titular abbess. Even after her marriage, Sancha seems to have retained something of her position and as the *Historia Silense* also tells us, it was Sancha who persuaded Fernando I to be buried at Leon and to build a new church for the purpose.

Within the infantado she had jurisdiction over a large amount of monastic property in the provinces of Leon, for by this time the infantados of Leon and Covarrubias had been joined. Apart from the monasteries and estates entrusted to her with the infantado, which might well be considered exempt from any vow of poverty as they were only in trust, she also retained property of her own. We can see this in a document of 1074 where Urraca and, her sister, Elvira gave land of their own, inherited from their father Fernando I, to the Bishop of Burgos. Urraca and Elvira also gave away a monastery belonging to the infantado and replaced it with Urraca's own villa of San Julian de los Oteros del Rey.

Urraca spent all the moments of her life in the realization of her most beloved task: adorning the sacred altars with gold and silver and precious stones and sacerdotal vestments while collecting every holy relic she could.

Fernando I, Urraca's father, was honored by the abbey of Cluny on the very same level as the German imperial family, and Urraca may have aspired to Adelbeid's status. This may also explain why she commissioned a chalice in a style which clearly belonged to a German imperial tradition. If my arguments are correct, and Urraca took responsibility for intercession for her father's soul on the scale of that conducted by imperial queens, she had an important liturgical role.

Urraca, was given by her father, Ramiro, in 1060 to the convent of Santa Cruz de los Seros which, it says, operated under the Rule of Saint Benedict. The convent lies near Jaca, just below the Pyrenees, and was a dependency of San Juan de la Pena.

It is interesting to note that Sancho and Sancha, as grandchildren of Sancho the Great, had Basque blood. It is difficult to prove, but the Basques are thought to have operated a matrilineal system of inheritance in which the sister's property passed to her brother's children not to her own. In such a background might also Sancha, Urraca and Elvira have made Fernando I, who had the same roots, sympathetic to the infantado in Leon. In any case, in Aragon we have found a woman deeply involved in church reform. Moreover, she achieved this without incurring any disapproval—indeed she received the highest papal approbation for it. Modern historians continue to speak well of Sancha, and in Aragon she is celebrated.

The most authentic of the blood relics of Jesus of Nazareth and Mary Magdalene seem to have ended up in southern France and northern Spain in churches and monastery belonging to the infantado of Spanish monarchies. The Chalice of Urraca of Leon is a good example of this rule, or the Chalice of Valencia. From Vezaley in France, where the remains of Mary Magdalene are found, to the endpoint of the Camino de Santiago, the church of Saint James of Compostela in western Spain, there are numerous holy blood relics that were venerated by pilgrims for centuries. From the "mother of the children of Jesus," Mary Magdalene to the "brother of Jesus," Saint James, there are many stops along the camino ("The Way") where the life and blood of Jesus merges with the grail traditions and the matrilineal culture of the Occitania.

Chapter 3

Holy Crusades and Pilgrimages

Few modern people can imagine what it meant to take the vow to be a pilgrim of Christ, whether going to the Holy Land of Jerusalem where Jesus had walked, or to one of the numerous churches on the Camino de Santiago that afforded direct contact with the holy blood relics and the holy blood line of Jesus. More than half of the people who began the pilgrimage of Camino died on the path. More than three fourths of the crusaders died in the process of their pilgrimage to the Holy Land. There were also numerous crusades in Europe that took the lives of countless Christians, whether during the Spanish Reconquista or the French crusades against the Cathars, Albigensian, or other heretics. Crusades promised spiritual indulgences and the hope of great discoveries of holy relics, but they often ended in death.

After the First Crusade, Raymond IV had the Spear of Antioch and numerous other relics from Jerusalem that were considered quite authentic. These findings began a resurgence of relic worship with a special focus on the importance of holy blood relics. Many subsequent relics were "made" from the most holy relics of that period and these "copies" became quite popular. Eventually, over one hundred chalices existed that were said to have been the authentic chalice that Jesus Christ used at the

Last Supper. The creation of relics became a "business" for the church. Believers literally put their lives at stake to witness a holy relic—particularly one that was associated with the blood of Christ that believers worshiped as the redemption of humanity.

There were many starting points for the Camino de Santiago throughout Europe, but all the paths led to Saint James of Compostela. For the pilgrim, seeing the relics of Saint James, the brother of Jesus, was proof that the divine truly had come down from heaven to earth. In those days, seeing one single relic could change a person's life forever. Even kings, queens, and popes would make the long and dangerous pilgrimage to see holy relics. Alfonso Jordan himself walked the Camino in honor of Mary Magdalene and Saint James even though he was the heir to these great pilgrimage sites. He humbled himself to revere these holy relics and afterwards joined the next Crusade to the Holy Land.

The Christian Camino (Way) as the Quest of the Grail

There were many star-paths across Europe that were said to be the path of the Holy Grail as it traveled from east to west. The Holy Grail was said to exist in the "ethers" where it appeared to the seeker to spark the quest to attain the elusive and mystical grail. The wisdom of the East that prefigured and announced the coming Jesus Christ described the grail as a "vision" of a spear dripping blood into a vessel giving forth light, nourishment, and blessings to the faithful. For many, the Holy Grail was not a tangible object, but a path to an etheric world, or a pilgrimage to a holy place, or a quest for their "blessed self"—the higher spiritual self of the individual. For others, the quest was to follow "The Way" of the early Christians as they traveled from east to west spreading the gospel of Jesus Christ along the pilgrim's path.

The ancient star-paths were an outward sign of an inward spiritual path of development. The physical pilgrim's path was the very same path of the holy blood relics—the grail—and the transmission and of disseminating of the early Christian teachings. Animism and star-knowledge had a part in the early understanding of this path of the grail by using pre-Christian beliefs. Worship of the Archangel Michael goes back to ancient times and still has an influence in the Catholic churches' dedication to the Archangel Michael and Saint George. Some Catholic churches were built upon older sites that also revered the fiery spear of Michael in the form of a fallen meteorite. The churches that are dedicated to the Archangel Michael make a star-path across Europe from east to west and constitute a Soldier of God's pilgrimage which replicates the path followed by Longinus and Joseph of Arimathea. This Michaelic star-path that pilgrims traversed went from Saint Michael Gargano in Italy to Mont-Saint-Michel in France and then across the channel to Mount Saint Michael in Cornwall and ends up at Glastonbury. Glastonbury was home to the first Christian church where Joseph of Arimathea brought the fallen stone of Lucifer (Solomon's Bowl) which he used to capture the blood of Jesus under the cross. Saint Peter's Basilica in Rome, and many other Roman Catholic churches also have meteorites that have been incorporated into statues of the Archangel Michael.

The path of Michael is the pilgrim's path of the Soldier of God—the path Longinus took from Jerusalem to Glastonbury as he accompanied Joseph of Arimathea. This path became "The Way" of Arthurian grail knights as they sought the grail through perfection of their soul and selfless service to the whole, especially the Maidens of the Wells, the Grail Maidens, and the Grail Queens. This star-path of Michael was the initial path of the quest for the Holy Grail from east to west. The Soldier of God, as seeker of the grail, can find the grail and then protect and guard it for the Grail Maidens. A few grail knights attained the goal of the quest and became a Grail King who served the Holy Grail and the Keepers of the Grail—the Grail Maidens and the Maidens of the Wells.

The path of the Soldier of God follows the Holy Grail as it passes from east to west, like a blazing meteor, to mark the pilgrimage road of the questing knight. It is the duty of the grail knight to move initially from west to east to find and guard the grail, just as Crusaders moved from west to east in response to calls to protect and guard the Holy Land. These etheric star-paths are spiritual paths that have come to be marked by churches and monasteries dedicated to the Archangel Michael that show the original movement of the grail from east to west and the response of the Arthurian knights to find the Maidens of the Grail/Wells as they traveled from west to east.

The Path of Mary Magdalene

Another path the early Christian pilgrims centered on were the travels concerning the life of Mary Magdalene. As we know from the numerous versions of the legendary life of Mary, many wonders and imaginative deeds have been attributed to her and sites mark where these occurrences happened. As in many saint legends, there is simply too much attributed to Mary to create a clear line of historical descent that is consistent and verified. Thus, numerous sites claim to have relics of Mary, or holy blood relics connected to her life, that have come to be revered over time. It is therefore not possible to create a clear and accurate biography of Mary Magdalene. What we do have are the many sites that are attributed to the Mary Magdalene's path of the Holy Grail. This star-path also includes Mary's daughter, Sarah, and her many wondrous deeds.

Some of the sites associated with Mary Magdalene are found on the Camino de Santiago and include: Les Saintes Maries-de-la-Mer, Vezelay, Somport, Puenta-la-Reine, Burgos, Leon, and Santiago de Compostela. There are many starting places for this pilgrimage, and there are many offshoots that the pilgrim may choose to add to the standard group of sites. Another set of sites is associated with the direct bloodline of Jesus and Mary Magdalene, which is much broader in its scope and number of sites. The first pilgrimage path went from southern France to western Spain. The second path went from southern France to Scotland and follows the descent of the French monarchy and its hidden history that ends up near Rosslyn Chapel in Northern Scotland.

Some of the sites associated with Mary Magdalene's holy blood pilgrimage path are the following: Les Saintes Maries-de-la-Mer, Vezelay, Toulouse, Orleans, Chartres, Paris, Amiens, Troyes, Odilienberg, London, York, Edinburgh, Rosslyn Chapel, and an unnamed site in Scotland.

Saintly Relics on the Camino de Santiago

The third pilgrim path ("The Way") we would like to point out is that of the Camino de Santiago. The four paths to Compostela included twenty-three reliquary shrines of saints. There were twenty-seven saints' relics in all, including Saint James and the Paladins of Charlemagne on the Camino de Santiago. The pilgrim could begin the path at many places throughout France and Spain, but all roads led to Santiago de Compostela and the relics of Saint James, the brother of Jesus. It is no coincidence that many of the holy blood relics also ended up being hidden and protected in cities near Santiago de Compostela.

The Road of Tours, another popular pilgrim's path, was replete with saintly relics. Beginning with Euvertius at Orleans, the pilgrim was exhorted to pass via the shrines of <u>Martin at Tours</u>, Hilarius at Poitiers, and the head of John the Baptist at Angely. At Saintes, along the path, was the tomb of Eutropius; <u>Roland</u> and Romanus's relics were found at <u>Bordeaux</u>. At <u>Belin</u> could be found a single grave said to contain the remains of Olivier, Ogier, Arastain, Garain, and other paladins of Charlemagne. All of these sites were in addition to the sites along the standard path to Santiago de Compostela.

Camino Santiago de Compostela

On the Spanish side of the Pyrenees there were also many paths that joined with the Camino Santiago de Compostela.

Along the path were found four shrines to Santo Domingo de la Calzada near Logrono, the relics of Facundus and Primitivo at the Cluniac abbey of Sahagun, and Saint Isidore at Leon, before the ultimate destination of the shrine of the Apostle James at Compostela. The idea that all these illustrious shrines were mere way stations on the road to the ultimate goal in Galicia could only serve to promote the prestige of Compostela and elevate the Apostle James to a status which superseded all others in the Communion of Saints except Mary.

Some of the other sites and saints associated with the Camino de Santiago were the following: Vezaley, Santo Domingo de la Calzada, Sahagun, Saint Facundus, Primitivus, Isidore at Leon, San Juan de Ortega, Statue of the Virgin at Cebreiro, San Juan de la Pena, Saint Cristina at the Somport, True Cross at Liebana, Covadonga, Zaragoza, Oviedo, and the Statue of the Virgin at Cebreiro, among others.

An important pilgrim route that was associated with Mary was the Via Tolosana, which led through Arles, Saint-Gilles, Saint-Guilhem-le-Desert and Toulouse, then crossed the Pyrenees to join other routes at Puenta-la-Reina, and then to Santiago along the Via Compostela to Santiago de Compostela.

The Camino de Santiago

Another route, the Regordane led from Le Puy-en-Velay to Saint-Gilles, by way of the Cevennes, Ales, and Nimes. Some pilgrims came only as far as Saint-Gilles, the fourth most important pilgrimage destination in Europe. Others went on to Santiago de Compostela along the Via Tolosana, possibly taking a detour to Saintes-Maries-de-la-Mer. While Compostela claimed the relics of Saint-James, Saintes-Maries-de-la-Mer claimed the relics of his mother, Mary.

These pilgrim paths were meant to stretch the pilgrim to their limit, and often they died on the journey. The pilgrim's path was created to replicate the "Via Dolorosa" or "Way of Suffering" that Jesus followed on his path to the cross. But to the pilgrim who completed the path, it was all worth the privilege of seeing the wondrous churches and monasteries and having their faith bolstered by witnessing the holy relics of those who knew Jesus or the saints who gave up their lives for His gospel of love. Completing one of the pilgrim paths would undoubtedly be the most significant experience of their life and would set the tone of their quest for the holy blood relics—the quest for the Holy Grail.

Chapter 4
Grail Queen Lineage

The Grail lore was itself denounced as a heresy by the Vatican. The sixth-century writings of Merlin were expressly banned by the Ecumenical Council, and the original Nazarene Church (The Way) of Jesus became an "underground stream," aided by such notable sponsors as Leonardo da Vinci and Sandro Botticelli. In those days, the Church policed and controlled most literature in the public domain; to avoid outright censorship, the grail tradition became allegorical.

Why should Grail lore and the writings of Merlin have posed such a problem for the Church? Because, within the context of their adventurous texts, they told the story of the "Grail Bloodline"—a bloodline that had been ousted from its dynastic position by the popes and bishops of Rome who had elected to reign supreme by way of "apostolic succession."

From the 1100s, the powerful Knights Templar and their influence posed an enormous threat to the male-only Catholic church by bringing the heritage of Jesus and Mary Magdalene to the fore in the public domain. It was at that time that Grail lore was itself denounced as a heresy by the Vatican.

Undaunted by the Inquisition, the Nazarene movement (The Way) pursued its own course, and the story of the bloodline was perpetuated in literature such as the *Grand Saint Grail* and the *High History of the Holy Grail*. These writings were largely sponsored by the grail courts of France (Champagne, Anjou, and others) and also by the Knights Templar. So, why was it that King Arthur, a Celtic commander of the sixth century, was so important to the Knights Templar and the grail courts of Europe? Because Arthur was unique due to his heritage in the line of descent from Jesus and Mary Magdalene.

King Arthur was by no means mythical, as many have supposed. The details of Arthur are to be found in the Scottish and Irish annals. He was "the High King of the Celtic Isle" and the sovereign commander of the British troops in the late sixth century. He was born in 559, and he died in battle in 603. His mother was Ygerna del Acqs, the daughter of Queen Viviane of Avallon, in direct descent from Jesus and Mary Magdalene. His father was High King Aedan of Dalriada from the Western Highlands of Scotland. Aedan was the British Pendragon (Head Dragon or King of Kings) in descent from Jesus's brother James. It is for this reason that the stories of Arthur and Joseph of Arimathea are so closely entwined in the Grail Romances.

The coronation records of Scotland's King Kenneth MacAlpin (a descendant of Aedan the Pendragon) specifically refer to his own descent from the dynastic Queens of Avallon. King Aedan's paternal legacy emerged through the most ancient House of Camulot (England's Royal Court of Colchester) in a line from the first Pendragon, King Cymbeline.

Messianic descendants of Jesus and Mary Magdalene founded kingdoms in Wales and across the Strathclyde and Cambrian regions of Britain. Arthur's father, King Aedan of Scots, was the first British monarch to be installed by priestly ordination; he was crowned and anointed by Saint Columba of the Celtic Church in 574. As a direct result of this coronation, Saint Augustine was eventually sent from Rome in 597 to dismantle the Celtic Church. He proclaimed himself Archbishop of Canterbury three years later, but his overall mission failed, and the Nazarene tradition (The Way) persisted in Scotland, Ireland, and Wales and across the breadth of northern England.

The descendants of Jesus were never known as governors of lands. Like Jesus himself, they were designated "guardians" of the people. The Merovingians of Gaul, for example, were Kings of the Franks—not Kings of France. King Aedan, Robert the Bruce, and their Stewart successors were Kings of the Scots—not Kings of Scotland.

Even into the Middle Ages, the Nazarene Church ("The Way") and the long-prevailing cult of Mary Magdalene were prominent in Europe. Women's rights of equality were upheld throughout the Celtic culture, which was an enormous problem for the male-only priesthood of orthodox Christianity.

Grail Queen Lineage

We would like to take you down the path that the Grail Queens have walked in their unending courage and devotion to guard and protect the sacredness of the grail and its mission to bring love into the world. We will start with the first "keepers" and make our way through the open and obvious "Queens of the Grail" and then into more obscure history, legend, and tradition. We will be referring to the most complete versions of the stories that are often found in *The Golden Legend* or *Lives of The Saints*, by Jacobus de Voragine, 1275.

Mary the Mother of Jesus (Blessed Virgin Mary) is mentioned in the Gospels of Matthew and Luke in the New Testament, where it is said that she conceived Jesus while a virgin, through the Holy Spirit. The miraculous conception took place when she was already betrothed to Joseph. She accompanied Joseph to Bethlehem, where Jesus was born. The Gospel of Luke tells of the Annunciation, when the Angel Gabriel appeared to Mary and announced her divine selection to be the mother of Jesus. Mary was present at the Crucifixion and is depicted as a member of the early Christian community in Jerusalem. According to Catholic and Orthodox teachings, at the end of her earthly life, her body was assumed directly into Heaven; this is known in the Christian West as the Assumption.

Mary has been venerated since early Christianity, and is considered by millions to be the most meritorious saint of the religion. She is claimed to have miraculously appeared to believers many times over the centuries. The Catholic Church holds distinctive Marian dogmas, namely her status as the Mother of God, her Immaculate Conception, her perpetual virginity, and her Assumption into heaven.

Mary is depicted as being present among the women at the crucifixion standing near "the disciple whom Jesus loved" along with Mary of Clopas and Mary Magdalene, to which list Matthew 27:56 adds "the mother of the sons of Zebedee," presumably Mary Salome. In Acts 1:26, Mary is the only one other than the eleven apostles to be mentioned by name who abode in the upper room, when they returned from Mount Olivet. The Gospel of John states that Mary went to live with the "Disciple whom Jesus loved," identified as John the Evangelist, in Ephesus.

The Three Marys refers to the women mentioned in the gospels who were present at the Crucifixion and the Resurrection, several of whom were named Mary. The Gospels give the name Mary to several individuals. At various points of Christian history, some of these women have been conflated with one another. The Three Marys are mentioned as present at the Crucifixion of Jesus; at the tomb of Jesus on Easter Sunday; and as daughters of Saint Anne. The Blessed Virgin Mary is not always considered part of this group, as her title as Mater Dolorosa is reserved to a singular privilege. The mother of Jesus was sometimes referred to as Sophia.

The Three Marys may refer to: Mary (Mother of Jesus), Mary Magdalene (John 20:1, Matthew 28:1, Luke: 23:55), Mary of Jacob mother of James the Less (Matthew 27:56; Mark 15:40; Luke 24:10), Mary of Cleopas (John 19:25), Mary of Bethany (Luke 10:38–42; John 12:1–3) (not at Crucifixion or Resurrection), and Mary Salome. According to a legend, Saint Anne had, by different husbands, three daughters, all of whom bore the name Mary and who are referred to as the Three Marys: Mary (Mother of Jesus), Mary of Clopas, and Mary Salome. In a medieval legendary account, Mary Magdalene, Mary of Cleopas and Mary Salome, with Saint Sarah (the child of one of them) were a part of a group who landed near Saintes-Maries-de-la-Mer in Provence where their relics are a focus of pilgrimage.

Mary of Clopas (Cleophas) the wife of Cleophas, was one of the Marys named in the New Testament. Mary of Clophas is explicitly mentioned only in *John* 19:25, where she is among the women present at the Crucifixion of Jesus: "Now there stood by the cross of Jesus His mother, and His mother's sister, Mary the wife of Clopas, and Mary Magdalene." According to some interpretations, the same Mary was also among the women that on Resurrection morning went to the tomb to anoint Jesus's body with spices. *Matthew* 28:1 calls her "the other Mary" to distinguish her from Mary Magdalene, while *Mark* 16:1 uses the name "Mary of James." The *Gospel of Philip* seems to refer to her as Jesus's mother's sister (her sister) and Jesus's own sister (his sister). An early tradition within the Roman Catholic Church identify Mary of Clophas being the sister (or sister-in-law) of Mary the Mother of Jesus. Clophas was a brother of Joseph which makes Mary of Clophas a sister-in-law of Mary, the mother of Jesus. Jerome identifies Mary of Clophas as the sister of Mary, mother of Jesus and as the mother of those who were called the brothers and sisters of Jesus.

Mary Salome was a follower of Jesus who appears briefly in the canonical gospels and in more detail in apocryphal writings. She is named by Mark as present at the Crucifixion and as one of the women who found Jesus's tomb empty. She is often identified as the wife of Zebedee, the mother of James and John, two of the Apostles of Jesus. In Roman Catholic tradition Mary Salome is, or at least was in the Middle Ages, counted as one of the Three Marys who were daughters of Saint Anne, making her the sister or half-sister of Mary, mother of Jesus. In *John*, three or perhaps four women are mentioned at the Crucifixion; this time they are named as Jesus's "mother, and his mother's sister, Mary the wife of Clophas, and Mary Magdalene." (*John* 19:25) A common interpretation identifies Salome as the sister of Jesus's mother, thus making her Jesus's aunt. Traditional interpretations associate Mary the wife of Clophas (the third woman in the *Gospel of John*) with Mary the mother of James son of Alphaeus (the third woman in the *Gospel of Matthew*). In the *Gospel of Mark*, Salome is among the women who went to Jesus's tomb to anoint his body with spices. "And when the sabbath was past, Mary Magdalene, and Mary the mother of James, and Salome, had bought sweet spices, that they might come and anoint him." (*Mark* 16:1)

They discovered that the stone had been rolled away, and a young man in white then told them that Jesus is risen, and told them to tell Jesus's disciples that he would meet them in Galilee. In *Matthew* 28:1, two women are mentioned in the parallel passage: Mary Magdalene and the "other Mary"—identified previously in *Matthew* 27:56 as Mary the mother of James and Joseph. The canonical gospels never go so far as to label Salome a "disciple," and so mainstream Christian writers usually describe her as a "follower" of Jesus per references to the women who "followed" and "ministered" to Jesus (*Mark* 15:41).

Legend of the Three Marys from *The Golden Legend* of Jacque de Voraigne

Mary Magdalene was of the district of Magdala, on the shores of the Sea of Galilee, where stood her family's castle, called Magdalon; she was the sister of Lazarus and of Martha, and they were the children of parents reputed noble, or, as some say, royal descendants of the House of David. On the death of their father, Syrus, they inherited vast riches and possessions in land, which were equally divided between them.

Lazarus betook himself to the military life; Martha ruled her possessions with great discretion, and was a model of virtue and propriety, though perhaps a little too much addicted to worldly cares; Mary abandoned herself to luxurious pleasures and became at length so notorious for her extravagant lifestyle that she was known through all the country round only as "The Sinner." Mary's discreet sister, Martha, frequently rebuked her for these disorders and at length persuaded her to listen to the exhortations of Jesus, through which her heart was touched and converted. The seven demons which possessed her, and which were expelled by Jesus, were the seven deadly sins common to us all.

On one occasion Martha entertained the Savior in her house, and, being anxious to feast him worthily, she was 'cumbered with much serving.' Mary, meanwhile, sat at the feet of Jesus, and heard his words, which completed the good work of her conversion; and when, sometime afterwards, be supped in the house of Simon the Pharisee, she followed him thither and she brought an alabaster box of ointment and began to wash his feet with tears, and did wipe them with the hair of her head, and kissed his feet, and anointed them with ointment—and He said unto her, 'Thy sins are forgiven.'

Tradition relates that after the Crucifixion, Mary traveled to Italy, met with the Emperor Tiberius (14–37 AD) and proclaimed to him about Christ's Resurrection. According to tradition, she took him an egg as a symbol of the Resurrection, a symbol of new life with the words: "Christ is Risen!" Then she told Tiberius that, in his Province of Judea, Jesus the Nazarene, a holy man, a maker of miracles, powerful before God and all mankind, was executed on the instigation of the Jewish High Priests and the sentence affirmed by the procurator Pontius Pilate. Tiberius responded that no one could rise from the dead, any more than the egg she held could turn red. Miraculously, the egg immediately began to turn red as testimony to her words. Then, and by her urging, Tiberius had Pilate removed from Jerusalem to Gaul, where he later suffered a horrible sickness and an agonizing death.

Legend continues Mary's story. Fourteen years after the ascension, Lazarus with his two sisters, Martha and Mary; with Maximin, one of the seventy-two disciples, from whom they had received baptism; Cedon, the blind man whom our Savior had restored to sight; and Marcella, the handmaiden who attended on the two sisters, were by the Jews set adrift in a vessel without sails, oars, or rudder; but, guided by providence, they were safely borne over the sea until they landed in a certain harbor which proved to be Marseilles, in the country now called France.

The people of the land were pagans, and refused to give the holy pilgrims food or shelter, so they took refuge under the porch of a temple and Mary Magdalene preached to the people, reproaching them for their senseless worship of idols; and though at first they would not listen, yet being after a time convinced by her eloquence, and by the miracles performed by her and by her sister, they were converted and baptized. And Lazarus became, after the death of the good Maximin, the first bishop of Marseilles.

These things being accomplished, Mary Magdalene retired to the cliffs not far from the city. It was a frightful barren wilderness, and in the midst of horrid rocks she lived in the caves of Sainte-Baume; there for thirty years she devoted herself to solitary penance for the sins of her past life, which she had never ceased to bewail bitterly. During this long seclusion, she was never seen or heard of, and it was supposed that she was dead.

Mary fasted so rigorously, that but for the occasional visits of the angels, and the comfort bestowed by celestial visions, she might have perished. She was given the Holy Eucharist by angels as her only food. Every day during the last years of her penance, the angels came down from heaven and carried her up in their arms into regions where she was blessed by the sounds of unearthly harmony and beheld the glory and the joy prepared for the sinner that repents.

One day a certain hermit, who dwelt in a cell on one of those wild mountains, having wandered farther than usual from his home, beheld this wondrous vision—the Magdalene in the arms of ascending angels, who were singing songs of triumph as they bore her upwards; and the hermit, when he had a little recovered from his amazement, returned to the city of Marseilles, and reported what he had seen.

Saintes Maries de la Mer—Marseille

A Provencal legend tells us that in the year 40 AD, a boat was launched from Jerusalem, without sails, oars or supplies, and drifted across the Mediterranean until it came ashore at Saint Marys of the Sea. Some think the disciples were forced into a boat without facilities, and then cast adrift, so that they would perish at sea.

In the dispersion Maximin, Mary Magdalene, her brother Lazarus, her sister Martha, Martha's maid Martillam, blessed Cedonius, and many other Christians were herded by the unbelievers into a ship without pilot or rudder and sent out to sea so that they might all be drowned, but by God's will they eventually landed at Marseille. Mary and the others destroyed the temples of the idols in the city of Marseille and built churches to Christ on the sites.

The refugees in the boat were: Mary Jacobi, "the mother of James and the sister of the Virgin"; Mary Salome, the mother of the apostles James and John; Lazarus and his two sisters, Mary Magdalene and Martha; Saint Maximinus; Cedonius, who was born blind and cured, and Sarah, the "servant" of the two Marys, who was also on the boat.

Another version of the legend tells us the town was named after only the three Marys who were in a boat; Mary the mother of Jesus, Mary Magdalene, and Mary the sister of Lazarus. With them was Mary Magdalene's small daughter—called Sarah.

After landing safely, the group built a small oratory to the Virgin. Some disciples went their separate ways; Mary Magdalene went to Sainte-Baume and Martha to Tarascon. Marie Salome, Marie Jacobe, and Sarah remained in the Camargue, and were later buried in the oratory. And yet another legend says that two Marys arrived around 43 AD, and a simple cross of weathered wood marks the exact place. The two Marys caused a spring of fresh water to appear at the site where the village now stands.

Pilgrims started coming to Saints Maries in the fifteenth century—the village was mentioned in pilgrims' itineraries, for

Mary Salome was the mother of Saint James of Compostela. The route to Compostela passed through Arles before continuing westwards and the pilgrims only had a short distance to go to see the shrine to Mary who was the mother of James, who they were going to worship in Santiago de Compostela.

Magdalene Myths and Legends

Vezelay in Burgundy is famous for its Basilica of Mary Magdalene, a majestic Romanesque church and a major stop on pilgrimage trails like the Camino de Santiago (The "Way" to Saint James of Compostela). A piece of Mary's thigh bone is allegedly embedded in a statue and more of her bones are encased in a golden reliquary in the Carolingian crypt. Pilgrims could visit a cave, now a gorgeous chapel, in the Sainte-Baume mountains where it is said she spent her last thirty years as a recluse, upheld and nourished by angels.

There is another legend that Mary Magdalene was married to Jesus, and that they began the holy bloodline of the Merovingian kings of France which is secretly still in existence today. The story belongs to the Sacred History of France. Its origin is found in a fragment from the gnostic *Gospel of Philip*. It calls Mary Magdalene Jesus's "companion" and states that he loved her more than the other disciples and He kissed her.

In the first century, the region of Gallia Narbonensis was inhabited by Romans, Greeks, and the indigenous Gauls—Celtic peoples. Celts were spread across Western Europe and goddesses were as prevalent as gods. There were many divine couples in pantheons and there was common worship of the Triple Goddess. Christian missionaries reached Gaul early, and churches and shrines to saints were built on the old sacred Celtic sites. Some deities became saints, and some saints were adopted as deities.

The Virgin Mary, who combined "loving mother" and "untouched maiden," was ideal as an object of devotion in man's domain. But the church declared that Mary Magdalene was a repentant sinner and a model for all "fallen womankind," the perpetrators of "original sin." Yet a much deeper level of myth was being poured into the legends that grew up around Mary. She was also a Maiden Goddess, ready to bloom like the buds of spring. She was goddess as sacred wife and as the bounteous mother with all Nature as her children. And she was the goddess in her dark crone aspect, ancient wisdom, and all knowing in her cave of secrets. Mary Magdalene has archetypal significance, as well as her mysterious relationship with Jesus and their alleged children.

Mary Magdalene, from *The Golden Legend* by Jacque de Voraigne

Mary Magdalene had her surname of Magdalo, a castle, and was born of right noble lineage and parents, which were descended of the lineage of kings. Her father was named Cyrus, and her mother Eucharis. With her brother Lazarus and her sister Martha, she possessed the castle of Magdalo, which is two miles from Nazareth, and Bethany, the castle which is nigh to Jerusalem, and also a great part of Jerusalem. All these things they shared among them.

In such wise that Mary had the castle Magdalo, whereof she had her name Magdalene. And Lazarus had the part of the city of Jerusalem, and Martha had to her part Bethany. And when Mary gave herself to all delights of the body, and Lazarus intended all to knighthood, Martha, which was wise, governed nobly her brother's part and also her sister's, and also her own, and administered to knights, and her servants, and to poor men, such necessities as they needed.

Nevertheless, after the ascension of our Lord, they sold all these things, and brought the value thereof, and laid it at the feet of the apostles. Then when Magdalene abounded in riches, and because delight is fellow to riches and abundance of things;

and for so much as she shone in beauty greatly, and in riches, so much the more she submitted her body to delight, and therefore she lost her right name, and was called customably a sinner. And when our Lord Jesus Christ preached there and in other places, she was inspired with the Holy Ghost, and went into the house of Simon leprous, whereas our Lord dined. Then she durst not, because she was a sinner, appear before the just and good people, but remained behind at the feet of our Lord, and washed his feet with the tears of her eyes and dried them with the hair of her head, and anointed them with precious ointments.

Jesus embraced her all in his love and made her right familiar with him. He would that she should be his hostess, and his procuress on his journey, and he ofttimes excused her sweetly; for he excused her against the Pharisee which said that she was not clean, and unto her sister that said she was idle, unto Judas, who said that she was a wastresse of goods. And when he saw her weep he could not withhold his tears. And for the love of her he raised Lazarus which had been four days dead and healed her sister from the flux of blood which had held her seven years.

This Mary Magdalene is she that washed the feet of our Lord and dried them with the hair of her head, and anointed them with precious ointment, and did solemn penance in the time of grace, and was the first that chose the best part, which was at the feet of our Lord, and heard his preaching. Which anointed his head; at his passion was nigh unto the cross; which made ready ointments, and would anoint his body, and would not depart from the monument when his disciples departed. To whom Jesus Christ appeared first after his resurrection, and was fellow to the apostles, and made of our Lord apostolesse of the apostles.

There was that time with the apostles Saint Maximin, which was one of the seventy-two disciples of our Lord, to whom the blessed Mary Magdalene was committed by Saint Peter, and then, when the disciples were departed, Saint Maximin, Mary Magdalene, and Lazarus her brother, Martha her sister, Marcelle, chamberer of Martha, and Saint Cedony which was born blind, and after illumined of our Lord; all these together, and many other Christian men were taken of the miscreants and put in a ship in the sea, without any tackle or rudder, for to be drowned. But by the purveyance of Almighty God, they came all to Marseilles, where, as none would receive them to be lodged, they dwelled and abode under a porch before a temple of the people of that country.

When the blessed Mary Magdalene saw the people assembled at this temple for to do sacrifice to the idols, she arose up peaceably with a glad visage, a discreet tongue and well speaking, and began to preach the faith and law of Jesus Christ and withdrew from the worshipping of the idols. Then were they amarvelled of the beauty, of the reason, and of the fair speaking of her. And it was no marvel that the mouth that had kissed the feet of our Lord so debonairly and so goodly, should be inspired with the word of God more than the other.

The blessed Mary Magdalene, desirous of sovereign contemplation, sought a right sharp desert, and took a place which was ordained by the angel of God, and abode there by the space of thirty years without knowledge of anybody. In which place she had no comfort of running water, no solace of trees, nor herbs. And that was because our Redeemer did show it openly, that he had ordained for her refection celestial, and no bodily meats. And every day at every hour canonical she was lifted in the air of angels and heard the glorious song of the heavenly companies with her bodily ears. Of which she was fed and filled with right sweet meats, and then was brought again by the angels unto her proper place, in such wise as she had no need of corporal nourishing.

Mary Magdalene as Wife of Jesus

There are at least three versions of how many children Jesus of Nazareth had with Mary Magdalene. The family trees presented below are examples of what legend tells us. All three traditions are quite different and give legendary descent from Jesus to people who were directly involved in the Holy Grail mysteries and the Mysteries of the Blood Relics. Modern books and movies have speculated on these traditions, and one such claim still believes the Merovingian lineage of French kings comes from Mary's daughter Sarah. Some theorists go so far as to say that the Holy Grail is the blood lineage of Jesus and Mary Magdalene. These modern ideas have deep roots in the Grail tradition and certainly carry the same spiritual content that is described in the variety of other grail stories.

We may never know if Jesus had children with Mary Magdalene. It is likely that since Jesus was called Rabbi, he was married. The descriptions of their relationship indicate that Mary was the likely candidate to be his wife. Remember that Mary had invited Jesus into her house, and she had become his "hostess" in all things. In those times, marriage was as simple as stepping across the threshold of a house, or tent, together holding hands to formalize the marriage.

According to one version of the descendants of Jesus and Mary Magdalene, Mary had two children before the Crucifixion and was pregnant with the third at that time. In another version, Mary was pregnant under the cross with Sarah, her only girl child, who became the legendary founder the French monarchy.

Whether we are looking at the Three Marys as the "keepers" of the holy blood relics of Jesus or at Mary Magdalene as the "keeper" of Christ's blood lineage, Mary Magdalene is still the principal carrier of the Holy Blood Mysteries. Whether as wife or chief disciple of Jesus, Mary Magdalene held the key position as the first Grail Maiden who carried in her soul the wisdom and understanding of the true meaning of the Holy Grail.

Saint Martha, hostess of our Lord Jesus Christ, was born of royal kindred. Her father was named Syro and her mother Encharia. The father of her was duke of Syria and places maritime, and Martha with her sister possessed by the heritage of their mother three places, that was, the castle Magdalen, and Bethany and a part of Jerusalem. It is nowhere found that Martha had ever any husband nor fellowship of man, but she as a noble hostess ministered and served our Lord, and would also that her sister should serve him and help her, for she thought that all the world was not sufficient to serve such a guest. After the ascension of our Lord, when the disciples were departed, she with her brother Lazarus and her sister Mary, also Saint Maximin which baptized them, and to whom they were committed of the Holy Ghost, and many others, were put into a ship without sail, which by the conduct of our Lord they came all to Marseilles, and after came to the territory of Aix, and there converted the people to the faith. Martha was right facound of speech, and courteous and gracious to the sight of the people.

There was that time upon the river of Rhone, in a certain wood between Arles and Avignon, a great dragon, half beast and half fish, greater than an ox, longer than an horse, having teeth sharp as a sword, and horned on either side, head like a lion, tail like a serpent, and defended him with two wings on either side, and could not be beaten with cast of stones nor with other armor, and was as strong as twelve lions or bears; which dragon lay hiding and lurking in the river, and perished them that passed by and drowned ships. And when he is pursued he casts out of his belly behind, his ordure, the space of an acre of land on them that follow him, and it is bright as glass, and what it toucheth it burneth as fire. To whom Martha, at the prayer of the people, came into the wood, and found him eating a man. And she cast on him holy water, and showed to him the cross, which anon was overcome, and standing still as a sheep, she bound him with her own girdle, and then was slain with spears and glaives of the people.

And there the blessed Martha, by license of Maximin her master, and of her sister, dwelled and abode in the same place after, and daily occupied in prayers and in fastings, and thereafter assembled and were gathered together a great convent of sisters, and built a fair church at the honor of the blessed Mary virgin, where she led a hard and a sharp life. She eschewed flesh and all fat meat, eggs, cheese and wine; she ate but once a day. An hundred times a day and an hundred times a night she kneeled down and bowed her knees.

Saint Sarah (Sara-la-Kali), is the patron saint of the Romani people. The center of her veneration is Saintes-Maries-de-la-Mer, a place of pilgrimage in southern France. Legend identifies her as the servant (or child) of one of the Three Marys, with whom she is supposed to have arrived. According to various legends, during a persecution of early Christians, commonly placed in the year 42 AD, Lazarus, his sisters Mary and Martha, Mary Salome (the mother of the Apostles John and James), Mary Jacobe, and Maximin were sent out to sea in a boat. They arrived safely on the southern shore of Gaul at the place later called Saintes-Maries-de-la-Mer. In some accounts Sarah, a native of Upper Egypt, appears as the black Egyptian maid of one of the Three Marys, usually Mary Jacobe. The tradition of the Three Marys arriving in France stems from the high Middle Ages.

Saint Maximinus of Aix was the (legendary) first bishop of Aix-en-Provence in the first century. According to his legend, he was the steward of the family at Bethany and one of the seventy-two disciples of Jesus. He accompanied Lazarus, Martha and Mary on their flight and began the evangelization of Aix-en-Provence together with Mary Magdalene. He is traditionally named as the builder of the first church on the site of the present Aix Cathedral. Mary Magdalene later left him to continue his apostolate alone when she withdrew to the solitude of a cave, which later became a Christian pilgrimage site named Sainte-Baume. On the day she knew she was to die, she descended into the plain so that Maximinus could give her communion and arrange her burial. Her sarcophagus is now at the Basilica of Saint Mary Magdalene at Saint-Maximin-la-Sainte-Baume.

The Queen of Sheba is mentioned in the Hebrew bible. The tale of her visit to King Solomon has undergone extensive Jewish, Islamic, and Ethiopian elaborations, and has become the subject of one of the most widespread and fertile cycles of legends. Sheba came to Jerusalem "with a very great retinue, with camels bearing spices, and very much gold, and precious stones"—and some say, the Holy Grail. (*I Kings* 10:2). "Never again came such an abundance of spices" (*II Chronicles* 9:1–9) as those she gave to Solomon. She came "to prove him with hard questions," which Solomon answered to her satisfaction. Sheba was the Queen of the South Arabian kingdom of Saba, centered around the oasis of Marib, in present-day Yemen. The Bible stories of the Queen of Sheba and the ships of Ophir served as a basis for legends about the Israelites traveling in the Queen of Sheba's entourage when she returned to her country to bring up her child by Solomon. One legend has it that the Queen of Sheba brought Solomon the same gifts that the Magi later gave to Christ. The subject of Solomon and the Queen of Sheba was not common until the twelfth century. Sheba enthroned represented the coronation of the virgin and her exchange of the Ark of the Covenant with her gift of the Bowl of Solomon prefigures the grail mysteries.

Saint Helena (250–330 AD) was an Empress of the Roman Empire, and mother of Emperor Constantine the Great. She became the consort of the future Roman Emperor Constantius Chlorus (reigned 293–306) and the mother of the future Emperor Constantine the Great (reigned 306–337). In her final years, she made a religious tour of Syria Palaestina and Jerusalem, during which she allegedly discovered the True Cross. Constantine was proclaimed Augustus of the Roman Empire in 306 by Constantius' troops after the latter had died, and following his elevation, his mother was brought back to the public life in 312, returning to the imperial court. Her conversion to Christianity followed her son becoming emperor. Constantine appointed his mother Helena as Augusta Imperatrix, and gave her unlimited access to the imperial treasury in order to locate the relics of Judeo-Christian tradition.

In 326–28, Helena undertook a trip to the Holy Places in Palestine. Jerusalem was still being rebuilt following the destruction caused by Titus in 70 AD. Emperor Hadrian had built, during the 130s, a temple over the site of Jesus's tomb near Calvary. According to tradition, Helena ordered a temple of Venus torn down and chose a site to begin excavating which led to the recovery of three different crosses. Helena had a woman who was near death brought from the city and when the woman touched the first and second crosses, her condition did not change, but when she touched the third and final cross she suddenly recovered. Helena declared the cross that the woman had touched and was healed to be the True Cross. On the site of discovery, Constantine ordered the building of the Church of the Holy Sepulchre. Helena also found the nails of the Crucifixion. To use their miraculous power to aid her son, Helena allegedly had one placed in Constantine's helmet, and another in the bridle of his horse. According to one tradition, Helena acquired the Holy Tunic on her trip to Jerusalem and sent it to Trier.

Several relics purportedly discovered by Saint Helena are now in Cyprus, where she spent some time. Among them are items believed to be part of Jesus Christ's tunic, pieces of the holy cross, and pieces of the rope with which Jesus was tied on the Cross. The rope, considered to be the only relic of its kind, has been held at the Stavrovouni Monastery, which was also founded by Saint Helena. Helena left Jerusalem and the eastern provinces in 327 AD to return to Rome, bringing with her large parts of the True Cross and other relics, which were then stored in her palace's private chapel. Her palace was later converted into the Basilica of the Holy Cross in Jerusalem.

Flavia Maxima Fausta (289–326 AD) was a Roman Empress, daughter of the Roman Emperor Maximianus. To seal the alliance between them for control of the Tetrarchy, in 307 Maximianus married her to Constantine I, who set aside his wife Minervina in her favor. Constantine and Fausta had been betrothed since 293. Empress Fausta was held in high esteem by Constantine, and in 324 she was proclaimed Augusta; previously she held the title of Nobilissima Femina. Her sons became Roman Emperors: Constantine II, reigned 337–340, Constantius II reigned 337–361, and Constans reigned 337–350. She also bore three daughters: Constantina, Helena, and Fausta. Of these, Constantina married her cousins, firstly Hannibalianus and secondly Constantius Gallus, and Helena married Emperor Julian.

Euphemia (died 520 AD), whose original name was Lupicina, was an Empress of the Byzantine Empire by marriage to Justin I. Empress Euphemia is credited with the ecclesiastical policies of Justin and she founded a Church of Saint Euphemia, where she was buried following her death. Justin was buried by her side in 527. The marriage of Euphemia and Justin is estimated to have occurred during the reign of Anastasius I (reigned 491–518) when Justin had a prosperous career in the Byzantine army. As Justin I, he was proclaimed emperor in the Hippodrome in accordance with tradition. Lupicina became his empress consort under the name Euphemia. The selection of this name is suspected to be an early indication of both Justin and Lupicina being fervent Chalcedonian Christians. The imperial couple attained the throne in the closing years of their lives. Being childless, their heir was Justinian I. He was the nephew and adoptive son of Justin.

Euphemia was martyred for her faith at Chalcedon in 304 AD. The governor of Chalcedon, Priscus, had made a decree that all of the inhabitants of the city take part in sacrifices to the pagan god Ares. Euphemia was discovered with other Christians who were hiding in a house and worshiping the Christian God, in defiance of the governor's orders. Because of their refusal to sacrifice, they were tortured for a number of days, and then handed over to the Emperor for further torture. She was subjected to particularly harsh torments, including the wheel, in hopes of breaking her spirit, but the wheel miraculously stopped, and an Angel of the Lord ministered to her wounds. The governor then ordered that the saint be cast into a fiery furnace. Two soldiers, Victor and Sosthenes, led her to the furnace, but seeing two fearsome angels in the flames, refused to carry out the order of the governor and became believers in the God whom Euphemia worshipped. Saint Euphemia was still cast into the fire by other soldiers and remained unharmed. Ascribing this to sorcery, the governor gave orders to dig out a new pit. After filling it with knives, he had it covered over with earth and grass so that the martyr would not notice the preparation for her execution, but here, too, she remained unhurt. Finally, they sentenced her to be devoured by wild beasts at the circus. Before her martyrdom, Saint Euphemia implored God to deem her worthy to suffer terribly for His name, but when she was cast into the arena, none of the wild beasts attacked her. Finally, one of the she-bears gave her a small wound on the leg, from which flowed the pure blood of the martyr, and immediately Euphemia gave her spirit to the Lord.

Theodora (500–548 AD) was empress of the Eastern Roman Empire by marriage to Emperor Justinian I. She was one of the most influential and powerful of the Eastern Roman empresses. Some sources mention her as empress regnant with Justinian I as her co-regent. Along with her spouse, she is a saint in the Eastern Orthodox Church. When Justinian succeeded to the throne in 527, two years after the marriage, Theodora became Empress of the Eastern Roman Empire. She shared in his plans and political strategies, participated in state councils, and Justinian called her his "partner in my deliberations." She had her own court, her own official entourage, and her own imperial seal.

Aelia Sophia (530–601 AD) was the Empress consort of Justin II of the Byzantine Empire, and regent during the incapacity of her spouse from 573 until 578. Sophia was a niece of Theodora, the Empress consort of Justinian I. During the reign of Justinian I (527–565), Theodora arranged for Sophia to marry his nephew Justin. The accession speech of Justin makes specific mention of Sophia co-ruling with her husband, the presumption being that she already exercised political influence over him. Sophia also influenced the financial policies of Justin. Having inherited an exhausted treasury, they set about repaying the various debts and loans of Justinian to bankers and money-lenders. Sophia oversaw financial records and payments and restored the credibility of the royal treasury. She was the first Empress consort depicted on Byzantine coinage with royal insignia equal to her husband. They were also depicted together in images and statues, while the name of Sophia alone was given to two palaces, a harbor, and a public bath built in her honor.

In 569, Justin and Sophia together reportedly sent a relic of the True Cross to Radegund; the event was commemorated in Vexilla Regis by Venantius Fortunatus. They also sent relics to Pope John III in an attempt to improve relations: the Cross of Justin II in the Vatican Museums, a crux gemmata, and a reliquary of the True Cross perhaps given at this point, has an inscription recording their donation and apparently their portraits on the ends of the arms on the reverse. Justin reportedly suffered from temporary fits of insanity and was unable to perform his duties, so Sophia assumed sole power over the Empire at this point.

Boudicca was a queen of the British Celtic Iceni tribe who led an uprising against the occupying forces of the Roman Empire in 60 AD. Boudicca's husband, Prasutagus, ruled as a nominally independent ally of Rome and left his kingdom jointly to his daughters and the Roman emperor in his will. However, when he died, his will was ignored, and the kingdom was annexed, and his property taken. When the Roman governor Gaius Suetonius Paulinus was campaigning on the island of Anglesey off the northwest coast of Wales, Boudicca led the Iceni, the Trinovantes, and others in revolt. They destroyed Camulodunum (modern Colchester), earlier the capital of the Trinovantes but at that time a colonia, a settlement for discharged Roman soldiers, and the site of a temple to the former Emperor Claudius. Upon hearing of the revolt, Suetonius hurried to Londinium (modern London), the twenty-year-old commercial settlement that was the rebels' next target. The Romans, having concluded that they lacked sufficient numbers to defend the settlement, evacuated and abandoned Londinium. Boudicca led 100,000 Iceni, Trinovantes, and others to fight Legio IX Hispana, and burned and destroyed Londinium and Verulanmium (modern-day Saint Albans). It is said that she carried the Spear of Longinus (which she took from Longinus after imprisoning him and Joseph of Arimathea) into battle.

Melusina is a figure of European folklore and mythology, a female spirit of fresh water from a sacred spring. She is usually depicted as a woman who is a serpent or fish from the waist down (much like a mermaid). She is also sometimes illustrated with wings, two tails, or both. Melusina is one of the pre-Christian water-faeries who were sometimes responsible for changelings. The "Lady of the Lake," who spirited away the infant Lancelot and raised the child was such a water nymph. Her legends are especially connected with the northern and western areas of France, Luxembourg, and the Low Countries. The House of Luxembourg (which ruled the Holy Roman Empire from AD 1308 to AD 1437), the Counts of Anjou and their descendants, the House of Plantagenet (kings of England), and the French House of Lusignan (kings of Cyprus from AD 1205–1472) are said in folk tales and medieval literature to be descended from Melusina.

The chronicler Gerald of Wales reported that Richard I of England was fond of telling a tale according to which he was a descendant of a countess of Anjou who was in fact the faery Melusina, concluding that his whole family "came from the devil and would return to the devil." The Angevin legend told of an early Count of Anjou who met a beautiful woman when in a far land, where he married her. He had not troubled to find out about her origins. However, after bearing him four sons, the behavior of his wife began to trouble the count. She attended church infrequently, and always left before the Mass proper. One day he had four of his men forcibly restrain his wife as she rose to leave the church. Melusina evaded the men and clasped the two youngest of her sons and in full view of the congregation carried them up into the air and out of the church through its highest window. Melusina and her two sons were never seen again. One of the remaining sons was the ancestor, it was claimed, of the later Counts of Anjou and the Kings of England.

Queen Melisende (1105–1161 AD) was Queen of Jerusalem from 1131 to 1153, and regent for her son between 1153 and 1161 while he was on campaign. She was the eldest daughter of King Baldwin II of Jerusalem, and the Armenian princess Morphia of Melitene. When Melisende bore a son and heir in 1130, the future Baldwin III, her father took steps to ensure Melisende would rule after him as reigning Queen of Jerusalem. Baldwin II held a coronation ceremony investing the kingship of Jerusalem jointly between his daughter, his grandson Baldwin III, and Fulk. Strengthening her position, Baldwin II designated Melisende as sole guardian for the young Baldwin, excluding Fulk. When Baldwin II died the next year in 1131, Melisende and Fulk ascended to the throne as joint rulers.

Urraca of Castile (1079-1126 AD) called the Reckless, was Queen of Leon, Castile, and Galicia from 1109 until her death in childbirth. She claimed the imperial title as suo jure Empress of All the Spains and Empress of All Galicia. She was noted as a caretaker of numerous holy blood relics.

Queen Adelaide of Aquitaine and Poitiers (945-1004 AD) was queen consort of France by marriage to Hugh Capet. Adelaide was the daughter of William III, Duke of Aquitaine and Adele of Normandy, daughter of Rollo of Normandy. Her father used her as security for a truce with Hugh Capet, whom she married in 969. In 987, after the death of Louis V, the last Carolingian king of France, Hugh was elected the new king with Adelaide as queen. They were the founders of the Capetian dynasty of France. Hugh apparently trusted in her judgement and allowed her to take part in government: he proposed her to negotiate for him with the regent of the German Empire, empress Theophanu, committing himself beforehand to their agreement.

Sancha of Leon (1018-1067 AD) was a Queen of Leon. Sancha was a daughter of Alfonso V of Leon by his first wife, Elvira Menendez. She became a secular abbess of the Monastery of San Pelayo. In 1029, a political marriage was arranged between her and count Garcia Sanchez of Castile. However, having traveled to Leon for the marriage, Garcia was assassinated by a group of disgruntled vassals. In 1032, Sancha was married to Garcia's nephew and successor, Ferdinand I of Leon and Castile. At the Battle of Tamaron in 1037, Ferdinand killed Sancha's brother Bermudo III of Leon, making Sancha the heir and allowing Ferdinand to have himself crowned King of Leon, Sancha thereby became Queen. Following Ferdinand's 1065 death and the division of her husband's kingdom, she is said to have played the role of peacemaker among her sons. She died in the city of Leon on 27 November 1067. She was interred in the Royal Pantheon of the Basilica of San Isidoro, along with her parents, brother, husband, and her children Elvira, Urraca, and Garcia.

Urraca of Zamora (1033–1101 AD) was a Leonese infantada, one of the five children of Ferdinand I the Great, who received the city of Zamora as her inheritance and exercised palatine authority in it. Her story was romanticized in the *Cantar de Mio Cid*, and Robert Southey's *Chronicle of the Cid*. Before his death in 1065, Ferdinand divided his widespread conquests in central Spain between his five children, charging them to live at peace with one another. Ferdinand's oldest son, Sancho II, received Castile and the tribute from Zaragoza; Alfonso VI received Leon and the tribute from Toledo; and Garcia II received Galicia. His daughters, Elvira and Urraca, received Toro and Zamora respectively. Sancho, however, resolved to rule over his father's entire kingdom and made war on his siblings. By 1072, Sancho had overthrown his youngest brother Garcia, and forced his other brother Alfonso to flee to his Moorish vassal city of Toledo. Toro, the city of Sancho's sister Elvira, fell easily. But in a siege of Urraca's better-defended city of Zamora, King Sancho was stalled, and was then mysteriously assassinated on 7 October 1072. It was widely suspected that the assassination was a result of a pact between Alfonso and Urraca. Alfonso was grudgingly acknowledged as heir to both Castile and Leon. *The Chronicle of the Cid* states that in his early years as king, Alfonso followed Urraca's advice in all respects. In her later years, Urraca gradually gave up her governing duties, finally retiring to a monastery in Leon, where she died in 1101. She is interred in the Chapel of the Kings at the Basilica of San Isidoro of Leon, along with her siblings Elvira and Garcia.

Queen Guinevere was the wife of King Arthur in Arthurian legend. Her story first appeared in Chretien de Troyes's *Lancelot, the Knight of the Cart* and became a motif in Arthurian literature, starting with the *Lancelot Grail* of the early thirteenth century and carrying through the *Post-Vulgate Cycle* and Thomas Malory's *Le Morte d'Arthur*. In Geoffrey of Monmouth's *Historia Regum Britanniae*, she is described as one of the great beauties of Britain, descended from a noble Roman family and educated under Cador, Duke of Cornwall. In Chretien de Troyes's *Yvain*, the *Knight of the Lion*, she is praised for her intelligence, friendliness, and gentility. The works of Chretien were some of the first to elaborate on the character Guinevere beyond simply the wife of Arthur. This was likely due to Chretien's audience at the time, the court of Marie of France, Countess of Champagne, which was composed of courtly ladies who played highly social roles. In French chivalric romances, and the later works based on them, including Thomas Malory's *Le Morte d'Arthur*, Guinevere is the daughter of King Leodegrance, who had served Arthur's father Uther Pendragon and was entrusted with the Round Table after Pendragon's death. In these histories, Leodegrance's kingdom typically lies near the Breton city of Carhaise. In the fields to the south and east of Carhaise, Arthur defends Leodegrance by defeating Rience, which leads to his meeting and marriage with Guinevere. This version of the legend has Guinevere betrothed to Arthur early in his career, while he was garnering support. When Lancelot arrives later, she is instantly smitten, and they have an affair that, in the end, leads to Arthur's fall.

Empress Matilda (1102–1169 AD) was the claimant to the English throne during the civil war known as the Anarchy. The daughter of King Henry I of England, she moved to Germany as a child when she married the future Holy Roman Emperor Henry V. She travelled with her husband into Italy in 1116, was controversially crowned in Saint Peter's Basilica and acted as the imperial regent in Italy. Matilda and Henry had no children when Henry died in 1125. In 1139, Matilda crossed to England to take the kingdom by force, supported by her half-brother, Robert of Gloucester, and her uncle, King David I of Scotland, while Geoffrey focused on conquering Normandy. Matilda was never formally declared Queen of England but was instead titled the "Lady of the English." Matilda returned to Normandy, now in the hands of her husband, in 1148, leaving her eldest son to continue the campaign in England; he eventually succeeded to the throne as Henry II in 1154. She settled her court near Rouen and for the rest of her life concerned herself with the administration of Normandy.

Eleanor of Aquitaine (1124–1204 AD) was queen consort of France (1137–1152) and England (1154–1189) and duchess of Aquitaine in her own right (1137–1204). As a member of the Ramnulfids (House of Poitiers), rulers in southwestern France, she was one of the most powerful and wealthiest women in western Europe during the High Middle Ages. She led armies several times in her life and was a leader of the Second Crusade. As duchess of Aquitaine, Eleanor was the most eligible bride in Europe. Three months after becoming duchess upon the death of her father, William X, she married King Louis VII of France, son of her guardian, King Louis VI. As queen of France, she participated in the unsuccessful Second Crusade.

Later, Eleanor became engaged to the duke of Normandy, who became King Henry II of England in 1154. Over the next thirteen years, she bore eight children: five sons, three of whom became kings; and three daughters. However, Henry and Eleanor eventually became estranged. When Henry died, their second son, Richard the Lionheart, ascended the throne.

Of all her influence on culture, Eleanor's time in Poitiers between 1168 and 1173 was perhaps the most critical, yet very little is known about it. Henry II was elsewhere, attending to his own affairs after escorting Eleanor there. Some believe that Eleanor's court in Poitiers was the "Court of Love" where Eleanor and her daughter Marie meshed and merged the ideas of troubadours, chivalry, and courtly love into a single court.

Saint Euphrosyne of Polotsk (1104–1167 AD) was the daughter of Prince Svyatoslav of Polotsk. She is one of the fifteen patron saints of Belarus, whose lives are celebrated in the Belarusian Orthodox Church. When she was young, Predslava refused all proposals of marriage and, without her parents' knowledge, ran away to the convent where her aunt was the abbess. She became a nun and took the name Euphrosyne. Around 1128, Bishop Elias of Polotsk entrusted Euphrosyne the task of organizing a women's monastery. At the newly constructed Savior Transfiguration monastery at Seltse, she taught the young women to copy books, sing, sew, and other handicrafts. Towards the end of her life, she undertook a pilgrimage to Constantinople and the Holy Land. Patriarch Michael II of Constantinople gave her an icon of the Theotokos, which is now called the Virgin of Korsun. The Crusader king, Amalric I of Jerusalem, also received her in the Holy Land. There she died about 1173. Her body, after the conquest of Jerusalem by Saladin in 1187, was carried by the monks to Kiev and deposited there in the Monastery of the Caves.

Countess Joan of Toulouse (1220–1271 AD), was the only child of Raymond VII, Count of Toulouse by his first wife Sancha, daughter of King Alfonso II of Aragon. Joan accompanied her spouse on both the Seventh Crusade in 1249 and the Eighth Crusade in 1270. In 1249, her father died, and she succeeded him as ruler of Toulouse with her spouse as co-ruler. Her mother-in-law installed a governor for them until their return to France. The couple took control over their lands in 1250 and made their official entrance as Countess and Count of Toulouse in May 1251.

Joan of Arc (1412–1431 AD), "The Maid of Orleans," is considered a heroine of France for her role during the Lancastrian phase of the Hundred Years' War and was canonized as a Roman Catholic saint. Joan received visions of the Archangel Michael, Saint Margaret, and Saint Catherine of Alexandria instructing her to support Charles VII and recover France from English domination late in the Hundred Years' War. The uncrowned King Charles VII sent Joan to the siege of Orleans as part of a relief mission. She gained prominence after the siege was lifted only nine days later. Several additional swift victories led to Charles VII's coronation at Reims. She was beatified in 1909 and canonized in 1920. Joan stated that she carried her banner in battle and had never killed anyone, preferring her banner "forty times" better than a sword. Many of the noblemen stated that Joan had a profound effect on their decisions since they often accepted the advice she gave them, believing her advice was divinely inspired. Historians agree that the army enjoyed remarkable success during her brief time with it.

The lineage of the grail queens presented above is only a small sampling of what has been ignored by most scholars of Grail lore. The primal position of the Maidens of the Wells, The Three Marys, the Maidens of the Grail, the Queens of Courtly Love, and the Spanish Infantados demonstrate that the female guardians of the grail were the true "keepers" of the holy grail blood Mysteries. Pre-Christian beliefs, symbology, and story-lines merged into the blood Mysteries surrounding Jesus of Nazareth and what arose was a cult of relics that created "The Way," followed by disciples of Jesus. The Mother of Jesus also created a devotional path that she called the Stations of the Cross that imitated the Via Dolorosis (Way of Suffering) that Jesus tread on the path to Calvary. Everything that touched the blood of Jesus was held sacred by his followers and were protected by Christians from that time forward. The central importance of the protection of the Queens of Spain, under the auspices of the "Infantado," which allow females to hold the power and the relics of their male family members. Thus, the holy blood relics of Jesus were hidden from invaders and protected by infantado, in the name of the Catholic church.

Throughout all Grail lore, holy blood Mysteries of Jesus, and pre-Christian beliefs, the important roles of females cannot be overemphasized. Often, historians practically ignore queens who, in many cases, are at least as powerful as the kings they are married to. In some cases, the matrilineal influence far outweighs the male monarchy. Numerous European royal houses are said to be derived from the Maidens of the Wells, or faeries of holy springs who enchant and marry human males. Through the female lineage, the realm of faery was brought into history; these Maidens became the keepers of the grail.

Chapter 5

Sophia and the Holy Grail

We have shown in the list of Grail Maidens and Grail Queens that the influence of the feminine is quite pronounced in the Grail tradition, beginning with the Maidens of the Holy Wells. One might even say that the principal figures in the Grail tradition show that the female grail attendants had already completed the quest for the grail and had become the "Keepers of the Grail." As kings and knights were fighting wars and questing after the grail, the Grail Maidens kept the belief alive by conducting the ritual of the Grail Procession three times a day. Many knights may find the Grail Castle and still not attain the grail unless the forces of compassion and love have been developed into "blessedness." This condition of blessedness was the prerequisite for the female Grail Keepers. From the Three Marys onward, the unending devotion to the blood relics of Jesus and his gospel were carried out by the women who knew and understood the blood Mysteries.

Generally, women in the Roman Catholic church were not held in high standing. The further east in the kingdom Christians traveled, the more they encountered Persian, Indian, and other teachings of the Gnostics that elevated the feminine to the highest prominence. Gnostic teachings from Alexandria and other parts of Egypt were well known in the time of Jesus. These teachings came to be folded into the new beliefs and practices of the Christians. The reverence for the Mother of Jesus (Sophia) was so profound that the Roman Catholic church eventually elevated her to a divine position sitting next to God and Jesus in heaven. Mary, the Virgin, was raised so high that the church believed she was "assumed" physically into heaven after three days of lying in "dormition." Mary ascended into heaven to her throne, just as Jesus had done.

Reading the works of the Gnostic writers clarifies the key roles of the Three Marys in the early church. Mary Magdalene was seen as the most faithful of the disciples of Jesus, and she was given many unique and special privileges. The Mother of Jesus (Sophia) was so important that she basically became a co-equal with the male Trinity of Father, Son and Holy Spirit. Many believe that Mary became the Holy Spirit after her Assumption into heaven. These ideas have a strong foundation in the beliefs of the Gnostics. The Mother of Jesus and Mary Magdalene became Gnostic goddesses in the minds of their followers due to their devotion to the holy blood Mysteries and the teachings of Jesus Christ.

We offer below a few selections of the Gnostics to demonstrate the atmosphere of belief that was prevalent at the time of the Three Marys. Many called the Mother of Jesus the name Sophia, even when she was alive, to show respect for and honor her wisdom and strength. The being of wisdom, called Sophia by the Gnostics, is a prefiguring of the profound deeds of love and sacrifice that the Mother of Jesus made as she participated in the Passion of Jesus Christ.

The following translation of *The Sophia of Jesus Christ* by Douglas M. Parrott, sometimes titled *The Wisdom of Jesus Christ*, is derived from two separately preserved copies of the text. The first copy is in the *Nag Hammadi Codex III*; a second copy of this text was preserved in the *Berlin Gnostic Codex*. A third fragment of the text in Greek was also found among the *Oxyrhynchus* papyrus documents.

The Sophia (Wisdom) of Jesus Christ

"I want you to know that First Man is called 'Begetter, Self-perfected Mind.' He reflected with Great Sophia, his consort, and revealed his first-begotten, androgynous son. His male name is designated 'First Begetter, Son of God,' her female name, 'First Begettress Sophia, Mother of the Universe.' Some call her 'Love.' Now First-begotten is called 'Christ.' Since he has authority from his father, he created a multitude of angels without number for retinue from Spirit and Light.

"Son of Man consented with Sophia, his consort, and revealed a great androgynous light. His male name is designated 'Savior, Begetter of All Things.' Her female name is designated 'All-Begettress Sophia.' Some call her 'Pistis.'

"All who come into the world, like a drop from the Light, are sent by him to the world of Almighty, that they might be guarded by him. And the bond of his forgetfulness bound him by the will of Sophia, that the matter might be revealed through it to the whole world in poverty, concerning Almighty's arrogance and blindness and the ignorance that he was named. But I came from the places above by the will of the great Light, I who escaped from that bond; I have cut off the work of the robbers; I have awakened that drop that was sent from Sophia, that it might bear much fruit through me, and be perfected and not again be defective, but be joined through me, the Great Savior, that his glory might be revealed, so that Sophia might also be justified in regard to that defect, that her sons might not again become defective but might attain honor and glory and go up to their Father, and know the words of the light.

"Now because the multitudes gather and come to a unity we call them 'Assembly of the Eighth.' It appeared as androgynous and was named partly as male and partly as female. The male is called 'Assembly,' while the female is called 'Life,' that it might be shown that from a female came the life for all the aeons. And every name was received, starting from the beginning.

"And the immortals, whom I have just described, all have authority from Immortal Man, who is called 'Silence,' because by reflecting without speech all her own majesty was perfected. For since the imperishabilities had the authority, each created a great kingdom in the Eighth, and also thrones and temples and firmaments for their own majesties. For these all came by the will of the Mother of the Universe.

"Thus, the aeons were completed quickly in the heavens and the firmaments in the glory of Immortal Man and Sophia, his consort: the area from which every aeon and the world and those that came afterward took their pattern for their creation of likenesses in the heavens of chaos and their worlds.

"I want you to know that Sophia, the Mother of the Universe and the consort, desired by herself to bring these to existence without her male consort. But by the will of the Father of the Universe, that his unimaginable goodness might be revealed, he created that curtain between the immortals and those that came afterward, that the consequence might follow.

"Behold, I have revealed to you the name of the Perfect One, the whole will of the Mother of the Holy Angels, that the masculine multitude may be completed here, that there might appear in the aeons, the infinities and those that came to be in the untraceable wealth of the Great Invisible Spirit, that they all might take from his goodness, even the wealth of their rest that has no kingdom over it."

As can be deduced from the above selection of the Gnostics, Sophia is as important as Jesus Christ and, in fact, he is her consort and the source of creation in Gnostic belief. This type of matrilineal descent of the divine was quite common in the ancient past. These types of traditions show the respect and reverence that the ancients had for the Being of Wisdom: Sophia. As we have noted, many called the Mother of Jesus the name Sophia during her life. It was her wisdom that guided the apostles after the Crucifixion. It was the Mother of Jesus that the apostles were gathered around in the upper room during Pentecost when the Holy Spirit descended and filled them with the power and words of God. It was always the Three Marys who served Jesus better than the apostles, and only the Three Marys and John the Beloved had the spiritual strength to witness the Crucifixion.

The Gnostic traditions were not strictly oriented to the feminine, but they offer a wonderful synthesis of teachings of the

East concerning the descent of the solar hero to the earth and the part Sophia played in that cosmic drama. The emphasis on the virgin birth and the highly developed spiritual nature of the Mother of Jesus made Mary-Sophia the "spiritual consort" of her son, not just his mother, in the eyes of the Gnostics, who tried to understand the secrets of the female and male true natures. In the Gospels, it was often for the sake of his Mother that Jesus performed miracles and accomplished his ministry. The Three Marys were with Jesus throughout and seemed to be much better at understanding Christ's ministry than the other disciples.

The Secret Revelation of John

We can see in the selection above that females were held as a co-equal with the male gods of the Gnostic. As a matter of fact, the feminine spiritual nature entered more fully into the world and thus is more accessible to the seeker of the divine. Or as Jesus said, "My Father's kingdom is not of this world." One can imagine how the Mother of Jesus came to be recognized as the Mother of God by the Roman Catholic church when she transcended this worldly plane and was physically assumed into heaven to sit beside her son. Mary eventually came to be seen as equally "divine" as Jesus her son. Worship of Mary gained more recognition over time, and thus we can see the influences of Gnostic thinkers in both the holy blood Mysteries of Jesus Christ and the Holy Grail traditions that are sprinkled with references to the divine nature of the feminine.

The text below shows again the primary place of Sophia in the creation of the world. Sophia is also seen not only as the perfect reflection of the divine male aspect, but also the force of wisdom that enters into the world to transform it. Sophia is as close as a person's conscience, and she lends help and support to all who are on the quest for their higher self. The being of Sophia, for the Gnostics, is much like the Mother of Jesus who ascends to the position of the "Mother of God."

This original translation of Marvin Meyer's book *The Secret Book of John* is presented in the *Gnostic Society Library* and reproduced in *The Gnostic Bible* (Willis Barnstone & Marvin Meyer, 2003). Dr. Meyer notes that this translation of *The Secret Book of John* is based largely on the Coptic text of the *Nag Hammadi Codex II*.

The Secret Book of John

The following gnostic text again shows the primary place of the feminine in the ancient worldview that was prevalent at the time of Jesus Christ. We quote from a selection of the Gnostic text *The Secret Book of John*.

Now, this father is the One who beholds himself in the light surrounding him, which is the spring of living water, and provides all the realms. He reflects on his image everywhere, sees it in the spring of the spirit, and becomes enamored of his luminous water, for his image is in the spring of pure luminous water surrounding him.

The father's thought became a reality, and she who appeared in the presence of the father in shining light came forth. She is the first power who preceded everything and came forth from the father's mind as the forethought of all. Her light shines like the father's light; she, the perfect power, is the image of the perfect and invisible virgin spirit.

She, the first power, the glory of Barbelo, the perfect glory among the realms, the glory of revelation, she glorified and praised the virgin spirit, for because of the spirit she had come forth.

She is the first thought, the image of the spirit. She became the universal womb, for she precedes everything, the mother-father, the first human, the holy spirit, the triple male, the triple power, the androgynous one with three names, the eternal realm among the invisible beings, and the first to come forth.

Barbelo asked the invisible virgin spirit to give her foreknowledge, and the spirit consented. When the spirit consented, foreknowledge appeared and stood by forethought. This is the one who came from the thought of the invisible virgin spirit. Foreknowledge glorified the spirit and the spirit's perfect power, Barbelo, for because of her, foreknowledge had come into being.

She asked again to be given incorruptibility, and the spirit consented. When the spirit consented, incorruptibility appeared and stood by thought and foreknowledge. Incorruptibility glorified the invisible one and Barbelo. Because of her they had come into being.

Barbelo asked to be given life eternal, and the invisible spirit consented. When the spirit consented, life eternal appeared, and they stood together and glorified the invisible spirit and Barbelo. Because of her they had come into being.

She asked again to be given truth, and the invisible spirit consented. Truth appeared, and they stood together and glorified the good invisible spirit and its Barbelo. Because of her they had come into being.

This is the father's realm of five. It is: the first human, the image of the invisible spirit, that is, forethought, which is Barbelo, and thought, along with foreknowledge, incorruptibility, life eternal, and truth.

The father gazed into Barbelo, with the pure light surrounding the invisible spirit, and its radiance. Barbelo conceived from it, and it produced a spark of light similar to the blessed light but not as great. This was the only child of the mother-father that had come forth, its only offspring, the only child of the father, the pure light. The invisible virgin spirit rejoiced over the light that was produced, that came forth first from the first power of the spirit's forethought, who is Barbelo. The spirit anointed it with its own goodness until it was perfect, with no lack of goodness, since it was anointed with the goodness of the invisible spirit. The child stood in the presence of the spirit as the spirit anointed the child. When the child received this from the spirit, at once it glorified the holy spirit and perfect forethought. Because of her it had come forth.

The child asked to be given mind as a companion to work with, and the spirit consented. When the invisible spirit consented, mind appeared and stood by the anointed, and glorified the spirit and Barbelo. All these beings came into existence in silence.

> Mind wished to create something by means of the word of the invisible spirit. Its will became a reality and appeared, with mind and the light, glorifying it. Word followed will. For the anointed, the self-conceived god, created everything by the word. Life eternal, will, mind, and foreknowledge stood together and glorified the invisible spirit and Barbelo, for because of her they had come into being.
>
> The holy spirit brought the self-conceived divine child of itself and Barbelo to perfection, so that the child might stand before the great, invisible virgin spirit as the self-conceived god, the anointed, who honored the spirit with loud acclaim. The child came forth through forethought. The invisible virgin spirit set the true, self-conceived god over everything, and caused all authority and the truth within to be subject to it, so that the child might understand everything, the one called by a name greater than every name, for that name will be told to those who are worthy of it.
>
> Our sister Sophia is the one who descended in an innocent manner to restore what she lacked. For this reason, she was called life, that is, the mother of the living, by the forethought of the sovereignty of heaven and by the afterthought that appeared to Adam. Through her have the living tasted perfect knowledge.

These two Gnostic texts above are very clear about the primal importance of the female divine and her place in creation and its continued sustenance. The Gnostics prefigured the emphasis on the female in the quest for the divine and described prophetically what would eventually become the Roman Catholic church's beliefs in the Virgin Mary and her Assumption into heaven as a reward for being the loving spiritual consort of Jesus Christ. Jesus and Mary go together as the Creator and Sophia are found united in these Gnostic creation stories.

We can see that the sacred reverence for the Three Marys and the long line of Grail Queens who were the Keepers of the Grail are part of a never-ending lineage of Grail Maidens who devotedly serve the grail and conduct the holy rituals that invoke the power and wonder that the grail holds for each seeker.

Chapter 6
Origin and Meaning of the Grail

Early scholarship on the grail story found that the disparate versions had an archetypal narrative concerning an otherworldly talisman that medieval romance authors never fully understood yet attempted to explain. The original myth/legend/stories multiplied a process of corruption during its transmission over the centuries. Yet, if the grail texts are examined in chronological sequence of publication, the material becomes more consistent over time.

The recurring theme of the grail is that it is a sustainer of life, in particular the health of a wounded king, the Rich Fisher King, the host of the Grail Castle. The grail object, in some versions, appears at the beginning of the tale as a mysterious vision amidst the intrigues at Camelot, King Arthur's court.

The grail is elevated in some renditions as the primary object of the quest, while other versions describe how it miraculously provides the food and drink at a banquet in the Grail Castle. The leitmotif established for the grail is that it is the sustainer of life, especially the wounded king or kings in the mysterious Grail Castle and the Grail Maidens. Robert de Boron, one of the earliest grail authors, equates this power to the Christian Holy Eucharist, linking the grail through Joseph of Arimathea to the mystery of the Last Supper. The earliest text written by Chretien de Troyes hints that the Rich Fisher King is sustained by sacred food, but simply describes the grail as a jeweled dish or cup, without mentioning any aspect of holiness.

The Grail Procession brought food on a kind of gradulus, a large, flat dish used to serve food to the table. The grail is described in subsequent stories as two dishes, a knight on a bier, a severed head on a salver, a wondrous stone, or a ciborium, among many other descriptions. In Robert de Boron's story, the grail was the cup used at the Last Supper and the bloody lance was the lance of Longinus, which pierced Christ's side and drew the last of his blood. The broken sword of the grail stories becomes identified with the sword that beheaded John the Baptist, who was executed by Herod Antipas at the request of Salome, who demanded that his head be brought to her on a platter.

An explanation for the increasing Christianization of the Grail Story is that it veiled heretical secrets from the cruel gaze of the Inquisition. Another suggests that the alleged discovery of Arthurian antiquities at Glastonbury in 1191, increased the interest in holy relics associated with biblical events located in the Holy Land. Several Christian relics associated with the story of Christ's Passion were brought into Europe at this period, such as the True Cross, the Lance of Longinus, Veronica's Veil, the Holy Shroud, and the Chalice of Valencia, among others.

The connection of the grail with Joseph of Arimathea and Glastonbury, although the latter is not clearly mentioned by Robert de Boron, have become just as compelling and enduring as the grail itself. Indeed, the two themes meld at many points.

The great body of grail romances that came into existence between the years 1180 and 1240 are mostly in French. These romances may be divided into two classes: Grail Quest and Grail History. The Grail Quest is found in the *Conte del Graal* of Chretien de Troyes and his continuators, a vast poetic compilation of some 60,000 verses, composed between 1180 and 1240, and the Middle High German epic poem *Parzival* of Wolfram von Eschenbach, written between 1205 and 1215. To these may be added the Welsh folk-tales or *Mabinogion* from manuscripts of the thirteenth century. Of grail histories, the oldest is the trilogy of Robert de Boron, composed between 1170 and 1212, of which only the first part (*Joseph d'Arimathie*) and a portion of the second (*Merlin*) still exist.

Robert de Boron's works and their subsequent prose redactions impacted later versions of the Arthurian legend and its prose cycles, particularly due to his Christian backstory for the Holy Grail. Boron merged the Holy Grail myth with a Christian dimension to produce a history of the grail. According to him, Joseph of Arimathea used the Grail (the Last Supper vessel) to catch the drops of blood from Christ's body as he hung on the cross. Joseph's family brought the Grail to Avalon, identified with Glastonbury, where they guarded it until the rise of King Arthur and the coming of Perceval.

The story, *Joseph d'Arimathie* was supposed to be the Grail History, with Joseph of Arimathea as the main character. Boron kept his story simple and very short, where Joseph was involved in bringing the Grail to Britain. Boron tells us that Joseph of Arimathea witnessed the Last Supper; though Joseph did not have a seat at the table with Jesus and the twelve apostles, he had secretly followed and loved Jesus and therefore shared bread and a cup of wine with the disciples.

Nicodemus helped Joseph take down Jesus's body from the cross. When blood poured from Jesus's wound, Joseph used the same cup (grail) that was used during the Last Supper to collect the blood. Joseph returned home and hid the cup with Jesus's blood in his house. When the body of Jesus was missing, the authorities accused Joseph of stealing Jesus's body from the tomb. Joseph was beaten and interrogated and thrown into a dungeon where he was deprived of light, freedom, food, and water.

Jesus appeared before Joseph, carrying the cup (grail) that brought radiance into his dark cell. Jesus gave the chalice, which eventually would be called the Holy Grail, into Joseph's safekeeping. The Holy Grail would provide Joseph with sustenance. Each day, a dove would deposit a wafer in the cup, and he would eat it.

Joseph was freed by Vespasian. The surviving Jews believed that it was miracle that Joseph had survived in the dungeon without food and water. Vespasian was converted to Christianity and Joseph and Vespasian became friends allowing Joseph to be free to continue his ministry.

In the New Testament of the Christian Bible, Joseph was a rich man from Arimathea, a town probably about thirty miles north-east of Jerusalem. Joseph was one of members of the Council (Mark 15:42), where Jewish priests and teachers had interrogated Jesus when Jesus was arrested. Joseph did not approve of his colleagues' action but was powerless to do anything to help Jesus. Joseph was secretly a follower of Jesus (Matthew 27:57; Luke 24:50-51; John 19:38) but was afraid of the Jewish authorities.

At the Crucifixion on the hill, called Golgotha (the Place of the Skull), Pontius Pilate, the Roman governor of Judaea, granted Joseph's request to entomb Christ's body in a nearby cave outside of Jerusalem (Matthew 27:57-60; Mark 15:42-47; Luke 23:50-56; John 19:38-42). With the help of Nicodemus, Joseph had anointed Jesus's body with spices (myrrh and aloes), before wrapping it in linen sheets around the body.

Only the Gospel of John mentioned Nicodemus assisting Joseph with the preparation of Jesus's body. Nicodemus was a Jewish leader among the Pharisees who had gone to speak with Jesus about the resurrection. Later, when the Pharisees were outraged over Jesus's preaching, Nicodemus tried to calm them down, saying that they couldn't condemn a man without a hearing. In the Arthurian legend, particularly that of the *Perlesvaus*, the Grail hero Perceval was a direct descendant of Nicodemus, while on his mother's side, he was descended of Joseph of Arimathea's sister.

Joseph also had another son who was named Galahad, king of the Hosselice (Wales). Lancelot and the Grail hero, Galahad, later found Joseph's tomb. These heroes were descendants of Joseph of Arimathea. When Joseph and son came to Britain initially, they were imprisoned by the pagan king but were rescued by

Origin and Meaning of the Grail

Mordrain. Joseph was wounded in the thigh by a broken sword. The Arthurian writers not only considered Joseph to be a saint, but also that he and his son were one of the earliest and greatest Christian knights—true Soldiers of God.

The story of Joseph of Arimathea is found in its fullest biblical expression in the disputed New Testament texts known as *Apocrypha*, specifically the *Acts of Pilate*, which is part of the *Gospel of Nicodemus*. Various versions of the legend of Joseph exist, but the most enduring is the assertion that Joseph and his sister and her husband left Jerusalem and sailed to France, where Joseph left his sister and his brother-in-law while he sailed on to England and established the first Christian church at Glastonbury. Some accounts tell us that Joseph left the cup in the care of his brother-in-law in France while others tell of him bringing the cup to Glastonbury.

Christian Blood Relics

The efficacy of the Roman Catholic blood relics is really a matter of personal belief and individual faith. The Holy Grail essentially is the wisdom of the East that prefigured Christ and the transformation of those beliefs into a living experience of the Cosmic Christ and the personal Christ (higher self) within our own spirit. The most common imagination of the Holy Grail is one of an "otherworldly" vision of a chalice and a spear that floats in a living realm (etheric) above the earth and calls the seeker (grail soldier/knight) to discover its nature and meaning and to ask the question: "Whom does the grail serve?" Seldom is the grail attained and even more seldom does the grail soldier become the grail keeper unless he awakens from his "dullness" and attains "blessedness" by understanding the meaning of the grail and who it serves.

The grail was not physical in the Arthurian grail quest, but the first grail stories tell about the physical grail of Joseph and the spear of Longinus. For some Christians, tangible proof like a cup, spear, or the bones of saints helped foster belief during the early days of Christianity. Now, the weekly Holy Eucharist can give the modern believer a touch-point for their beliefs through the chalice of wine and water and the physical bread of the host. Many believe that as they eat and drink these "symbols," they transubstantiate into the actual body and blood of Jesus Christ that redeems their soul and feeds their spirit.

Are these modern ritual practices, which replicate the procession of the Grail Maidens, meant to physically draw down from heaven the same forces that were active during the War in Heaven, the expulsion from Eden, and the Crucifixion of Jesus Christ? Does the physical Christ actually descend, like a dove from above, to bring the body and blood of Christ into the Eucharist? Where do the myths and legends end and modern "faith" begin?

Combining mythological gods, spiritual practices, and the use of animistic forces is common in Tibetan Buddhist practices that have a strong influence from the ancient Bon Po religious practices. Two deities stand out as being good examples of Grail lore mixed with religious practice. The first is the being of compassion named Avilokateshvara whose great love for humanity caused him to seek out the suffering of others and try to heal it. He was so overwhelmed with all the suffering that he witnessed that his head split open and became twelve heads that could see in all directions. Through the great vision of the top-most head, he could also see the most precious thing in existence, the "Wish-fulfilling Stone." Avilokateshvara sought after the stone and finally grasp it to his heart and wished with all his might to be able to help and heal all the suffering he witnessed. At that moment, a thousand arms sprung from his body, and in the palm of each hand was a spiritual weapon or tool that could help defeat the source of suffering for each person that he reached out to help.

There is only one Wish-fulfilling Stone, and it fell from heaven as a gift of grace to humanity. Once Avilokteshvara gained the stone and transformed into a many-armed deity, he rose into the luminous, living realm around the earth (etheric realm) and works from that realm to bring compassion, love, and the relief of suffering to all who seek his help. Among the spiritual tools that he holds are the principal elements we find in many grail narratives: a flaming sword, a mighty spear, a bowl that overflows with life, the rosary (mala), the book of wisdom, a platter of offerings, a dorge or lightning-bolt spear, and various other items that show that Avilokteshvara is similar in many ways to Jesus Christ. When you examine the elements and symbols involved in the Crucifixion of Jesus, you find many poignant correspondences and similarity.

Another deity who also has many corollaries to the Christian grail is Vajrayogini, the female deity worshiped in the Tibetan highest yoga tantra practices as the inspirer and consort of all ten thousand Buddhas. She is another being of compassion who has conquered pride and is stripped naked and burning in the flames of transcendental wisdom. She carries a cross (spear or club) over her shoulder and a knife/sword in her hand to cut her own body into pieces as an offering to mitigate the suffering of humanity. She has a rosary (mala) of skulls around her neck and she wears a crown with Buddha jewels. In her left hand, she holds a cup of blood into which she throws her cut-up body as it cooks into an elixir that brings eternal life to those who drink it. She sacrifices her body and blood in a skull-cup (grail) as the redemption for those whose consciousness does not stay focused on looking with their spiritual eye directly into heaven. Worship of Vajrayogini is the highest spiritual practice in Tibetan Buddhism. It mixes animism and primal female wisdom of Bon Po with the Hindu and Buddhist traditions of India into an amalgamation of spiritual practices that go back to the beginning of history. These practices unite the ancient matriarchical cultures with the grand rituals of five thousand years of Hindu pantheism.

The similarity we find in these Eastern practices shows us that spiritual development may take on different flavors over time, but the essential message and the heart of the practices have common themes and use the same powers and forces in the human body and the archetypes found in ancient beliefs. The same spiritual evolution happens whether you practice ten-thousand-year-old obscure rituals or the grail-like Holy Eucharist of the Catholic church.

The insights and beliefs of the East filtered into Europe and were transformed into symbols and teachings that were appropriate for a new audience. Asia means "light," and Europe means "darkness." As the light of the East traveled to the dark of Europe, the Holy Grail was part of the living imagination that inspired the grail romances and a grail-interpretation of the Passion of Jesus Christ. Spiritual realities are cloaked in many symbols and images that tell the same story in different words. Knowing these different paths that have similar signposts is confirmation of the efficacy of the spiritual content of the teachings.

Another direct analogy to the grail story of Jesus Christ was pre-figured in the myths of Odin, the Norse Father God who lived in Asgard, inside the world tree Yggdrasil and ruled the nine-realms of heaven and earth. Odin's wife, Frigg, sits on her throne next to Odin, who sometimes rides a flying eight-legged horse and wields a mighty spear (Gungnir) that never misses its mark and always returns to Odin's hand. Odin plucked out his eye and dropped it into the well of wisdom so that he could understand everything. Next to his throne is a great cup that is filled with the draught of immortality and wisdom. The severed head of Mimir (the wise one) also sits next to his throne; Odin can ask any question, and Mimir's head will give the correct answer.

Odin pierced his own side with his spear and hung himself for three days on the world tree to gain the insight he needed to help humanity. After three days, Odin figured out that the twigs of the world tree that had fallen on the ground made shapes that could be turned into a written language (runes) that would help humans grow and evolve. Thus, "Odin sacrificed unto Odin" to redeem his creation of humanity. Frigg witnessed Odin's sacrifice and offering to humanity and supported him with her great wisdom gleaned from the Well of Wisdom of the Nornies. Odin often disguised himself, walked among humans, and visited

Origin and Meaning of the Grail

them in their homes as a wanderer. This tradition became so prominent that the Norse always welcomed visitors with unconditional hospitality because they believed that any wandering guest might be Odin in disguise. Ultimately, Odin instilled great compassion and love for all people in the Norse people, and his stories prepared them for the teachings of Jesus Christ.

Many other beliefs are corollaries to what came to be the Christian doctrines that are folded into the legends of the Holy Grail. Pre-Christian beliefs added to the new impulses that Christ brought, and they were mixed together because the same spiritual truths were being told in a variety of ways. Each new version combined what had been added in the interim by the actions of the spiritual world. The Tibetans ended up with rituals that are very similar to the Christian Holy Eucharist, even though the creators of those rituals were not aware of one other.

Throughout all true spiritual practices around the world, we find references to a solar hero who brings the grail that provides nourishment and eternal life to those who seek and find it. It may be described in many different forms and fashions of the time, but the same spiritual archetypes lead the seeker to discover our original home through eating and drinking the body and blood of a deity, god, or solar hero. The death and resurrection of these female and male deities exemplify what the grail seeker must do to become a guardian of the grail.

The Celtic and Irish grail stories added an extra dimension to the grail adventure, which was often seen as a chivalric quest of a courageous knight. The grail quest evolved into a spiritual pilgrimage. Though many of the tales have Celtic motifs and symbolism, the grail quest was painted with Christian overtones. The focus of the grail quest had changed to the development of the hero himself. To succeed in the quest, the criteria became purity of heart, chastity, and love. The new story says that the hero not only needed to be a knight, but also a type of Christian monk—a Soldier of God.

Perceval, the first grail knight in the legend, was no longer sufficient. Perceval was not the true grail knight in the new tale;

his role was taken over by Galahad, the illegitimate son of Lancelot and Elaine, who was the daughter of the Rich Fisher King. Galahad, who attained the grail, was something like a saint. He had the ability to perform miracles, such as banishing demons and healing the sick. The Celtic and Irish motifs had even larger Christian overtones that transformed the grail history with a new grail quest.

In Wolfram von Eschenbach's *Parzival*, the dark adept Klingsor is the black magician who has grievously wounded the leader of the grail knights, King Anfortas, in a battle. The Grail King lies bleeding in the Grail Castle of Montsalvasche, yet no one can alleviate his suffering.

Klingsor is an earthly tool of the dark powers, the demonic realm, which seeks to pervert God's creation into a hideous reflection of their own evil image. The dark powers and principalities have thus empowered Klingsor. They have enabled him to build a blasphemous mockery of the Grail Castle in a nearby valley. Klingsor had transformed a once poisonous wasteland into a seductive counterfeit of paradise in which self-indulgence, carnality, and the satisfaction of lusts were lauded over the very things that characterized the search for the Holy Grail. Klingsor's "Garden of Delights" was populated with lustful maidens who wove spells to trap the unwary and so was an evil mirror image kingdom of the Maidens of the Wells and the realm of faery.

The Grail King, Anfortas, had gone forth against Klingsor in an attempt to end his power and dark reign on Earth, carrying the Holy Spear: the lance of the Lord that had pierced the side of Christ on the cross. Klingsor, by a ruse, seizes the spear from Anfortas and strikes him his terrible blow, wounding him in the groin.

Into this situation rides the innocent, questing knight called Parzival. Parzival is the future grail hero who vows to avenge Anfortas, regain the holy spear, and vanquish Klingsor and his evil minions. Parzival sallies forth and enters the seductive realm of Klingsor, the beautiful disguised hell filled with temptations of every kind.

Parzival almost succumbs to its temptations but overcomes his lower instincts through a supreme spiritual effort. He masters his lower self and transmutes the energizing potency of his lower instincts into his higher spirituality, which makes him invincible.

Parzival then confronts Klingsor, seizes the holy spear, and makes the Sign of the Cross, whereupon the black magician instantly disappears, and his false edifices and illusions quickly melt away. Parzival, the grail hero, now makes his journey home, back to the real Grail Castle of Montsalvasche, and there heals the bleeding wound of Anfortas with the tip of the holy spear.

The main tenet of all the direct experiences, visions, revelations, and legends communicated to the initiates of the Holy Grail questing for the Grail Castle was the principle of the sanctity of blood, especially of the Mysteries of the blood and the existence of a royal bloodline.

Chapter 7

Many Forms of the Holy Grail

Some followers of the grail legend will say that there is only one special chalice that is the Holy Grail. Others point out that the Holy Grail legends composed in Europe during the twelfth to fifteenth centuries enumerate more than ten different Holy Grails. Others contend that holy grails have existed around the globe for thousands of years. In truth, holy grails have been everywhere in every age. They have taken the form of chalices, spears, skulls, platters, stones, swords, cauldrons, books, and even children. What makes an object a holy grail is its possession of a special power that has been called the Holy Spirit by Christians, the Alchemical Force by Alchemists, and Kundalini by Hindu Yogis, among many others. Legend has it that if you drink or eat from a holy grail, or even just touch it, its power will enter you and initiate a process of alchemical transformation that will subsequently heal you, enlighten you, and possibly even make you immortal.

The most famous historical holy grail is the cup/bowl/chalice of Christ, which was called Joseph of Arimathea's Bowl of Solomon. This is the vessel in which Joseph of Arimathea caught the blood and "water" of Jesus after he was taken down from the cross, which is the same cup that Jesus had previously passed among his disciples during the Last Supper. It is said that the

Archangel Gabriel instructed Joseph and eleven other missionaries to travel with the cup and two flasks, or cruets, containing Jesus's blood and water to Glastonbury. Once settled in their new homeland, Joseph and his companions constructed Saint Mary's Chapel, which became the chalice's reliquary and the first Christian church in Europe. Joseph hid the Holy Grail in Chalice Well in Glastonbury, where blood-colored water (symbolizing the blood of the Messiah) continually flows out to nourish and heal all who drink or bathe in it.

According to an alternate legend regarding the cup of Christ, after the Ascension, Joseph's chalice was taken by Saint Peter to Rome where it became the principal chalice used by the early popes during Holy Communion. Then, in approximately 258 AD, when the Roman Emperor Valerianus was regularly persecuting bishops and other high-ranking Catholic church officials, a Vatican soldier took the chalice to Spain. It eventually made its way to the Cathedral of Valencia where it became famous as the Holy Chalice of Valencia. According to the Vatican, this is the true cup of Christ.

Although the cup of Christ (Chalice of Valencia) is indeed special, it is just one of many holy grails dating from the time of the Passion of Jesus. Known collectively as the Arma Christi, these are the articles of the Passion that became saturated with the spiritual power of Jesus while touching his body and blood. The holy grails of the Arma Christi include the True Cross that Jesus was nailed upon during the Crucifixion, the Crown of Thorns, the Veil of Veronica (the cloth that briefly covered his head), and the Shroud of Turin (the cloth that covered Jesus's corpse). Legend has it that the Knights Templar possessed all the articles of the Passion at one time or another. Most of them were discovered by the warrior monks during the Fourth Crusade when they entered a small chapel in the Boukoleon Palace in Constantinople and discovered many articles of the Passion along with the head of John the Baptist. The Knights would later claim that John's Head, which they called Baphomet, emanated the same spiritual power it did when it was on the body of the

Baptist, thus making it a true holy grail. Since John had become known at that time by the inner circle of Templars as the "Savior and Maker of the Order," his head immediately became the most cherished holy grail of the knights.

An earlier holy grail from the Holy Land, the Bowl of Solomon was made from a huge emerald discovered in the Mediterranean Sea and given to the King of Tyre. The gem was brought to King Solomon by Hiram Abiff, the builder of Solomon's Temple, and Solomon had it carved into a drinking bowl.

Another ancient holy grail associated with Sumer is the Sumerian Grail. A fragment of the Sumerian Grail was discovered in the foundations of a tower belonging to "the oldest Sun Temple in Mesopotamia." In ancient times, the vessel had been hidden there by King Udu of Kish, the great-grandson of King Dur, the first Sumerian king and original owner of the chalice, who had apparently captured the cup from "aboriginal Chaldean serpent-worshippers" when he replaced dragon worship with a sun cult. King Dur then engraved the vessel with "the oldest known historical inscription in the world," which contained a genealogy of the ancient Sumerian kings.

Persia's contribution to the list of holy grails includes the Jami-Jamshid, the Cup of Jamshid, which was discovered by the legendary Persian King Jamshid when he was excavating an ancient city in central Asia. Jamshid's radiant chalice, which was made of pure turquoise, could both reveal the future and transform a human being into an immortal god. Another famous Persian holy grail resided at the court of King Kay Khosrow. Known as the Nartmongue, meaning the "Knights' Cup," this chalice was passed among Persian knights for at least a thousand years before Arthurian knights pursued their magical Holy Grail.

In the Far East, the existence of an ancient holy grail called the Chalice of Buddha was contained within a *Jataka*, an anecdotal story extracted directly from the life of Buddha, which stated: "from the four lands came the four guardians of the world ... they offered four bowls made of black stone and the Buddha, full of compassion for the four wise men, accepted the four bowls. He placed one inside the other and ordained, 'Let there be one!' And the edges of the four became visible as outlines. All the bowls formed into one bowl. The Buddha accepted food in the newly formed bowl and, having partaken of food, he offered thanks."

China's Royal Cauldron is a large golden pot known to have once brought long life and prosperity to some of the early Chinese emperors. The Royal Cauldron was renowned for its alchemical properties and for magically manifesting within itself the elixir of immortality for righteous emperors, including the Emperor Hung-ti and the beneficent Emperor Wu of the Han Dynasty. But the Royal Cauldron would only assist righteous emperors. Otherwise, as in the case of the evil Emperor Shi Huang-ti of the Chin Dynasty, the Royal Cauldron would mysteriously disappear and remain hidden until a more well-disposed ruler ascended the throne of China.

The Hebrew Holy Grail has many forms. When Noah entered the Ark, he brought precious stones and jewels with him to keep track of day and night. When the jewels shone dimly, he knew that it was daytime, and when they shone brightly, he knew that it was night. Noah needed the jewels because the celestial bodies—including the sun—did not shine their light during the year of the Flood; no sunlight entered the Ark.

According to the Talmud, Jacinth was the Light of Noah's Ark. According to the Talmud Genesis 6:16a, God said: "A light [*tsohar*—also translated here as "window"] shall you make for the Ark" and so Noah gathered luminous stones and jewels, that they might give light as bright as the noonday sun. Noah used the light from the jewels as a lantern to safely steer his Ark through the darkness of the night. These stones provided the only source of light inside the Ark.

Elsewhere in the Talmud, there is another tradition that Abraham also had a miraculous stone: Rabbi Shimon ben Yochai has said, "Abraham had a precious stone hung round his neck which brought immediate healing to any sick person who looked on it, and when Abraham our father left this world, the Blessed Holy One hung it from the wheel of the sun." (*Baba Batra* 16b)

Those who possessed the *tzohar* not only had illumination, but access to the secrets of the Torah and all its powers. Thus, God created it, but then hid it away for the sole use of the righteous. The Angel Raziel gave it to Adam after the Fall and Adam passed it down to his children all the way to Noah. Abraham returned the *tzohar* to heaven and hung it on the sun, but other traditions track its continued use by the righteous of each subsequent generation. For example, Joseph used it for his dream interpretations, and Moses recovered it from the bones of Joseph and placed it in the Tabernacle.

Writers like Wolfram von Eschenbach, who wrote *Parzival* (1210), say that the grail was a stone fallen out of the sky. This stone or grail was called "Lapis Exillas." The essence of the Lapis Exillas was so pure that it was able to nourish a person who stands before its presence, as well as sustain a mortally wounded person for at least a week and slow the aging process.

Perlesvaus or *Le Haut Livre du Graal* (1212) says that the Holy Grail and Bleeding Lance had vanished when the Fisher King died, before Percival could complete his quest. The quest had changed to where the hero must find a golden circlet, instead of the grail. This golden circlet was known as the Circle of Gold, but it was actually the crown of thorns that the Romans placed on Jesus's head before crucifying him. The Holy Grail, the Bleeding Lance and other holy relics reappeared when Perceval's wicked uncle, the King of Castle Mortal, had died.

In the Bible, the Holy Grail was associated with the cup used by Jesus during the Last Supper (*Matthew* 26:26–29; *Mark* 14:22–26; *Luke* 22:14–20). Jesus shared bread and wine with his apostles, saying that this was his last meal with them. Jesus broke the bread and said, "This is my body, which is given to you" (*Luke* 22:19). With the wine in the cup, he said, "This cup is God's new covenant sealed with my blood, which is poured out to you" (*Luke* 22:20). After the Last Supper, the cup was never mentioned again.

In Irish myth, the Cauldron of Dagda was a large vessel on wheels that had some powerful magical properties. The cauldron was always full of food that would satisfy a person's hunger and refresh and renew his strength. It also had the magical ability of healing.

In the Welsh myth "*Preiddiau Annwfn*" ("Spoils of Annwfn") from the *Book of Taliesin*, Arthur and his companions went to Annwyn to steal a magic cauldron. Annwyn was the Welsh form of the Otherworld—the land of faery.

In the Welsh myth "Branwen the Daughter of Llyr" in the *Mabinogion*, Bran was the legendary king of the Land of the Mighty, who possessed the magic cauldron of rebirth. The cauldron brought nourishment and restored life to the dead.

Another form of the Holy Grail arises from a different interpretation of the words Sang Real (Royal Blood), in support of the contention that Jesus Christ had a child(ren) by Mary Magdalene. This lineage of the Royal Blood continued and (in some theories) exists to the present day. The grail, in this case, is a person rather than a thing—that is, a lost royal heir in whose veins course the blood of Jesus. This is a modern retelling of a legend which was detailed in Jacobus de Voragine's *The Golden Legend*, who also linked it to king Dagobert the Great and the Merovingians, the first Frankish dynasty reigning from about 500 to 751 AD. The story asserts that the Merovingian rulers, through king Dagobert, were the descendants of Jesus Christ and Mary Magdalene, and that certain families today are the heirs of Dagobert.

Chretien de Troyes was the first author to write about the Grail. In the *Le Conte du Graal*, Perceval was the hero who witnessed the procession of grail maidens carrying mystical objects. When Perceval saw the grail for the first time, he noticed a "holy host" in the vessel illuminated the room brightly and was able to sustain life. Though Chretien says that the vessel was holy, he did not make an explicit connection between Jesus Christ and the grail.

Later, Arthurian authors were more concerned with the Holy Grail itself than the contents in the grail. Some of the forms of the grail described by varying authors include:

Conte du Graal—Chretien de Troyes—dish
Joseph d'Arimathie—Robert de Boron—chalice (cup of Christ)
Didot Perceval—Anonymous—chalice (cup of Christ)
Perlesvaus—Anonymous—chalice (cup of Christ)
Peredur—Mabinogion—platter with a severed head
Parzival—Wolfram von Eschenbach—stone—Lapis Exillas
Diu Krone—Heinrich von dem Turlin—crystal vessel, later a golden bowl
Queste del Saint Graal—Vulgate Cycle—platter
Roman de Graal—Post-Vulgate—silver basin
Le Morte d'Arthur—Sir Thomas Malory—chalice (cup of Christ)

Robert de Boron says that the Holy Grail was the cup used by Jesus Christ at the Last Supper, and later at the Crucifixion, when Joseph of Arimathea used it to catch the blood of Christ. However, the Bible places no special emphasis on the cup. There was no connection between Joseph and the grail in the gospels. Boron also says that it was the Rich Fisher King, named Bron, who was the brother-in-law of Joseph, and that it was he who brought the grail to Britain. In other versions, it was Joseph and his son Josephus, who brought the grail to Britain. In Boron's second work, called *Merlin*, the tale linked the first book with the last, where the wizard Merlin created the Round Table, using "Joseph's Grail Table" as a model. The third book, called *Perceval*, recounts the adventures of Perceval's quest of the grail, where he eventually became the successor of the Rich Fisher King (who happened to be his grandfather, Bron). The Holy Grail and the Holy Lance vanished with Perceval's death.

The Holy Grail in Wolfram von Eschenbach's *Parzival* is a wondrous stone of the purest kind, called the Lapis Exillis, which was brought to the earthly plane by angels who were neutral during the War in Heaven. The Grail Family, who are sustained and given immortality by it, guards this stone with great care. The Lapis Exillis, the Grail stone, shows a message saying that Anfortas' successor will come, but this knight must ask a specific question on the first night. Parzival observes the procession and the bleeding spear, but out of misplaced modesty says nothing and asks no questions.

The Cauldron of Awen had a potion brewed in it which could bestow all knowledge. The goddess Ceridwen obliged a youth, Gwion, to stir this magic potion until three drops spilled onto his fingers. He put his fingers into his mouth and thereby gained all knowledge.

In the Christian tradition, the Grail Cup is always carried or guarded by women and has life-restoring capabilities, whilst the grail in Arthurian legend could bestow knowledge. Thus, many authors have tried to show that Celtic cauldrons are in some sense a precursor to the modern Grail image.

There are many traditions that indicate that the grail is a luminous stone that is intimately connected to the fall from grace and is some type of help and assistance in the quest for the grail. Lucifer's brilliant green stone, that was the jewel of his crown, fell from heaven to earth and was fashioned into a bowl used by Jesus at the Last Supper. This stone became the Holy Grail after the blood of Jesus Christ had filled it. Lucifer's stone was redeemed by this act of Joseph of Arimathea, indicating that someday Lucifer himself may turn from darkness and reunite with the bright worlds of heaven surrounding the throne of God.

Hebrew legends tell us about a stone called the *tzohar* which an angel brought out from the Garden of Eden and gave to Adam and Eve as a help and comfort. It gave forth light, warmth, and nourishment to the suffering couple, who found the cold world a hard place to live. This stone was cherished by Adam and Eve and was passed down from father to son. The *tzohar* was described as a stone but also as a "bright window to heaven" that brought light in the day and warmth at night. It was this *tzohar* that God told Noah to place in the Ark to give light and sustenance to all humans and animals throughout the flood.

Another story of the *tzohar*, sometimes called the Stone of An, is about the death of Adam. When Adam knew he was about to die, he sent his son Seth back to the Garden of Eden to find three seeds from the Tree of Life. Seth found the path back to Eden by following the footprints of Adam and Eve, which were burnt into the stone they had walked upon while leaving. Seth was a highly developed soul who was pure of heart, therefore he was able to convince the angel with the flaming sword to let him pass. Once Seth found the Tree of Life, he picked a fruit and found the three seeds he needed. But when Seth arrived back home, Adam had already died. Seth placed the three seeds upon the tongue of Adam and his entire head began to glow and shine like the sun. From then onward, the head of Adam (Stone of An) continued to shine brightly while nourishing and healing anyone who came near it. It was the Stone of An that was passed down to Noah and used as the grail of the Ark, the *tzohar*.

Another tradition tells that the *tzohar* of the Garden of Eden was passed down to Abraham who wore it on a necklace for all to see. Anyone who came near the stone was amazed by its powers to heal and nourish. The "Stone of Abraham" is yet another version of the Holy Grail that insinuates that some type of shining stone is connected to the quest for the holy grail that brings the keeper of the grail great powers of wisdom and healing.

Alchemists also have their version of the Holy Grail as a stone they call the "prime material" or the original substance of creation. Another name they give it is the Philosopher's Stone, which is purported to exist everywhere and nowhere, a substance that is transcendent. Once this stone is attained, the alchemist can then turn base metals into gold. It can also become the elixir of life, the heavenly dew, or the fountain of youth. Again, with the help of a "magical stone," we find that consciousness is developed, nourishment is given, and the path to the grail is attained.

The question of whether any of these stones existed is debatable and falls into the category of miracles and wonders. Did Solomon believe that he had the stone that fell from Lucifer's crown? Did Abraham really wear a grail around his neck? Did the head of Adam become a shining stone? Did Joseph of Arimathea catch the blood of Christ in a Holy Grail?

These types of imaginations, traditions, and legends call into question whether these beliefs and stories are analogies for soul and spiritual stages of development and not physical objects. Can these ideas be taken for face value or are we to use a "science of the grail" to understand the true nature of the Holy Grail? Is belief in the Holy Grail necessary to "see" the vision of the grail that calls the seeker to the path (The Way)? Can we look for the answers to these questions within our own physical body as a study of esoteric anatomy? Can the Grail Castle be found in the mysterious ventricles of the brain and its "glowing" and "shining" activity created by the minerals and metals (stones) that accumulate there? Are the pineal gland's "crystals" of calcium carbonate the "grail stones" we are developing along the path? Is the fourth ventricle, where the pineal gland resides, the inaccessible castle of the Grail King and Queen? Is the grail knight also a seeker of the higher self—the Grail King or Grail Queen?

Whether the grail stone is real or whether the holy blood relics have sacred powers may be completely up to the individual person on the graded path towards the grail. Even witnessing the Grail Procession does not guarantee that the seeker will have developed enough moral strength and insight to ask the question: "Whom does the grail serve?" Perhaps even seeing the Holy Grail in all its glory may not awaken the dull soul enough to receive the grace and gifts that could nourish them into blessedness. The blinders of materialism may make the seeker unable to experience the grace and glory that exist right in front of him. We can see how the blindness of Longinus was healed by contact with divine blood and the love of a divine sacrifice. The Holy Grail, like Christ's sacrificial deed, is real but the ability to witness it and understand its meaning is not a given. Only the awakened ones have "ears to hear" and "eyes to see." When the Holy Grail floated before Arthur and his Knights of the Round Table, only a few saw the grail, but they all vowed to seek after it.

Does understanding the holy grail require faith in the unseen and belief in holy blood relics? Does the search for the grail predicate belief in Jesus Christ? Is the grail an exclusively Christian belief?

As we have mentioned, the grail legends, myths, and beliefs existed long before Christianity and, in fact, can be found in almost every tradition. A magic cauldron, a giving bowl, a cornucopia of harvest, the helix of creation, or an ocean of being are part and parcel of explaining the origins of the world and the cosmos. In some creation stories, a divine spear comes down from heaven and stirs the bowl of creation until some type of trinity is born (sun, moon, stars). This original container of creation is often depicted as female, while the spear is seen as male. Between the male impulse of creation and the female receptacle of creation—the gods and humans arise. This impregnation of creation is a divine impulse and it can be found as close as the human heart and the circulation of the blood and its mysteries.

We need not look any further than the human body if we wish to lift the blinders of materialism to find the grail. Science has found miraculous wonders in every cell that show that the Garden of Eden might be replicated in human nucleic DNA (Tree of Life) and mitochondrial DNA (Tree of Knowledge of Good and Evil). Embryonic cells appear to "not die" and live forever, as though they had eaten from the Tree of Life. Certain enzymes also take on miraculous characteristics and do not die; they just transform and move at speeds that are incomprehensible. The open and awakened eyes and ears of the grail seeker can see these wonders as miracles of the grail found in the human body. From the pineal gland's "stones" to the corpus quadra gemini's cube-like structure below it, the human body presents us with images analogous of grails and grail castles.

We have described above the possibility that the flaming sword of human consciousness needs to strike from the "crown" the sin of jealousy and pride until it falls into the heart as a vessel to hold grail wisdom. Once human blood has been offered as a humble sacrifice to the spirit through breathing, it suffers both oxygen and carbon dioxide to be carried throughout the body as a labor of love and nourishment. The iron in our blood helps in this process like the iron in the flaming sword and the heavenly spear of consciousness. When the heart/grail receives an overabundance of light (consciousness) it begins the pilgrim's path (grail quest) back to the Grail Castle in the head. What is conquered through perception of the outside world (the dragon) is transformed in the heart/grail and sent up the spear of consciousness (human spine) to bathe the pineal gland with the warmth, light, and nourishment refined in the process. Carbon (the philosopher's stone) is transformed through the pilgrim's path (the route from heart to head) and calcium (death) is transformed into calcium carbonate, a living piezoelectric crystal that can spark piezoelectrical charges through the fourth ventricle and down to the pituitary gland. When this spark of light passes through the third ventricle, it is passing through the Holy Grail vessel in the brain and is enhanced with energy and special substances from the first and second ventricle that focus the fiery tip of the spear (the spine) into a bio-electrical charge that reaches the pituitary. When the pituitary gland is stimulated in this process, it excretes pituitrin, a hormone that nourishes the nerve and blood systems. A type of "grail nourishment" arises from in this process of digesting perception with love.

We can find the Holy Grail manifesting in many fashions based upon our belief system. We can use the "science of the grail" to find physical correspondences for the effects of the "Holy Grail phenomena" acting upon our nerves, glands, blood, and bones. We can focus the devotion to the grail that is displayed by the Maidens of the Wells, the Grail Maidens, and the King/Queen of the Grail to acquire a deeper understanding of human physiology and the development of soul and spirit.

Often, those who follow the path of devotion find solace and comfort in seeing a reenactment of the grail mysteries during the Holy Eucharist, as performed in Catholic churches during Holy Communion. The more ornate and mysterious the pageantry of the Holy Eucharist, the more the devotional seeker of the grail is reminded of the procession of the Grail Maidens and are inclined to "willingly suspend their disbelief." Many Christians believe in their hearts that they are consuming the body and blood of their lord and savior during Holy Communion. Faith is the key factor for these devoted seekers who live out their beliefs through modern spiritual rituals.

Does the belief of the faithful change a relic so that it is more powerful over time because of the devotion of the faithful? Take, for instance, the Chalice of Valencia, which is said by the Catholic church to be the cup Jesus used at the Last Supper. It has been revered and worshiped for two millennia, and many have died to guard it from invading Moors in Spain. It is still seen today in Valencia and it has been dated to the first century, just like another chalice in Leon, Spain. The question can rightly be asked: Is either one or both made more "holy" by the worship of the faithful?

There is a tradition in the Catholic church that if a substance touches a "first-class" relic (directly connected to holy blood relics or saint relics) it takes on the characteristics of the first-class relic. Thus, if an ordinary nail were to touch holy nail of the cross, it would take on some of the "holiness" of that first-class relic. This explains why there are so many churches that claim to have the cup of the Last Supper. Perhaps those cups touched the chalice of Valencia or Leon. The many pieces of the Holy Cross found in churches across Europe were also created in this fashion, as were many, many other relics. To the devoted believer, contact with a relic of any sort supports the path to belief and devotion. This is the justification for the many Holy Grail chalices found in hundreds of churches throughout Europe.

Chapter 8

Fiery Spear from Heaven

In Hebrew legends, Lucifer's fall from the War in Heaven was like a mighty fireball streaking from heaven, trailing a tail like a fiery dragon. The Fall from Heaven resembled a falling meteor that came from the "Fiery Eye of God's Throne" like a falling star. Lucifer was cast out from the presence of the fiery eye of God by the Archangel Michael while the Archangel Gabriel protected the souls that were not swept down to earth by the dragon's great tail. Meteors were a powerful symbol for the ancient Hebrews, who revered their splendor and usefulness. Meteorites brought the gift of fire from the sky and the precious metals and crystals inside. These substances aided the advancement of metalwork a great deal and provided the exact substances the Bronze Age needed to become the Iron Age.

Tubal-Cain was the son of Cain who was noted for his brilliance in fashioning tools for living. He was known as the first smithy who forged metal, even from the iron and nickel found in meteorites. Iron meteorites gave direct access to the hardest metals without having to separate them from their matrix. They also contain carbon, which tempers iron into steel. Cobalt, nickel, white gold, arsenic, and other elements and metals useful in forging were also found in meteorites. A speck of the right meteorite mixed with bronze makes the metal harder and makes bronze as hard as steel. Other meteorites, called palladiums, are filled with a green crystal called olivine. In some cases, the entire meteorite may be principally olivine crystal. Using meteorites helped Tubal-Cain create strong swords and spears and provided crystal that could be ground and made into vessels and jewelry.

Legend has it that Tubal-Cain found a great meteorite that God told him to forge into a very special sword and spear. As long as the bearer of the weapons never separated the sword and spear, they were undefeatable. Tubal-Cain was instructed to hide the weapons deep among rocks at the top of a mountain until the time when they would be needed would come. They were found again much later and used by kings and leaders of the Hebrew people to bring many victories. Unfortunately, the sword and spear were jealously desired by rulers who fought over and separated them. Eventually, the spear came be to owned by Phinehas, the grandson of Aaron. This same spear was still used at the time of Jesus of Nazareth and was carried out to the Mount of the Skull (Golgotha) by the Sanhedrin during the Crucifixion. This spear was considered to be the "authority" and "witness" when the Sanhedrin condemned someone to death.

Roman Catholics also revere meteorites and have built churches at the site of numerous meteor falls. These churches were dedicated to the Archangel Michael, and the meteorite is often incorporated into a statue of Michael holding Lucifer (a dragon) at bay. It is generally the shield of Michael that has been forged from a meteorite. Often, this shield is rather small, compared to standard shields, because the meteorite was limited in size. The shield is usually not very prominent and is forged into the shape of a bowl or dish, not the shape of a standard shield. These beliefs are most interesting and show that whether as sword, spear, or shield, meteorites from "heaven" play a large part in the protection of a Soldier of God, of whom the Archangel Michael is the primary archetypal example.

Whether an olivine crystal carved into a bowl or one of Tubal-Cain's forged swords or spears with meteorites folded into the mix, the ancient Hebrews understood both the potential of meteorites to advance metalwork and the value of olivine and the other precious substances found within them. Even during Roman times, a centurion's spear (*hasta novio magus*) was forged with meteorite to strengthen the spearhead. It is likely that Longinus's spear would have been forged with meteorite. The Spear of Phinehas was likely also forged with meteoric metal, as was common with blades made in Palestine. The spiritual spear of Longinus was the opposite of the Hebrew spear of Phinehas that had seen so much death and war.

Animistic belief in the living nature of meteorites is most pronounced in Indonesia, particularly Java. It was tradition that every male Javanese had a special knife or spear called a cris (kris or keris) that was revered as a living god if it contained meteorite. These knives and spears were made of three parts that were often fashioned by three different artists. The blade was forged, and then the smithy would determine if the blade had a good or bad spirit to it. Generally, a cris with meteorite was seen as good and filled with dragon force that could be seen in the tail of the meteor as it fell to earth.

Every cris was considered alive and was treated as a god or a demon. Javanese religious worship centers around these sacred cris. The legends and myths concerning these double-edged daggers shaped like serpents continue to this day. Miraculous powers and phenomena accompany these blades and their scabbards, which are also considered sacred. The scabbard is seen as the "vessel" that holds the power of the "blade of heaven." The handle of the cris is also considered holy and has the power of a human spirit—a sort of "I am," or individualized personality. Some cris are ancient, and the beings associated with them are believed to be ancient, wise beings who communicate and speak directly to Javanese priests.

Finding the meteorite connection to the Christian grail legends does not belittle the belief of ancient animism or the Quest for the Holy Grail. Knowing the living nature of substance is a part of "grail science." Meteorites advanced metallurgy through a quantum leap that didn't require faith. Believing that an olivine bowl caught the blood of a god that redeemed the dead nature of the earth and the human spirit still takes great faith. Using living tools that become spiritual tools does not detract from the cosmic meaning and power of the Mystery of Golgotha (the life, death, and resurrection of Christ). In fact, using living substances that carry powerful symbolic value for the believer may enhance religious experience. Christians absorbed many prior beliefs and ritual practices because those practices had inherent power and aligned perfectly with the clairvoyant prophecies that prefigure Jesus Christ.

Christ was like a meteor descending from the throne of God. The flaming sword of Michael was present at the Crucifixion because the spear of Longinus was made with meteoric metal and the vessel of Joseph of Arimathea was a green stone that fell from heaven. None of these legendary and historical stories detract from the Mystery of Golgotha; in fact, they enhance and enrich these beliefs.

The Holy Lance of Love

It may surprise some Christians that a weapon of war, a mighty spear, is part of a spiritual path that leads to compassion and love. Perhaps it is appropriate that a spear (and sword) is given to the Archangel Michael to defend the throne of God from the assault of Lucifer, who desired to sit on the throne of God and take his place. Certainly, defending God from this attack justified the War in Heaven and Lucifer being cast out of the presence of God. The fiery spear of Michael was a spiritual tool that was used to hold Lucifer (dragon) at bay so that his evil might be transformed into good. This type of outcome makes the spear and sword of Michael into spiritual weapons that vanquish evil in the battle for good. But to apply that type of spiritual logic to the spear that pierced the side of Jesus on the Cross is difficult for some to understand.

It is good to remember that Jesus of Nazareth was a spiritual warrior who directly confronted and defeated the evil of his time with courage that was unmatched. Jesus consciously sacrificed his life for the good of humanity as a divine being descending from the throne of God into the dark realm of humanity's earth. Christ said to "turn the other cheek," but He also stood up to the evil Sanhedrin and fought for the gospel of "The Way, the Truth, and the Life." Jesus overturned the tables of the money changers in the temple and faced off against the Roman Empire's stranglehold on the Hebrew people's freedom. Jesus is quoted in the *Gospel of Matthew*: 10:34: "Do not suppose that I have come to bring peace to the earth. I did not come to bring peace, but a sword."

These words are seldom quoted by Christians, but they indicate that Jesus was a radical spiritual warrior who was grappling with Lucifer and Satan to ransom the spiritual heart of humanity from the grip of evil. The Archangel Michael is a mighty warrior for God, but Christ is the conqueror of evil in this material world. Jesus was a soldier of God, like the Archangel Michael who is called the *face* or *continence* of Christ. Christ and Michael work together in the battle for the soul and spirit of each human. Michael is clad with the flaming sword given to him by God and the fiery spear that rent the curtain of heaven. Christ is gird with compassion, love, and the grace and mercy of the divine. These spiritual weapons of Christ conquered Lucifer and Satan and hold them at bay like the Archangel Michael binds the dragon so that it will not consume the child who is born of the Virgin "surrounded by the sun and stars with the moon beneath her feet" that we read about in the *Apocalypse of John the Beloved*.

The *Book of Wisdom* (5:17–20) tells us:

> "The Lord will take his zeal as his whole armor and will arm all creation to repel his enemies; he will put on righteousness as a breast plate and wear impartial justice as a helmet; he will take holiness as an invincible shield, and sharpen stern wrath for a sword, and creation will join with him to fight against his frenzied foes."

Whether we use the heavenly armor of righteousness, impartiality, holiness, and wrath or the soldier's tools of a spear, a sword, a shield, a breast plate, a helmet, and a swift and mighty horse, the battle must be engaged. Conquering one's lower self is the prerequisite for the questing knight longing to find the grail (higher self). It may seem like an analogy or a metaphor of spiritual fancy, but the war against evil within and without is raging and the Holy Grail of love is the source of victory. It is incumbent upon the seeker of the grail to pass through the stages of purification, renunciation, and dedication to the quest, and then to evolve to the perfection of the soul as a worthy vessel (grail) that receives the outpouring of the spirit.

We are given a further injunction by the apostle Paul's *Letter to the Ephesians* (6:10–18) that sounds like a call to battle:

> Finally, my brethren, be strong in the Lord, and in the power of his might. Put on the whole armor of God, that ye may be able to stand against the wiles of the devil. For we wrestle not against flesh and blood, but against principalities, against powers, against the rulers of the darkness of this world, against spiritual wickedness in high places. Wherefore take unto you the whole armor of God, that ye may be able to withstand in the evil day, and having done all, to stand. Stand therefore, having your loins girt about with truth, and having on the breastplate of righteousness; and your feet shod with the preparation of the gospel of peace; above all, taking the shield of faith, wherewith ye shall be able to quench all the fiery darts of the wicked. And take the helmet of salvation, and the sword of the Spirit, which is the word of God: praying always with all prayer and supplication in the Spirit and watching thereunto with all perseverance and supplication for all saints.

We are told to take the "sword of the Spirit, which is the word of God" to withstand the evil. This is a fight to the finish that will take all the seeker's moral development to withstand the assault of evil. Truth, righteousness, peace, faith, salvation, the word of God, and prayers create the armor of the Soldier of God. Each spiritual weapon is seen as a preparation for the encounter with evil in our day. We must make the commitment to fight evil with every part of our beings and not surrender to the onslaught of the dragon. This war must be fought to make our way through the world to the place where the Grail Castle (Garden of Eden, Paradise) is found. Once we find our inheritance, the Grail Castle, we can lay down our weapons and finally rest as we assume our role as the Queen/King of the Grail—the master of our lower self and witness to our spiritual higher self.

The archetypal grail soldier is Longinus, who was the first one to say aloud that "surely, this must be the Son of God" and was then healed of his blindness. It is said that the Archangel Michael guided the spear of Longinus so that it would pierce the heart of Jesus Christ and release the blood and water to fall into the earth to redeem humanity. Longinus's deed was an act of compassion to keep the Sanhedrin from breaking the legs of Jesus to accelerate his death. Longinus knew that Jesus had already died, so he pierced his side so that his legs would not be broken. The lance of the centurion Longinus thus became the "Lance of Love" that resembles the spear of Michael.

We are told of the merciful deed of Longinus in the *Gospel of John* (19:34-37) in the following words: "But one of the soldiers with a spear pierced his side, and forthwith came there out blood and water. And he that saw it bare record, and his record is true: and he knoweth that he saith true, that ye might believe. For these things were done, that the scripture should be fulfilled, 'A bone of him shall not be broken.' And again, another scripture saith, 'They shall look on him whom they pierced.'"

When Longinus had pierced Jesus and the blood and water touched his eyes and healed him, Longinus became the first grail knight—Soldier of God—to convert from outward war and fighting to the inner battle for the heart of the spirit. Longinus became the first grail knight to seek after the grail, find the grail, and ask whom the grail serves. Longinus found Christ in Jesus (The Truth), dedicated his life to protecting Christ's mission (The Way), and then participated in the grail procession (The Life) of

Jesus Christ (Via Dolorosis). Longinus became a Grail King—one who knows his higher self through the holy blood Mysteries.

Longinus was a spiritual tool of the Archangel Michael, and he realized that letting the divine work through him was the path he was always seeking. Longinus immediately converted to Christianity and served the Mother of Jesus like she was his own mother. Longinus helped Joseph of Arimathea take down the body of Jesus from the cross to clean and prepare it for burial. The next day, Longinus resigned his position as a Roman centurion and turned in his horse, sword, and shield. Longinus gave the spearhead of his Roman centurion hasta to the Mother of Jesus for safe keeping. He then stayed with Mary for the next eleven years until her Assumption into heaven at Ephesus.

The Roman Catholic church, which celebrates the feast of Saint Michael the Archangel on September 29, tells us about the nature and work of the Archangel Michael, who was so closely over-lighting Longinus. Let's examine the cosmic battle between Michael and Lucifer and explore how Michael could cast out Lucifer (Satan) and his cohort of fallen angels.

In *Revelation* (12:1-9), we hear about the battle between Michael and the dragon:

> And a great sign appeared in heaven: A woman clothed with the sun, and the moon under her feet, and on her head a crown of twelve stars:
>
> And being with child, she cried travailing in birth, and was in pain to be delivered.
>
> And there was seen another sign in heaven: and behold a great red dragon, having seven heads, and ten horns: and on his head seven diadems:
>
> And his tail drew the third part of the stars of heaven and cast them to the earth: and the dragon stood before the woman who was ready to be delivered; that, when she should be delivered, he might devour her son.
>
> And she brought forth a man child, who was to rule all nations with an iron rod: and her son was taken up to God, and to his throne.

And the woman fled into the wilderness, where she had a place prepared by God, that there they should feed her a thousand two hundred sixty days.

And there was a great battle in heaven, Michael and his angels fought with the dragon, and the dragon fought and his angels:

And they prevailed not, neither was their place found any more in heaven.

And that great dragon was cast out, that old serpent, who is called the devil and Satan, who seduces the whole world; and he was cast unto the earth, and his angels were thrown down with him.

In *Luke* (10:18–20), Jesus refers to this "fall from heaven" when speaking to his apostles in the following words:

The seventy-two returned with joy and said, "Lord, even the demons submit to us in your name." He replied, "I saw Satan fall like lightning from heaven. I have given you authority to trample on snakes and scorpions and to overcome all the power of the enemy; nothing will harm you. However, do not rejoice that the spirits submit to you, but rejoice that your names are written in heaven."

In *Isaiah* (14:12-15) we find a reference to Lucifer:

How art thou fallen from heaven, O Lucifer, who didst rise in the morning? how art thou fallen to the earth, that didst wound the nations? And thou saidst in thy heart: "I will ascend into heaven, I will exalt my throne above the stars of God, I will sit in the mountain of the covenant, in the sides of the north. I will ascend above the height of the clouds, I will be like the most-High." But yet, thou shalt be brought down to hell, into the depth of the pit.

We have another powerful description of the War in Heaven in *Ezekiel* (28:11-18):

Moreover, the word of the Lord came to me: "Son of man, raise a lamentation over the king of Tyre, and say to him, thus says the

Lord God: You were the signet of perfection, full of wisdom and perfect in beauty. You were in Eden, the garden of God; every precious stone was your covering, sardius, topaz, and diamond, beryl, onyx, and jasper, sapphire, emerald, and carbuncle; and crafted in gold were your settings and your engravings. On the day that you were created they were prepared. You were an anointed guardian cherub. I placed you; you were on the holy mountain of God; in the midst of the stones of fire you walked. You were blameless in your ways from the day you were created, till unrighteousness was found in you. In the abundance of your trade you were filled with violence in your midst, and you sinned; so, I cast you as a profane thing from the mountain of God, and I destroyed you, O guardian cherub, from the midst of the stones of fire. Your heart was proud because of your beauty; you corrupted your wisdom for the sake of your splendor. I cast you to the ground; I exposed you before kings, to feast their eyes on you. By the multitude of your iniquities, in the unrighteousness of your trade you profaned your sanctuaries; so, I brought fire out from your midst; it consumed you, and I turned you to ashes on the earth in the sight of all who saw you."

We can see from these passages that Satan was once called "Lucifer" or "light-bearer" and sought to usurp God, exalting himself above all. Yet, he was cast down from heaven by Michael the Archangel along with a third of the other angels who rebelled against God.

The Roman Catholic Church affirms that Lucifer/Satan was once a good angel and that he (and many other angels) freely chose to reject God. Lucifer knew exactly what he was doing when he chose to rebel against God, and he knew its implications. This rebellion was accomplished at the beginning of time, shortly after the creation of the angels and before the full creation of humans. This can be deduced simply by the fact that Lucifer/Satan (the old dragon, the father of lies) was already present in the Garden of Eden.

Traditionally speaking, all angels were created at the very beginning of creation. On the first day, when God made light, the light He made was the angels (*Genesis* 1:3). This is further confirmed when God "divided the light from the darkness," referring to the rebellion of the angels led by Lucifer (*Genesis* 1:4). Tradition also tells us that Lucifer was created by God as a "Seraphim," in the highest choir of angels, while Michael was an "Archangel."

In Roman Catholicism, the Archangel Michael has four distinct roles. First, he is the enemy of Lucifer/Satan and the fallen angels. He defeated Lucifer and ejected him from Paradise and will achieve victory at the hour of the final battle with Lucifer. Secondly, he is the Christian angel of death; at the hour of death, Michael descends and gives each soul the chance to redeem itself before passing. Michael's third role is weighing souls; hence, the Archangel Michael is often depicted holding scales on Judgment Day. And finally, Michael is the Guardian of the Church.

Archangel Michael is viewed as the commander of the Army of God. From the time of the apostles, he has been invoked and honored as the protector of the Church. Scripture describes him as "one of the chief princes" and the leader of heaven's forces in their triumph over the powers of hell.

Archangel Michael defeats Satan two times, first when he ejects Lucifer from Paradise, and then in the final battle at the end-times when the Antichrist will be defeated by him. "Who is like God?" was the cry of Archangel Michael when he smote the rebel Lucifer in the conflict of the heavenly hosts.

Archangel Michael is one of the angels presumed present at the hour of death. Traditionally, he is charged to assist the dying and accompany their souls to their judgement where he serves as an advocate. Cemetery chapels are often dedicated to him and masses are offered in his honor on behalf of the departed. In Catholic tradition, on Judgment Day, Archangel Michael weighs souls based on their deeds during their life on earth. Michael has long been recognized as the protector and guardian of the Church itself and the angel of the Blessed Sacrament (Holy Grail Mysteries).

The emperor Constantine built the Michaelion at Chalcedon dedicated to the Archangel Michael. Other sanctuaries were located at healing springs in Anatolia, Antioch, Castle of the Holy Angel in Rome, and Egypt. Legends include reported appearances of Archangel Michael, where sanctuaries or churches were later built or dedicated to him. These include Monte Gargano in Italy early in the sixth century, where the Sanctuary of Monte Sant'Angelo, the oldest shrine in Western Europe is dedicated to Saint Michael. Early in the eighth century, Archangel Michael reportedly appeared three times to Saint Aubert, the bishop of Avranches in Normandy, France, and instructed him to build a church on the small island now known as Mont-Saint-Michel. Several healings were reported when the church was being built and Mont-Saint-Michel remains a major Catholic pilgrimage site.

The role of Archangel Michael as protector and guardian has also led to the design of statues that depict him and the construction of churches and monasteries at specific locations. Because most monastic islands lie close to land, they were viewed as forts holding demons at a distance against attacks on the church. Monasteries such as Mont-Saint-Michel, off the coast of France, and Skellig Michael, off the coast of Ireland, are dedicated to the Archangel Michael. Another notable structure is that of Saint Michael's Mount, located in Mounts Bay, near Penzance, Cornwall—a stunning island castle that resembles Mont-Saint-Michel and can only be reached on foot and at low tide.

Archangel Michael and the War in Heaven

In the early Eighth Century, on a wild inhospitable rock, the cult of the Archangel Michael became an important place of Christian pilgrimage and led to the development of an Abbey. The cult of Archangel Michael goes back to the Fifth Century. In Italy, the Monte Gargano is a site dedicated to Archangel Michael that has been recognized since the end of Antiquity, before the cult of the Archangel Michael extended to the whole of medieval Western Europe.

According to the *Revelatio ecclesiae sancti michaelis*, the oldest text recording the origins of Mont-Saint-Michel, the first foundations of the Abbey were laid in the year 708, when Aubert, Bishop of Avranches, built the first sanctuary dedicated to the Archangel Michael on Mont-Tombe, now Mont-Saint-Michel. According to the legend, the Archangel appeared to Aubert three times in a dream, asking him to establish a sanctuary in his name. As tradition has it, on the third attempt, the Archangel went as far as poking his finger into Aubert's skull to get him to perform his wishes. Aubert sent messengers to the Monte Gargano in Italy, to bring back relics to the Mont-Tombe. Once completed, the sanctuary was finally dedicated to Archangel Michael on 16 October 709.

Flaming Sword

There is no end to the stories of flaming swords in myths, legends, and religious belief. The flaming sword, or fiery spear, is the initiator of the holy blood Mysteries and is a crucial element for the Procession of the Grail by the Grail Maidens. A spear, or sword, is responsible for shedding the blood that fills the Holy Grail. Spear and chalice, or sword and cup, belong together as the spiritual tools to find the holy blood that redeems the seeker and nourishes their soul. Together, Archangels Michael and Gabriel hold the sword, spear, and chalice that are the key elements of the Holy Grail Mysteries.

Michael in the Hebrew language means "Who is like God?" or "Who is equal to God?" Archangel Michael has been depicted from earliest Christian times as a commander, who holds in his right hand a spear with which he attacks Lucifer/Satan, and in his left hand a green palm branch. At the top of the spear, there is a linen ribbon with a red cross. The Archangel Michael is especially considered to be the Guardian of the orthodox faith and a fighter against heresies.

Gabriel means "God is my strength" or "Might of God." He is the herald of the mysteries of God, especially the Incarnation of God and all other holy blood Mysteries related to it. He is depicted as holding in his right hand a lantern with a lighted taper inside, and in his left hand, a mirror of green jasper or the Holy Grail as a chalice. The mirror signifies the wisdom of God, known as Sophia.

Uriel means "God is my light," or "Light of God" (*II Esdras* 4:1, 5:20). He is depicted holding a sword in his right hand, and a flame in his left.

In Sumerian mythology, the deity known as Asaruludu is "the wielder of the flaming sword" who "ensures the most perfect safety."

According to the Bible, a cherub (or the Archangel Uriel) with a flaming sword was placed by God at the gates of Paradise, Garden of Eden, after Adam and Eve were banished from it, as told in *Genesis* 3:24: "The Lord God made garments of skin for Adam and his wife and clothed them. And the Lord God said, 'The man has now become like one of us, knowing good and evil. He must not be allowed to reach out his hand and take also from the Tree of Life and eat and live forever.' So, the Lord God banished him from the Garden of Eden to work the ground from which he had been taken. After he drove the man out, he placed on the east side of the Garden of Eden a Cherubim and a flaming sword flashing back and forth to guard the way to the Tree of Life." Eastern Orthodox tradition says that after Jesus was crucified and resurrected, the flaming sword was removed from the entrance to the Garden of Eden, making it possible for humanity to re-enter Paradise.

In Welsh mythology, the Dyrnwyn (White-Hilt) is said to be a powerful sword belonging to Rhydderch Hael, one of the "Three Generous Men of Britain" mentioned in the *Welsh Triads*. When drawn by a worthy or well-born man, the entire blade would blaze with fire. Rhydderch was never reluctant to hand the weapon to anyone—hence his nickname Hael "the Generous"—but the recipients, as soon as they had learned of its peculiar properties, always rejected the sword. Its fire would burn the man who drew it for an unworthy purpose.

The sword wielded by the Norse god Surtr, a jotunn of Muspelheim, is a flaming sword with immense destructive power that appears in Norse mythology. This sword was the key to the last battle of the Aesir gods.

There is no end to the stories, myths, legends and tales that highlight a heavenly spear or sword. The selections above are a sampling of the many references found in every tradition and religion throughout the world and down through history, but they are not a comprehensive picture of all mentions of holy weapons.

Archangels of the Grail

According to some traditions, Ratziel (Samael, Azriel) was the holy guardian angel of Adam in the Garden of Eden, and thus is said to be the guardian and guide of the elect. Although Gabriel is considered the "keeper" of the Holy Grail and Michael has been called the "guardian" of the grail, Ratziel is said to know the inmost secret mystery of the Holy Grail, for Ratziel is the angel of the Gnostic being of wisdom, Sophia.

In the Gnostic tradition, Sophia, or the "Shekinah Consort of the Messiah," is considered to be the physical embodiment of the Holy Grail. The "Pistis Sophia" (Wisdom) represents all souls who are a holy vessel into which Christ pours divine light. The soul transformed or transfigured by that holy light is the Holy Grail. The Christian apostle is a grail-bearer or light-bearer. Purification, renunciation, and consecration opens "The Way" for receiving the light from the divine for the nourishment of our soul and spirit.

The following selection describing the work of the archangels in from the *Pistis Sophia* (Book 2), translated by GRS Mead.

> "And Gabriel and Michael led the light-stream over the body of the matter of Pistis Sophia and poured into her all the light-powers which they had taken from her. And the body of her matter became shining throughout, and all the powers also in her, whose

light they had taken away, took light and ceased to lack their light, for they got their light which had been taken from them, because the light was given them through me. And Michael and Gabriel, who ministered and had brought the light-stream into the chaos, will give them the Mysteries of the Light; it is they to whom the light-stream was entrusted, which I have given unto them and brought into the chaos."

We can see the primal place of Michael and Gabriel in relationship to the being of Wisdom, Pistis Sophia. It is said that Mary, the Mother of Jesus, was the physical incarnation of Pistis Sophia. The Archangel Gabriel came to Mary and brought the Holy Spirit to fill her with the Son of God. Archangel Michael was there at the Crucifixion and became the protector of the holy blood relics and the Mystery of Golgotha. Throughout and beyond the life and mission of Jesus Christ, the influence of the heavenly archangels is found as a profound support and help.

Meteors as Michael's Flaming Sword/Spear

In Celtic mythology, stones fall from the sky frequently and are often seen as a holy sign. The most famous example of a stone that fell from the sky is the "Lapsit Exillis" from Wolfram von Eschenbach's *Parzival* (1215). This is the jewel that comes from the stars and was struck from the crown of Lucifer. In *Parzival*, the hermit Trevrizent says that only the chosen can obtain the grail and the name of the chosen seeker can be found written on the stone. In the *Book of Revelation of Saint John* (2:17) it says: "He who has an ear, let him hear what the Spirit says to the churches. To him who overcomes, I will give some of the hidden manna. *I will also give him a white stone with a new name written on it*, known only to him who receives it."

Sometimes the alchemical Philosopher's Stone is said to have fallen from the sky or is described as a cubic stone. Alchemists began looking for the "stone of the wise" by finding the "prima materia" and transforming it into the "lapis philosophorum"—imagination into the grail.

Philosophical alchemists believe that the Philosopher's Stone is a metaphor for the process of enlightenment, to find what was lost when we fell from our original state of being. Sometimes this state is symbolized by a stone, or crystal, pure water, blood, fire, or spiritual light. When we redeem the emerald of the crown, we restore humanity's ability to embody wisdom, love, and beauty. The fall from paradise was a darkening of our inherent imagination and the Philosopher's Stone reopens our capacity for living imagination—living thoughts.

Imagination is omnipresent thought—a realm of living mental images that is beyond time and space. Oscar Wilde describes it in these words: "the imagination is itself the world of light. The world is made by it, and yet the world cannot understand it. That is because the imagination is a manifestation of love, and it is love and the capacity for it that distinguishes one human being from another."

The prima materia (Imagination/Living Thought) is the same thing as the Philosopher's Stone, but through the results of the expulsion from paradise we have lost the ability to see the innate substance of that "stone." Polish the stone and restore it to its original, pristine condition, and miraculously you can see the thoughts and imaginations that hold the world together.

The Philosopher's Stone is the ultimate ground of being and is sometimes called a diamond because it is the indestructible primal substance. In Tibetan Buddhism, it is referred to as the diamond thunderbolt (dorge), the Greeks described it as the hardest substance known to humans named *adamant*. In the Judeo-Christian Bible (*Psalm* 118:22, *Matthew* 21:42), the grail is referred to as "the stone the builders rejected that has become the cornerstone. This is from the Lord, and it is marvelous in our eyes."

Meteorites

Understanding meteorites was very important to the ancients as they tried to meld animism into their religious and philosophical ideas about the divine. The second century Christian historian Clement of Alexandria is said to have concluded about meteorites that "the worship of such stones was the first, and earliest idolatry in the world."

Edward King's book *Remarks Concerning Stones said to have Fallen from the Clouds* points out that many sacred stones worshipped by the ancients were conical or pyramidal in shape:

> "The learned Greaves leads us to conclude the famous image of Diana at Ephesus to have been nothing but a conical, or pyramidal stone, that fell from the clouds. For he tells us, on unquestionable authorities, that many others of the images of heathen deities were merely such."
>
> "Herodian expressly declares that the Phoenicians had ... a certain great stone, circular below, and ending with a sharpness above, in the figure of a cone, of black color. And they report it to have fallen from heaven, and to be the image of the sun."

Tacitus says, that at Cyprus, the image of Venus was not of human shape, but a figure rising continually round, from a larger bottom to a small top, in conical fashion. And it is to be remarked, that Maximus Tyrius says the stone was pyramidal. And in Corinth, we are told by Pausanias that the images both of Jupiter Melichius and of Diana were made with little or no art. The former was represented by a pyramid, and the latter by a column.

Many believe that the image of Aphrodite (Venus) in the sanctuary at Paphos was simply a white cone or pyramid, that the emblem of Astarte at Byblus was a cone, and that the image of Artemis (Diana) at Perga in Pamphylia was also a cone. The images of the sun god, Heliogabalus, at Emesa in Syria was a cone of black stone with small knobs on it, as it appears on coins of Emesa. The sacred stone of Cybele, brought from Pessinus to Rome during the second Punic war, was a rugged, small black stone.

Conical stones, considered sacred, have been found at Golgi in Cyprus, in the Phoenician temples at Malta, and in the shrine of the Mistress of Turquoise in Sinai. Similarly, Book V of Herodian's *Histories* describes the "Black Stone of Elagabalus," a Phoenician temple dedicated to the sun god:

"In this shrine there is no statue sculpted by the hand of man ... but there was an enormous stone, rounded at the base and coming to a point on the top, conical in shape and black ... worshipped as though it were sent from heaven."

While in most cases these sacred stones have disappeared, we have depictions of some of them recorded on ancient coins that show that the stones were the shape of typical meteorites. This conical or pyramid shape is similar to another sacred stone revered by the ancient Egyptians: the black, cone-shaped "Ben-Ben" stone kept in the temple of Ra at Heliopolis. The shape of this stone is thought to have acted as the model for the capstones found on many of Egypt's pyramids and obelisks.

Thus, stones that fall from heaven have been worshiped by the ancients since history began, and often connected to the feminine goddesses and the importance of wisdom, the being of Sophia. The goddesses and maidens associated with the "stones that fall from heaven" constitute a continuous stream of wisdom that has created and informed the Mysteries throughout all ancient cultures.

Raining Blood from the Sky

"The first angel sounded his trumpet, and there came hail and fire mixed with blood, and it was hurled down on the earth. A third of the earth was burned up, a third of the trees were burned up, and all the green grass was burned up. The second angel sounded his trumpet, and something like a huge mountain, all ablaze, was thrown into the sea. A third of the sea turned into blood, a third of the living creatures in the sea died, and a third of the ships were destroyed."

Revelation 8:7–9

"In the year of grace 541 AD, there appeared a comet in Gaul, so vast that the whole sky seemed to be on fire. In the same year, there dropped red blood from the clouds, and a dreadful mortality ensued."

Geophysical Memoirs No. 70, 1937

One of the most unusual and inexplicable phenomena associated with a "fiery spear from heaven" is blood rain. What appears to be actual blood, rains down from above after a fiery spear (meteor) has passed overhead. Many people throughout history have witnessed blood rain and written about it. In almost all cases, blood rain occurred after a meteor/comet was seen in the sky directly before the "burning hot blood rain" falls everywhere. Blood rain could last from a few moments to a few months with a variety of effects from good to bad. Both the "fiery heavenly spear" and "blood rain" were sometimes seen as great signs of victory; or conversely, evil omens of death and destruction.

Just as the bleeding tip of the holy grail spear drips blood, so too this heavenly spear of fire (meteor) is accompanied by blood raining down after its appearance in the sky. Blood rain was collected by the ancients and described as being similar to human blood in texture, smell, and all other properties. Most ancients associated blood rain with the death of a heavenly god or a curse upon an enemy. Often blood rain would turn rivers and lakes red and poison them. Generally, the appearance of blood rain was considered a bad omen foreshadowing dramatic events, but it is described differently by the cultural motifs of the people observing it.

Cases of blood rain have been recorded throughout history and around the world. Over eighty accounts of blood rain and twenty references to rivers and lakes turning into blood have been documented. Before the seventeenth century it was generally believed that blood rain was actually blood. Recorded instances of blood rain usually cover small areas lasting several days. In the nineteenth century, blood rains were scientifically examined, and theories that dust gave the water its red color gained ground. Today, the dominant theories are that the rain is caused by red dust suspended in the rain or by the presence of micro-organisms.

Perhaps the Grail mythos points us in the direction of an answer to the question of meteors and blood rain. If we recall the events in the great hall of the Rich Fisher King of the Holy Grail, we will find many similarities. Percival, the grail knight, is first presented with a sword. Next, the Grail procession enters the hall led by maidens carrying a candelabra; followed by a lance dripping blood; followed by the Grail itself, too brilliant to look at directly; followed by a maiden bearing a chalice (bowl or platter) catching the blood. Many of the elements of the Grail Procession and blood rain are similar and make sense of these strange stories. Some of the similarities are striking: The Grail Castle itself was round and had a dome "covered with blue sapphires strewn with carbuncles that shone like the sun"—like the starry night sky. The Grail is sometimes too bright to look at and floats through the air as if a cloth of white samite covered it—just as a meteor/comet might appear. Blood drips from the tip of the brilliant spear—like blood rain accompanies the fiery spear of the meteor. Blood rain can burn and devastate the land—the land around the Grail Castle had become a wasteland.

Could the descriptions of the Grail procession and the appearance of a meteor/comet that brings blood rain be one and the same?

Recorded Instances of Blood Rain

The descriptions of meteors/comets and blood rain are cloaked in the cultural motifs of the people writing the accounts below. A fiery spear, sword, dragon, or fireball are all describing a meteor or comet. Those descriptions are understandable to the modern thinker, but when it comes to blood rain, the imagination runs wild and cannot find a simple explanation for the phenomena. Blood rain stretches the imagination to its limits.

Let's hear a few historic descriptions of these most interesting and somewhat terrifying experiences.

From the *Mahabharata*:

"The air was filled with the shouting of men, the roaring of elephants, the blasts of trumpets, and the beating of drums: the rattling of chariots was like to thunder rolling in heaven. The Gods assembled in the clouds and saw the hosts which had gathered for mutual slaughter. As both armies waited for sunrise, a tempest arose and the dawn was darkened by dust clouds, so that men could scarce behold one another. **Blood dropped like rain out of heaven**, while jackals howled impatiently, and, kites and vultures screamed hungrily for human flesh."

Chinese Mythologist Mo Tzu:

"Heaven decreed their destruction. The sun came out at night and **for three days it rained blood**. A dragon appeared in the ancestral temple and dogs howled in the marketplace."

Homer's *Iliad*, chapter 16, verse 459:

"Zeus **poured bloody drops earthwards**, honoring his own beloved son, whom Patroklos was soon to destroy in fertile Troy far from his homeland."

The Reign of Synin (29 BC):

"In the thirty sixth year of his reign, it rained Stars from Heaven in Japan. In the 40th year of his reign, on a clear and serene day, there arose all of a sudden in China, a violent storm of thunder and lightning: comets, fiery-dragons and uncommon meteors appeared in the airs, and it **rained fire from Heaven**."

From Josephus (69 AD):

"Amongst other warnings, a comet, one of the kind called Xiphias, because their tails appear to represent the *blade of a sword*, was seen above the city for the space of a whole year."

Fiery Spear from Heaven

From: *Roman History: The Reign of Augustus*, by Cassius Dio (Book 51, 2nd Century):

"Not only did rain fall in places where no drop had ever been seen before, **but blood besides**, and the flash of weapons appeared from the clouds, **as the showers of blood mingled with water poured down**. In other places the clash of drums and cymbals and the notes of flutes and trumpets were heard, and a serpent of enormous size suddenly appeared and uttered a hiss of incredible volume. Meanwhile comets were observed in the heavens."

Obsequens, Book of Prodigies (4th Century):

"An uproar in the sky was heard and *javelins* seen to fall from heaven; **there was a rain of blood**; at Rome in daylight a torch was seen flying high."

Census of Ireland 1851—under an entry for the year 1017 AD:

"There appeared a most frightful comet for four months. **The same year it rained blood.**"

Anglo-Saxon Chronicle (DC.LXXXV):

"In this year there was **a bloody rain** in Britain and milk and butter were turned to blood."

Irish Book of Leinster (12th Century):

"**Showers of blood were poured**, and clots of gore were found."

Chronicum Scotorum (878 AD):

"It **rained a shower of blood**, which was found in lumps of gore and blood on all the plains."

Brennu-Njalssaga (Chapter 156):

"Heard a great noise, so that they all awoke and started up and got into their clothes. There with it **rained boiling-hot blood upon**

them. Then they sheltered themselves with their shields, but many were burned; that marvel lasted till broad day."

Polychronicon, by Ralph Higden (14th Century):
"In the same time there came a strange token, such as before never came, nor never hitherto since. From heaven here came a marvelous flood; **three days it rained blood**, three days and three nights. That was exceeding great harm!"

Modern Examination of Blood Rain

On November 14, 2012, a red rain was seen to fall over several provinces of Sri Lanka. About ten days before the actual rainfall, there were numerous meteor and fireball sightings in the area. Initial analysis of this rain seemed to indicate that the red color was caused by unicellular micro-organisms, presumed to be terrestrial in nature. Subsequent analysis, however, disclosed the presence of high concentrations of uranium in the outer layers of these cells. In addition, the cells lacked phosphorous in the nuclear region, which led the scientists studying them to call them "extremely unusual organisms."

In an April 2013 article in the *Journal of Cosmology* entitled *Discovery of Uranium in Outer Coat of Sri Lankan Red Rain Cells,* the authors state: "The microbial content of the red rain that fell over central Sri Lanka in November/December 2012, shows generic similarities to that of the Kerala red rain."

The Kerala red rain the author refers to was a similar event that took place in Kerala, India in May of 2001. It is estimated that during the occurrence over 50 thousand tons of red, blood-like rain fell over an area of a few thousand square kilometers. However, in this case, there was something more. The rainfall was preceded almost immediately by massive sonic booms of the kind that would be generated by a bolide or large meteor exploding in the atmosphere.

The red cells that were conveyed to Earth in the red rain of Kerala were truly extraordinary. Among their unexpected properties were not only survivability but the ability to reproduce at temperatures up to and exceeding 600 degrees Fahrenheit. In addition, the cells have a double-wall structure, which serves to protect the nucleus from damage, including from ultraviolet radiation. In other words, these cells are ideally suited to survive a journey through space and a fiery passage through Earth's atmosphere.

Patrick McCafferty, a chemical engineer and archeologist, has made an in-depth study of the red rain phenomenon throughout history. He authored an article on red rain for the *International Journal of Astrobiology* in 2008 in which he writes:

> "It was concluded that the red particles probably had an extraterrestrial origin, the result of a meteor airburst event on July 25, 2001, just hours before the red rain first started to fall. This conclusion raises the possibility that, in space, there are objects that contain red, blood-like cells. In other words, comets/meteors possibly harbor life. Such an image of a comet/meteor, containing a liquid interior teeming with red cells, is difficult to imagine and even harder to accept."

Imaginative Descriptions of Natural Phenomena?

Finding out about the mythical and scientific nature of blood rain begs the question: Is the Holy Grail actually a celestial phenomenon described in imaginative pictures or a story that is fiction? Do the myths and legends of the ancients insinuate a cosmic phenomenon brought down to earth through stories that try to explain a most mysterious cosmic occurrence? Does blood rain insinuate a golden thread running throughout all ancient myths, legends, and beliefs?

There are no simple answers to the questions above. Obviously, meteors/comets accompanied by blood rain do create a similar experience as the Grail Procession in many respects, albeit in a cosmic fashion. But we shouldn't fall prey to accepting a simple answer to a complex question. The uniting of numerous streams of mythology, folklore, legends, and ancient clairvoyant beliefs all combine to form the complex narrative of the Holy Grail and the holy blood relics of Jesus Christ. A natural phenomenon that supports and enhances the beliefs of one religion or another is quite common, but that does not dilute the truth or any expression of that truth, whether in the celestial or terrestrial domain. Truth finds its reflection everywhere in many forms and manifestations, and yet it does not change truth, nor does it make any particular description of that truth incorrect because it does not exactly match the cultural motifs used in another version of that truth. Thus, blood rain was not the sole source of the Holy Grail lore, but certainly might have affected the celestial confirmation of the earthly deeds that were the archetypal manifestations of a heavenly spear (meteor/comet) bringing forth heavenly blood raining down on the earth. The one does not preclude the other—they work together to form a complete picture of 'as above, so below.'

Sacred Places Dedicated to Archangel Michael

As we have read above, meteorites were worshiped in the past and believed to be divine gifts from heaven or even divine beings. Thus, the place where a meteorite landed was also considered holy and often a shrine or church was built in honor of the stone that fell from heaven. Christians believed in the divine nature of meteorites and attributed them to the Archangel Michael and often built a church dedicated to him at the site of the meteorite impact.

Mont-Saint-Michel

One church that was well-known as a meteorite impact site was Mont-Saint-Michel in France. In 966, the Duke of Normandy, Richard I, established a community of Benedictine monks there. They followed the Order of Saint Benedict, staying on the Mount for over eight hundred years.

By the year 1000, the fame of Mont-Saint-Michel had made it a primary destination for pilgrims. The original sanctuary was expanded by several new buildings in order to welcome the increasing number of pilgrims following the star-path of the Archangel Michael. Following the creation of the Duchy of Normandy in 911, Mont-Saint-Michel Abbey became a location of strategic importance for both the church and the military.

Sanctuary of Monte Sant'Angelo sul Gargano

The Sanctuary of Monte Sant'Angelo sul Gargano, sometimes called simply Monte Gargano, is a Catholic sanctuary on Mount Gargano, Italy, part of the commune of Monte Sant'Angelo, in the province of Foggia, northern Apulia. It is the oldest shrine in Western Europe dedicated to the Archangel Michael and has been an important pilgrimage site since the early Middle Ages. The earliest account of the foundation of the Sanctuary is a composite Latin hagiographical text known as *Liber de apparitione Sancti Michaelis in Monte Gargano*.

According to the legend, around the year 490, the Archangel Michael appeared several times to the Bishop of Sipontum near a cave in the mountains, instructing that the cave be dedicated to Christian worship and promising protection of the nearby town of Sipontum from pagan invaders. These apparitions are also the first appearances of Saint Michael in western Europe.

It is said, the first apparition manifested in 490 when a rich lord's prized bull wandered off and was later discovered kneeling at the mouth of the old Mithraeum. Unable to get the beast to leave, the man shot an arrow at it, but instead of striking the bull, the shaft turned around and wounded him. Mystified by the event, the injured man went to consult San Lorenzo, who instructed the citizens to fast and pray for three days. At the end of the third day, the Archangel Michael appeared to the Bishop and said, "I am Michael the Archangel and am always in the presence of God. I chose the cave that is sacred to me. There will be no more shedding of bull's blood. Where the rocks open widely, the sins of men may be pardoned. What is asked here in prayer will be granted. Therefore, go up to the mountain cave and dedicate it to the Christian God." Confused and doubting his faculties, San Lorenzo dismissed the vision.

Two years later, Siponto came under attack by a barbarian host. At the brink of capitulation, Saint Michael (with flaming sword in hand) again visited the Bishop, promising to break the siege and save the city if the Sipontini would take the fight to the invaders. Heartened by the news, the defenders abandoned the safety of their walls and charged their foe on the field of battle. A violent storm of hail and lightning miraculously whipped up in support and the enemy were completely routed.

Revealing himself for a third time, the Archangel Michael commanded San Lorenzo to go into the cave. Upon entering, the Bishop discovered an altar with a scarlet cloth, a cross, and a footprint in the stone, said to be Saint Michael's.

Monte Sant'Angelo was a popular pilgrimage site on the way the way to Jerusalem; pilgrims travelled from as far as the British Isles to visit the "Celestial Basilica." Among the pilgrims who visited the Saint Michael Archangel Sanctuary were many popes, emperors, kings, queens, and princes. Francis of Assisi visited the Sanctuary, but, feeling unworthy to enter the grotto, stopped in prayer and meditation at the entrance, kissed a stone, and carved on it the sign of the cross in the form.

Sacra di San Michele (Turin, Italy), Mount Pirchiriano

Roman Legions used Mount Pirchiriano as a fortress, and later the Lombards occupied the strategic outpost before Saint Giovanni Vincenzo, a hermit, was commanded by Saint Michael to build a shrine at the top of the mountain in the tenth century. Located on the terrible steep Mount Pirchiriano, the task to build a shrine so far up such a steep mountain seemed practically impossible to the Saint. By a miracle, however, all of the necessary building materials appeared precisely where the shrine stands today. Not surprisingly, the site quickly attracted pilgrims from throughout Italy and beyond who were traveling one or another star-path as a pilgrimage.

Chapter 9

Guardians of the Grail: The Michaelic Knights

The first "guardian of the grail" was a soldier named Longinus who, at first, was tasked with spying on Jesus and his disciples to find a good reason to condemn Jesus for some offense. Longinus, the Roman centurion, traveled alongside the followers of Jesus for two years, listened to what Jesus taught, and beheld many miracles and wonders. It may be hard to imagine how this "enemy" of Jesus became one of his first converts and most faithful protector and guardian of the holy blood Mysteries that were only fully understood by the Mother of Jesus. Longinus was the archetypal "Soldier of God" who devoted his life to the preservation of the Holy Blood Mysteries and the followers of Jesus Christ.

A close examination of the life of Longinus shows us that his example became the model for many saints who came after him and that his life and story are similar to many other traditions that existed at that time. His conversion from war to love and his change of heart made him one of the first to exclaim, "Surely this is the Son of God." He became the living example of the power of Christ to transform the soul and enkindle the spirit. Longinus stayed true to his calling to Jesus Christ throughout his many travels and much suffering, even until the end of his life in England. After his death, his children became leaders in the Arthurian grail Mysteries, and an entire "movement" of warrior saints and Soldiers of God developed into an entire path of grail lore described as the "quest of the holy grail."

Legend tells us that Longinus was nearly blind, and that after he thrust his spear into the side of Jesus, some of the blood and water from the wound fell into his eyes, and he was healed. He then exclaimed, "Indeed, this was the Son of God!" as recorded in *the Gospel of Mark* (15:39).

Longinus, now converted, left the army and studied under the Apostles until he ran afoul of the law because of his new faith. One story tells us that the authorities tortured him by pulling all his teeth from his mouth and cutting off his tongue, and yet he continued to speak clearly. While being tortured, Longinus picked up an axe and smashed several idols as the governor watched. The demons that had resided in the idols attacked the governor, depriving him of his sight and driving him mad. The soldiers continued to torture Longinus in every way they knew, but he would not die until after a dozen tortures, they cut off his head.

Longinus stayed true to the Mother of Jesus throughout his life and often visited her in Ephesus as he traveled throughout Cappadocia and Anatolia. He did not carry his spear with him because it reminded him of the time when he was blind to the spirit. He left the spearhead with the Mother of Jesus until she was assumed into heaven before his eyes. After that, Longinus carried the spear with him everywhere in honor of what he had witnessed. Later legends tell us that he traveled to England and established what would become the Knights of the Round Table. Longinus was the archetypal "Soldier of God" who converted to "The Way" of love taught by Jesus Christ. Longinus left his life of killing and war behind once Christ's blood touched his eyes. He could no longer harm others or fight mindlessly for the Roman Empire. Longinus fought for the ideals of the Christian family and seemed to be invulnerable and unconquerable. He became the guardian of the holy blood relics that Mary and her maidens kept and tended and protected the spear and the chalice until his death.

The path of Longinus is the basis for melding together many living imaginations of the Archangel Michael conquering the dragon. The cosmic image of the knight conquering the dragon (or beast) became mixed into the imaginations of many Christian knights who are depicted conquering a dragon; a Soldier of God fighting the devil. Often the Soldier of God is seen riding a horse and piercing a dragon with a spear. Usually, the "Michaelic Knight" is equipped with spear, sword, horse, helmet, shield, and a flame (candle) burning near his heart. The spear often transforms into a Christian banner with a cross at the top and the base holding the enemy at bay. The flaming sword is frequently drawn and held high, ready to strike but held back as a warning. The shield is often disc-shaped and quite small, like a dish or bowl. The helmet usually has a fiery plume like the descending tongues of flame of the Holy Spirit.

The Christian Soldier of God is a transformed Archangel Michael. In the stories, Michael is eventually transformed into a human being called Saint Michael who then becomes Saint George, who is part angel and part human. Saint (Archangel) Michael conquers Lucifer the dragon, whereas Saint Longinus conquers the dragon of his lower self, the war-like soldier he had been as a centurion. The path of Longinus is the same path of many seekers of the Holy Grail. The seeker starts out as a dull, unaware person who cares little for anyone but himself. The untamed soldier is a killer who is usually selfish and ignorant. Once the love of Christ fills the heart of the seeker of the grail, a new path that turns toward selflessness, kindness, compassion, and love begins. This is no easy path for the soldier of war who must conquer the lower desires of hatred, selfishness, greed, and the other deadly sins that turn him into a dragon of vile desire and a tool of war.

The Soldier of God (of Christ) needs to strike the stone of pride from the crown of selfishness and turn this stone into a vessel that can receive the descending grace and mercy of the divine. The fiery, bloody spear of war must be turned into the "lance of love and mercy" that defends the higher self of every person—especially the higher self of the Soldier of God. The sword transforms into the sword of wisdom and the spear brings love by holding back evil. The helmet can be removed to directly experience the rain of spiritual fire from the sky as the shield turns upward and becomes the bowl of mercy that catches the descending fire which feeds every need. The horse of the soldier becomes the vehicle with which to ride into the sky where the divine resides—the sky-dwellers. The earthly "soldier" of war transforms into the "maiden" of the Holy Grail—from seeker to keeper/protector. This path is sometimes depicted as the Soldier of God taming the dragon and turning the dragon's great power into a fountain of compassion, love, and mercy that the new Soldier of God, (Michaelic Knight) uses to seek, protect, and become the Holy Grail—the higher self. Taming one's lower nature is the lesson we learn from following the path of Longinus—from selfishness to selflessness.

Another tradition of the Soldier of God is that they become so impervious to pain, torture, and suffering that they can endure witnessing the flaming sword of paradise that blocks re-entry into Eden. Once the grail knight has attained the grail, death is conquered and the ability to redeem the Fall from Paradise becomes possible. One Soldier of God, known as Saint Phanorious, is depicted as a Michaelic Knight who tamed the dragon and re-enters paradise to pick an apple from the Tree of Life. Phanourios is clearly demonstrating that if you can tame your own dragon and attain the Holy Grail, you can also reclaim your divine inheritance and eat of the Tree of Life to gain immortality. This is the goal of the Michaelic Knight who turns from evil and embraces the highest elements of the quest for the Holy Grail that leads to eternal life.

Saint George Conquers the Lower Self

Another Michaelic Knight who followed the path of Longinus is Saint George (died 303) who, according to legend, was a Roman soldier of Greek origin and a member of the Praetorian Guard for Roman emperor Diocletian. He was sentenced to death for

Refusing to recant his Christian faith. He eventually became one of the more venerated saints in Christianity and was especially venerated by Crusaders, soldiers, and entire countries. As one of the Fourteen Holy Helpers and one of the most prominent military saints, England, Greece, and several other nation states, cities, professions, and organizations all claim Saint George as their patron.

The core of the legend is that George was a Roman officer of Greek descent from Cappadocia who was martyred. The legend can be traced to the fifth century and the addition of the dragon legend dates to the eleventh century. Saint George's martyrdom involved more than twenty separate tortures over seven years. Over the course of his martyrdom, it is said that 40,900 pagans were converted to Christianity.

The legend is first recorded in the eleventh century, in a Georgian source and reaches Europe in the twelfth century. *The Golden Legend* by Jacobus da Voragine gives an historicized narration of George's encounter with a dragon that was very influential in medieval romances.

Saint George is included in some Muslim texts as a prophetic figure. The Islamic sources state that he lived among a group of believers who were in direct contact with the last apostles of Jesus. Saint George may also be portrayed with Saint Demetrius, another early soldier saint. When the two saintly warriors are together and mounted upon horses, they may resemble earthly manifestations of the Archangels Michael and Gabriel. During the early second millennium, Saint George became a model of chivalry in works of literature, including medieval romances and sets the stage for the other Soldiers of God that arose from the model of Longinus.

Saint Phanourios

A perfect example of a Soldier of God who follows the story-line of Michael, Longinus, and Saint George is the mysterious and mythical Saint Phanourios. There is no literature available prior to discovering his little church in Rhodes, so not much is known about Saint Phanourios's life other than the images of his martyrdom on his icon. The main way of familiarizing oneself with the life of the saint is by studying the story of the life shown in the images on his icon.

A discovery by nomadic pagans brought to light this previously unknown saint when a roving band of Arabs uncovered, amid the ruins of an ancient church, a group of icons including one of Saint Phanourios. Drawn around the saint on his icon were twelve frames showing Phanourios enduring cruel forms of torture. Archbishop Milos of Rhodes concluded that the unblemished icon itself was testimony enough to prove that Phanourios was a man of divine grace, and he petitioned the archbishop to convene a synod which would officially proclaim Phanourios a saint, after which a cathedral which enshrined the holy icon was erected in the saint's memory.

Phanourious's Twelve Tortures

The original icon of Phanourios is quite large. In the center is a portrait of the saint holding a candle in his right hand and around this are twelve smaller images showing each stage of his martyrdom. The portrayal of each illustration is as follows:

1. The saint is standing in front of a Roman magistrate defending his Christian faith.
2. Soldiers beat the saint on the head and mouth with rocks to force him to deny his faith.
3. The saint remains patient which angers the soldiers. They are shown in this illustration, throwing him to the ground and beating him with sticks and clubs in a further attempt to force him to deny his faith.
4. The saint is now in prison. He is illustrated completely naked with the soldiers ripping his flesh apart with an iron implement.

5. The saint is still in prison. In this station, he is shown praying to God, perhaps to give him strength to endure his tortures.
6. Next, the saint is standing in front of the Roman magistrate again defending his position. The expression on the face of the saint is calm.
7. In this image, it is obvious that the Roman magistrate has sentenced the saint to the executioners for remaining unmoved. The saint is again shown naked with executioners burning his body.
8. At this station, he is tied to an apparatus that rotates to crush his bones. Though his body is truly suffering intensely for God, the look on his face is peaceful and patient.
9. His executioners watch as the Saint is thrown into a pit with wild beasts. The wild beasts circle around him as if they are lambs and share companionship with him.
10. The saint is removed from the pit to be crushed under the weight of a huge boulder.
11. The executioners now place hot coals into his palms to force the saint to sacrifice at their pagan alter. In this image, there is an image of a dragon, representing the devil, flying away, and crying at the saint's victory over this torture.
12. The final scene shows his martyrdom. He is in a large kiln, standing on a stool with flames and smoke all around him. The Saint is shown in prayer.

We can see by the story of Phanourious that death has little power over the true Soldier of God. No torture can sway the belief of the saint and he seems to have some magical powers of immortality. Perhaps it is the apple that he picked from the Tree of Life when he re-entered the Garden of Eden that gives him the strength to endure so many tortures. Death is conquered by Phanourious, and so is the devil (dragon) as he takes refuge in his Christian belief. He is truly an archetypal example of Michael gaining victory over the dragon who also suffers the terrible fate of torture that Longinus endured.

Saint Mercurius

Another Soldier of God on the Christian path of "The Way"—the quest for the holy grail—is a saint much like Saint George and Saint Phanourios. Saint Mercurius was a Christian saint and a martyr born in the city of Eskentos in Cappadocia, in the same area where Longinus, George, and Phanourios lived. Saint Mercurius is also known by the name Abu-Seifein, which in Arabic means "the holder of two swords," referring to a second sword given to him by the Archangel Michael.

The Emperor Decius began his persecution of Christians, compelling everyone to offer sacrifices to his pagan gods. The Archangel Michael appeared to Mercurius and told him to remember God and not be fearful of persecution. The Emperor tried to persuade him to give up his faith but failed. He then ordered Mercurius to be stripped of his rank and tortured. Mercurius was beheaded on December 4, 250 AD, at the age of 25 years old.

Again, with so many Soldiers of God, Mercurius was a faithful warrior who killed for his king. But when Jesus Christ became his king, he was willing to die for his beliefs. The killer becomes the killed for the sake of faithfully following "The Way" of Christ, which seems to take away any fear of death or the power it has over a non-believer. Michaelic Knights, as Soldiers of God, are willing to defend the sacred and sacrifice their lives, just as Jesus Christ did to gain eternal life. The example of Longinus was again shown in the life of Mercurius.

Saint Menas

The pattern of Roman soldiers converting to Christianity and becoming martyrs is found once again in Saint Menas (285–309), the martyr and wonder-worker. Minas was an Egyptian soldier in the Roman army who was martyred because he refused to recant his Christian faith. Menas is recognized as a minor saint in Western churches under the name of Saint Christopher, as one of the legends associated with Menas has him, like Christopher, carrying the Christ Child.

In the story of Menas, we have the warrior becoming the healer once again. This tradition of the saintly warrior-healer was replicated again and again through the lives of many Soldiers of God. Those who take lives then learn to heal lives, and by doing so gain eternal life. Once again, the seeker turns from war and becomes the loving protector and guardian of the sacred out of selflessness and pure love. This is obviously a Christian quest for the Holy Grail through the holy blood of Jesus Christ.

Saint Expeditus

There are seemingly endless examples of the pagan warrior becoming the Christian seeker who later becomes the protector and healer of the Christian blood mysteries. Another example is Saint Expeditus (died 303), who is said to have been a Roman centurion in Armenia who was martyred in what is now Turkey, for converting to Christianity.

Expeditus was born in Armenia and very little is known about his life. He was a Roman centurion in Armenia who became a Christian and was beheaded during the Diocletian Persecution in AD 303. The day he decided to become a Christian, the Devil took the form of a snake and told him to defer his conversion until the next day. Expeditus stamped on the snake and killed it, declaring, "I'll be a Christian today!"

We can see the theme of Michael putting Lucifer "under his foot" with Expeditus conquering the snake (dragon). Again, this Soldier of God is a centurion in the Roman army and is depicted with spear, sword, shield, horse, and dragon just as so many other early warrior saints. This theme is so often repeated that it is obviously describing the process of becoming a devoted Soldier of God who treads the "Way" of the holy blood mysteries of Jesus Christ, the path of Longinus.

Demetrios of Thessaloniki

Saint Demetrios of Thessaloniki was a Christian martyr of the early fourth century AD. During the Middle Ages, he came to be revered as one of the most important Orthodox military saints, often paired with Saint George. He was initially depicted in icons and mosaics as a young man in patterned robes with the distinctive tablion of the senatorial class across his chest. Miraculous military interventions were attributed to him during several attacks on Thessaloniki, and he gradually became thought of as a soldier.

The most common depiction is of Demetrius, bearded, rather older, riding a dark horse together with Saint George who is unbearded and on a white horse. Both are dressed as cavalrymen. Also, while Saint George is often shown spearing a dragon, Saint Demetrios is depicted spearing the gladiator Lyaeos, who according to the story, was responsible for killing many Christians.

The life of Demetrios shows high rank and the position of a Roman Senator converting to Christianity. This demonstrates that anyone in the Roman Empire could be spontaneously converted to Christianity. The lowly soldier, high-ranking officer, senator, or ruler could be converted to becoming a seeker of the blood mysteries of Jesus Christ. Christ was seen as the ruler of heaven and the angels who fight in the ranks of the hierarchy to defeat Lucifer, Satan, and the fallen evil ones. Calling on these Soldiers of God, who became saints, gave courage to the common soldier, and brought the support of the Archangel Michael and his host of heavenly warriors to the common believer.

The Beginning of the Soldiers of Christ

The early traditions of Longinus and Saint George started a movement of Roman soldiers converting to Christianity that became a tradition called "Miles Christianus," or the "Soldiers of Christ." The Soldier of Christ was seen as equipped with the Armor of God, including the Shield of the Trinity, and is crowned by an angel. In the other hand, the Soldier of Christ holds a list of the seven beatitudes, matched with the seven gifts of the Holy Spirit and the seven heavenly virtues, which in turn are set against the seven deadly sins.

The idea of the Soldier of Christ is a Christian allegory based on New Testament military metaphors, especially the "Armor of God" metaphor of military equipment standing for Christian virtues. By the fifth century, the Church had started to develop doctrines that allowed for Christian participation in battle, though this was limited by a requirement that the fighting must be undertaken to convert infidels or spread the glory of Christ. Christians were not to fight for conquest or personal glory.

The concept of Soldiers of Christ can be traced back to the first century AD. The phrase "Miles Christi" (Soldiers of Christ), derived from a letter from Paul the Apostle. Chivalry, as the idealized image of knighthood, was a common moral allegory in early Christian literature, whereas knighthood emerged much later as a concept during the time of Charlemagne. During the Saxon Wars, Charlemagne's Christian knights attended mass, surrounded by relics, before battles, and Charlemagne was said to possess holy blood relics of Jesus Christ. The concept of knighthood that was grounded in religion saw the nobility as defenders of the faith, which was later made even more explicit with the actual military expeditions of the crusades. The love and peace of Jesus Christ became lost as the Christian military orders started to focus Church efforts on the physical world instead of the spiritual world.

The Soldiers of God become Military Orders

The individual Soldier of God that models his life upon the that of Longinus, was that of a warrior turning into a guardian of the grail, a follower of "The Way" of Jesus Christ. Their mission was to conquer their lower selves, the dragon of evil that prevents them from finding, seeing, and serving the grail. Like Arthurian knights, they fought their battles alone and out of devotion for the grail and the Grail Maidens, the Keepers of Grail, the Maidens of Wells. There was no group experience, it was a lonely path that was different for each Soldier of God who sought to become a guardian of the grail, a protector of the Maidens of the Grail and the Grail Queen and King.

After the fifth century, the Roman Catholic Church subsumed the role of the Soldiers of God, who followed the example of Longinus and Saint George and made them into a variety of "orders" whose mission was to become literal warriors. Instead of being spiritual soldiers (conquering their lower self), these soldiers fought wars for the Church under the auspices of crusades. The example of Longinus was no longer the model for the Soldiers of God, who became warriors of the Church in military orders that were now allowed by the Church to fight and kill anyone named as an infidel.

Through the Church, monastic societies became military orders with a slight chivalric element to them that gave them the authority to fight and kill for the Church. Some western military orders were originally established as Catholic religious societies. The first orders originated during the medieval Reconquista and Crusades with the stated purpose of protecting Christians against violent persecution by Islamic conquests in Spain and the Holy Land. This impulse later evolved into the creation of a standing army that defended the Kingdom of Jerusalem for the Pope of Rome. Most members, often titled knights, were laymen, but they frequently took religious vows such as poverty, chastity, and obedience, according to monastic rules. The original features of the military orders were the combination of religious and military ways of life. Some of them, like the Knights Hospitaller and the Knights of Saint Thomas, also had charitable purposes and cared for the sick and poor. However, they were not purely male institutions, as nuns could attach themselves as convents of the orders. Prominent examples of these military orders include the Knights Hospitaller and the Knights Templar, as well as the later Teutonic Knights.

The Knights Templar, the largest and most influential of the military orders, was suppressed in the early fourteenth century; only a handful of orders were established and recognized afterwards. However, some persisted longer in their original functions, only later evolving into purely honorific and/or ceremonial chivalric orders with charitable aims in modern times, such as the Sovereign Military Order of Malta and the Order of the Holy Sepulchre, both of which are still conferred as Papal orders of knighthood.

In response to the Islamic conquests of the former Byzantine Empire, numerous Catholic military orders were set up following the First Crusade. The founding of such orders suited the Catholic Church's plan of channeling the devotion of the European nobility toward achieving the Church's temporal goals. The foundation of the Knights Templar in 1118 provided the first in a series of tightly organized military forces for the purpose of opposing Islamic conquests in the Holy Land and in the (the Reconquista) as well as Islamic invaders and pagan tribes in Eastern Europe which were perceived as threats to the Church's supremacy.

Through these truly "military" orders, the original examples of Longinus and Saint George and the other Soldiers of God were completely lost to the greed of the crusaders who became the antithesis of the path of suffering of Longinus who followed

"The Way" of Christ. Pure evil, through war and killing, transplanted the love and devotion to the holy blood relics of Jesus Christ and his teachings. The crusaders longed for the holy blood relics and agreed to return all relics to the Pope in Rome. Accordingly, the many fake relics that the Roman Catholic military orders "found" in the Holy Land now fill the churches of Europe. There are hundreds of grails and holy blood relics that are simply the confabulation of "soldiers" who desired to conquer the grail and not guard and serve it.

Spanish Soldiers of God

During the Middle Ages, there were early military orders in Spain that arose due to the confrontation between Muslims and Christians, the Reconquista. In Spain, the military orders exercised a political and economic role similar to that of a feudal manor that was defending itself from Muslim invaders. These Christian military orders were fighting for their lives on their own homeland and took on a very serious warrior-like quality. These Soldiers of God were fighting for territory and not just lofty ideals. The social implementation of the military orders within the Spanish noble families was very significant, extending through related female orders like the Comendadoras de Santiago.

The Christian Spanish military orders arose in the context of the Reconquista, the most important orders arising in the twelfth century in Leon and Castile (Order of Santiago, Order of Alcantara and Order of Calatrava) and in the fourteenth century in Aragon (Order of Montesa); preceded by many others that have not survived, such as the Aragonese Militia Christi of Alfonso of Aragon and Navarre, the Confraternity of Belchite (founded in 1122), or the Military order of Monreal (created in 1124), which became integrated into the Knights Templar after being refurbished by Alfonso VII of Leon and Castile.

Within these military orders, the master was the highest authority, with an almost absolute military, political, and religious power. The master was chosen by the council, made up of thirteen members, just as Christ and his twelve Apostles or Arthur and his twelve knights of the Round Table. The office of Master is lifelong, and on his death, the council chose the new master. In each of the various kingdoms there was a "greater commander" based in a town or fortress. The priors of each convent were elected by all the members including both knights and professed monks who taught and administering the sacraments.

After the turbulent period of the late medieval crisis, in which the position of Grand Master of the orders was the subject of violent disputes between the aristocracy, the monarchy, and the office of the "infantado" that managed to politically neutralize the military orders. The monarchy obtained the papal concession for the unification of all of the military orders. The later Spanish Catholic monarchy administered the kingdom through the Royal Council of the Military Orders. Thus, any last remnants of a pious Soldier of God that was contained in the Christian military orders dissolved into the temporal power of kings. Catholic monarchs managed to hold the mastership of all military orders in perpetuity. With their descendants, this mastership became hereditary. Thus, the line between divine and physical became blurred and turned in the opposite direction than that of the example of Longinus; the redemption of the soldier who becomes the guardian and protector of the grail.

Through the organization of Spanish military orders, that bled over into monarchical battles for control of kingdoms, the entire purpose of a Soldier of God was desecrated and turned into a mockery of the pious Christian devotion that is based upon conquering the dragon within. The battle for control of Spain mixed the prior traditions of France and England into a physical reclamation of Spain for the Roman Catholic Church and the Pope, who had become a warrior "general" with his own army. Church and chivalry mixed, and the traditions of the grail and the holy blood relics went "underground" while the physical battle for life and country went on. Fortunately, again, the female line of Grail Maidens (infantado) stepped in and protected the holy blood relics in strongholds throughout Northern Spain and the teachings of Longinus continued through the Arthurian grail traditions.

Warrior Monks Become Bankers

During the Crusades, the Templar Knights earned a reputation for bringing home treasures that had been hidden away in both Jerusalem's Temple of Solomon and Constantinople. No one denies the Templars were fierce in battle, frequently facing enemies vastly superior in size and often victorious on land and sea, and they brought back jewels, bullion, spices, and holy relics. It has been claimed that the Templars returned to France with the Ark of the Covenant, the Holy Grail, the Mandylion (which may have been the Shroud of Turin), and the skull of John the Baptist.

During the reign of the Roman Emperor Constantine, relics were moved everywhere by the Templars. Constantinople had been accumulating the relics of Christianity since Constantine's mother, Helena, traveled there after her visit to the Holy Land. The most sacred relics were protected and preserved in Constantinople from that time on, while great churches were built to house them. The management of holy relics was handled by the Templars as they protected the relics brought back from Jerusalem and the Holy Land.

It was said that over one hundred churches were destroyed, and their sacred and precious relics stolen from the fifth century to the fifteenth. The True Cross, the crown of thorns, and heads and bones of other saints were plundered. It is believed by many that the Templars brought the skull of the John the Baptist to the Cathedral of Notre Dame of Amiens along with many other holy relics. But the Templars not only got into the business of relics of all sorts, they also established fortresses throughout Europe and along the crusader/pilgrim paths to the Holy Lands. The Templars became the warrior monks who protected pilgrims but also held their gold, silver, and valuables in one of their "banks" and wrote a "note" that could be cashed at any other Templar bank. Through the Templars, who became warrior bankers, the noble example of Longinus was almost extinguished. Instead of devotion to "The Way" of the Cross and the love of Jesus, Templars became fierce warriors and powerful bankers. Their banks often became the center of what would become the cities of Europe and their power was unmatched.

The Templars spent as much time in the Middle East learning as they did fighting. Exposed to the texts and beliefs of the ancients, they brought home knowledge of science, medicine, astrology, and architecture. They were also exposed to the religions of the people among whom they lived and were the first adopters of many Eastern ideas which later were considered heresy. The King of France, Philip the Fair, lusted after the Templar riches and all but destroyed them to steal their gold. A fitting end to supposed "Soldiers of God" who seemingly became "Soldiers of Profit." Killing in the name of a Roman Catholic Pope who is also a military general is anathema to the spirit of Longinus and the teachings of "The Way."

Ancient Soldiers of God

As we have seen in the legends and stories of Longinus, many ancient traditions have been folded into the mix of what becomes Saint George and the Dragon, or Archangel Michael and Lucifer. These stories go back to the earliest times in human history and often are at the heart of the teachings of myths, religions, beliefs, legends, and fairy tales. There is an archetypal significance to the inner battle of the good warrior with his/her lower desires that must be kept at bay since this archetype can be found in almost all traditions.

The tradition of "spiritual soldiers" riding divine horses that conquer dragons is a theme found ubiquitously throughout the world. These marvelous stories of knights fighting on the side of good are found in almost every ancient tradition. The spiritual knight riding his horse with his sword and shield at his side and a magical spear in his raised hand is common. Whether archangel, deity, god, hero, or saint, the image of the rider conquering evil is an instructive motif that is similar to the Christian Soldier of God, military saint, and other Eastern gods.

In Hindu mythology, the *Rigveda*, there are divine twins named Ashwini Kumaras who are Vedic gods depicted as horsemen who ride through the sky. They symbolize the shining of sunrise and sunset and appear in the sky before the dawn in a golden chariot pulled by divine horses as they bring treasures to humans which aid in averting misfortune and sickness. They are the doctors of gods (healers) and are devas of Ayurvedic medicine who are often represented as horse-headed humans.

Another "divine rider," whose attributes were folded into the elaborations of Longinus and his miraculous life, is found in Phrygian myths. Sabazios is the sky-horseman and father-god of the Phrygians and Thracians—like the Greek Zeus. Sabazios is always on horseback, as a nomadic horseman god, wielding his characteristic spear of power.

Migrating Phrygians brought the belief in Sabazios with them when they settled in Anatolia and thus many Soldiers of God from the Christian tradition are found in Anatolia. Phrygians latter settled in Macedonia and became noted horsemen, horse-breeders, and horse-worshippers before the time of Philip II, whose name signifies "lover of horses."

The iconic image of the god or hero on horseback battling the chthonic serpent or dragon, on which his horse tramples, is also found throughout Celtic Europe. With the coming of Christianity, these Celtic ideas were quickly transformed into the image of Saint George and the Dragon, whose earliest known depictions are from tenth- and eleventh-century Cappadocia and Anatolia, the original home of the Christian Soldiers of God. Sabazios and the other horsemen (riders) prefigure Longinus, who is often seen on a horse as he spears Jesus on the cross with his upturned spear.

The Thracian Horseman (Thracian Rider or Thracian Hero) is the name given to a recurring motif of a horseman depicted in reliefs of the Hellenistic and Roman periods in the Balkans. The Thracian Horseman is depicted as a hunter on horseback, riding from left to right. Between the horse's hooves is depicted either a hunting dog, a boar, or a lion. Inscriptions found in Romania identify the horseman as Heros (also Eros, Eron, Herron). The motif of the Thracian Horseman was continued in Christianized form in the equestrian iconography of both Saint George and Saint Demetrius and the many other saints who were Soldiers of God.

These examples of divine soldiers on horseback battling with evil show that the example of Longinus is the archetypal example of self-development that turns the warrior from evil to good. On the path, divine help is given symbolically as the weapons, horses, armor, and war gear that must be stripped from the cold-hearted soldier and replaced with virtues that come from the divine, whether Jesus Christ or Vishnu. In all cases, the divine world is ready to help the "seeker" find the higher life that is found by renunciation of the worldly affairs of battling for physical, material things. It is divine intervention and transcendence of the physical that should be the focus of the spiritual warrior, the grail knight who is seeking "The Way" and ready to become a guardian and protector of the grail and not remain a warrior in the physical world.

From Warrior to Guardian

We have seen in the many stories of the Soldiers of God, from Longinus to military Pope's with their own standing armies, a transformation from the divine to the temporal. From war to peace, and then to war again seems to be the path that the Christian Soldier of God has taken within the Church itself.

The pious and devoted life of Saint Longinus is a clear example of the path of the seeker who desires to understand and serve the grail, the holy blood relics of Jesus Christ. Longinus turned from war and evil and witnessed the Son of God in Jesus and stayed true to him through trials, tortures, and suffering. He served the Christian maidens of the holy blood relics faithfully and protected them and the sacred relics. His life became an example of the path to the grail through a commitment to serve the first Grail King and Queen—Jesus and Mary. Together with Joseph of Arimathea, Longinus guarded the spear and chalice throughout the rest of his life. These devoted guardians became the source of the endless literature of grail tradition and lore that has never stopped inspiring writers.

Chapter 10

Holy Blood Mysteries

Throughout the unravelling of the holy grail stories and the Blood Mysteries of Jesus Christ, we find relics that relate to the Passion of Christ. These relics were spread throughout Christendom and ended up in places that are little known. Following the diaspora of the 72 followers of Christ, some relics ended up at Glastonbury, in the southwest region of England. It was there that the co-mingling of Christ's Blood Mysteries united with the Arthurian legends and cross-pollinating the twelfth century stories commissioned by Marie of France, Countess of Champagne, the daughter of Eleanor of Aquitaine. Marie had her court poet Chretien de Troyes invent the story of Lancelot to add to his grail legends. Chretien also wrote the unfinished poem *Perceval le Gallois*, about Perceval who became the keeper of the grail and was very important in many grail romance stories.

If we were to follow other Christian holy blood legends, we might end up in Constantinople. During the Fourth Crusade it is said that the Holy Blood of Christ made its way from Constantinople to the Basilius chapel in Bruges in 1150. This relic consists of coagulated blood kept in a twelfth century style rock-crystal flask. Since 1303, the relic has been carried around the city walls in a procession called the Holy Blood Procession, which is still celebrated today and is quite similar to the images of some Grail Processions found in grail lore.

In 1247, Westminster Abbey was presented with Christ's blood by King Henry III of England. The king had received this holy blood relic from the Masters of the Knights Templar and the patriarch of Jerusalem. The holy blood was encased in a crystal vase and is said to liquefy once a year. The Bishop of Norwich preached indulgence to anyone who venerated the relic, but unfortunately, it never made Westminster the pilgrim stop that Henry had desired. In Hailes Abbey, not too far from Westminster, larger crowds did come to see the vial of Christ's blood. King Henry was desperately trying to compete with the French king who a year later, dedicated his Sainte Chapelle with holy blood relics from the Holy Land, among them the Crown of Thorns, the Holy Lance, a portion of the sponge soaked with vinegar, purple vestments with which Jesus was mocked, and a sepulchral stone.

The phenomenon of blood and water flowing from the side of the crucified Jesus of Nazareth was considered a miracle by the church father Origen. Catholics, while accepting the biological reality of blood and water as emanating from the pierced heart and body cavity of Christ, also acknowledge the allegorical interpretation: it represents one of the main key teaching of the Church, and one of the main themes of the *Gospel of Matthew*, which is the interpretation adopted by the First Council of Nicaea, that "Jesus Christ was both true God and true man."

The blood of Jesus symbolizes his humanity, the water his divinity (the ichor of the gods). A ceremonial remembrance of this is done by a Catholic priest during Mass: Holy Eucharist/Holy Communion. The priest pours a small amount of water into the wine before the Consecration, an act which acknowledges Christ's humanity and divinity and recalls the issuance of blood and water from Christ's side on the cross. There have also been three or four major relics that are claimed to be the Holy Lance that pierced the side of Jesus and became a holy blood relic that was revered by Christians.

Blood of Christ

The "Blood of Christ" in Christian theology refers to the physical blood shed by Jesus Christ primarily on the Cross, and the salvation which Christianity teaches was accomplished thereby. The sacramental blood present in the Holy Eucharist, or Lord's Supper, is considered by Catholic, Orthodox, Anglican, and Lutheran Christians to be the same blood of Jesus of Nazareth shed on the Cross which is changed from the physical substance of wine and water into the divine blood and body of Christ. The Roman Catholic Church, Greek and Russian Orthodox Churches, Oriental Orthodox churches, the Assyrian Church of the East, and Lutherans, together with some Anglicans, believe in the "Real Presence of Christ" in the Eucharist. The Roman Catholic Church uses the term "Transubstantiation" to describe the change of the bread and wine into the body and blood of Christ.

In the early Church, the faithful received the Eucharist in the form of consecrated bread and wine. Saint Maximus explains that in the Old Law the flesh of the sacrificial victim was shared with the people, but the blood of the sacrifice was merely poured out on the altar. Under the New Law, however, Jesus's blood was the drink shared by all of Christ's faithful.

The Orthodox teach that what is received in Holy Communion is the actual resurrected body and blood of Jesus Christ. In the West, the "Words of Institution" are considered to be the moment at which the bread and wine become the body and blood of Christ. But for the Orthodox, there is no one defined moment; rather, all that Orthodox theology states is that by the end of the Epiklesis, the change has been completed.

The Orthodox also do not use the Latin theological term transubstantiation to define the conversion from bread and wine into the Body and Blood of Christ; they use the word "metaousia" without the precise theological elaboration that accompanies the term transubstantiation.

All of these current doctrines, found in major Christian religions, truly believe that the wine/blood that fills the chalice in a ritual re-enacting of Jesus Christ's Last Supper will bring them eternal life much like the Holy Grail will re-enliven the wasteland surrounding the Grail Castle. The body and blood of a God must be offered from a chalice that is filled by blood bleeding from a divine heart from above that brings eternal life.

As we can see, the Holy Eucharist of the Christians is quite similar to the basic ideas found in grail lore. In both Christian and Grail traditions, it is the blood itself overflowing the chalice that brings eternal life, spiritual nourishment, and the fulfillment of the quest for the grail. The blood (ichor) of the divine is the healing factor while the spear represents the suffering of "The Way," and the grail itself is the heart of the seeker questing for the grail.

Devotion to the Sacred Heart of Jesus

The devotion to the Sacred Heart (also known as the Most Sacred Heart of Jesus) is one of the most widely practiced and well-known Roman Catholic devotions, taking Jesus Christ's physical heart (grail) as the representation of his divine love for humanity. The devotion is especially concerned with what the Church deems to be the longsuffering love and compassion of the heart of Christ towards humanity.

The Sacred Heart is often depicted in Christian art as a flaming heart shining with divine light, pierced by the lance-wound, encircled by the crown of thorns, surmounted by a cross, and bleeding. Sometimes, the image is shown shining within the bosom of Christ with his wounded hands pointing at the heart. The wounds and crown of thorns allude to the manner of Jesus's death, while the fire represents the transformative power of divine love.

Historically, the devotion to the Sacred Heart is an outgrowth of devotion to what is believed to be Christ's sacred humanity. The revival of religious life and the zealous activity of Saint Bernard of Clairvaux and Saint Francis of Assisi in the twelfth and thirteenth centuries, together with the enthusiasm of the Crusaders returning from the Holy Land, gave rise to devotion to the Passion of Jesus Christ and particularly to practices in honor of the Five Sacred Wounds.

Devotion to the Sacred Heart developed out of the devotion to the Holy Wounds, in particular to the Sacred Wound in the side of Jesus. The first indications of devotion to the Sacred Heart are found in the eleventh and twelfth centuries in the fervent atmosphere of the Benedictine or Cistercian monasteries.

Saint Bernard (d. 1153) said that the piercing of Christ's side revealed his goodness and the charity of his heart for us. From the thirteenth to the sixteenth centuries, the devotion was propagated but it did not seem to have been embellished. It was everywhere practiced by individuals and by different religious congregations, such as the Franciscans, Dominicans, and Carthusians. Among the Franciscans, the devotion to the Sacred Heart of Jesus has its champion in Saint Bonaventure (d. 1274). In his *Mystical Vine* Saint Bonaventure wrote: "Who is there who would not love this wounded heart? Who would not love in return Him, who loves so much?"

Saint Mechtilde of Helfta (d. 1298) became an ardent devotee and promoter of Jesus's heart after it was the subject of many of her visions. The idea of hearing the heartbeat of God was very important to medieval saints who nurtured devotion to the Sacred Heart. Mechtilde reported that Jesus appeared to her in a vision and commanded her to love Him ardently, and to honor his sacred heart in the Blessed Sacrament as much as possible. He gave her his heart as a pledge of his love, as a place of refuge during her life and as her consolation at the hour of her death.

Thus, the devotion to the Sacred Heart resembles the quest for the Holy Grail in that it depicts the Holy Spirit descending into a chalice as a representation of the heart of Jesus Christ. The blood of Christ becomes the healing substance that radiates from the Christ's sacred heart—a Christian grail. The devotion of Christians to the Sacred Heart also includes reverence for the Holy Lance of Longinus.

Relics of Jesus of Nazareth

A number of relics associated with Jesus have been claimed and displayed throughout the history of Christianity. Some people believe in the authenticity of relics; others doubt the authenticity of various items. For instance, the sixteenth century Catholic theologian Erasmus wrote sarcastically about the proliferation of relics and the number of buildings that could have been constructed from the wood claimed to be from the cross used in the Crucifixion of Jesus. Similarly, while experts debate whether Christ was crucified with three or with four nails, at least thirty Holy Nails were venerated as relics across Europe in the early twentieth century.

Some relics, such as purported remnants of the Crown of Thorns, receive only a modest number of pilgrims, while others, such as the Shroud of Turin, receive millions of pilgrims. As Christian teaching generally states that Christ was assumed into heaven corporeally, there are few bodily relics, unlike with relics of saints. A notable exception, from long before the ascension, is the Holy Foreskin.

In the Christian tradition, the term "True Cross" refers to the actual cross used in the Crucifixion of Jesus. Today, many fragments of wood are claimed as True Cross relics, but it is hard to establish their authenticity. The spread of the story of the fourth century discovery of the True Cross was partly due to its inclusion in 1260 in Jacob de Voragine's very popular book *The Golden Legend*.

Tradition and legend attribute the discovery of the True Cross to Saint Helena, mother of Constantine the Great who went to Palestine during the fourth century in search of relics. Eusebius of Caesarea was the only contemporary author to write about Helena's journey in his *Life of Constantine*. But Eusebius did not mention the finding of the True Cross, although he dwelt heavily on the piety of Helena and her finding the site of the Holy Sepulchre. Texts that tell the story of the finding of the True Cross and its identification through a miracle date to the fifth century, and include writings by Socrates Scholasticus, Sozomen, and Saint Theodoret.

Pieces of the purported True Cross, including the half of the INRI inscription tablet, are preserved at the ancient basilica Santa Croce in Gerusalemme in Rome. Very small pieces or particles of the True Cross are reportedly preserved in hundreds of other churches in Europe and inside crucifixes. Their authenticity is not accepted universally by those of the Christian faith, and the accuracy of the reports surrounding the discovery of the True Cross is questioned by many Christians. The acceptance and belief of that part of the tradition that pertains to the Early Christian Church is generally restricted to the Catholic and Eastern Orthodox Churches. The medieval legends of its provenance differ between Catholic and Eastern Orthodox tradition.

A number of images reported to be of the face of Jesus or have impressions of his face or body on a piece of cloth have been written about or displayed over the centuries. The Shroud of Turin is the best-known relic of Jesus and one of the most studied artifacts in human history. Various tests have been performed on the shroud, yet both believers and skeptics continue to present arguments for and against the validity of the tests.

Sudarium of Oviedo

The Sudarium of Oviedo is a bloodstained cloth, measuring 84 × 53 cm, kept in the Camara Santa of the Cathedral of San Salvador, Oviedo, Spain. The Sudarium is claimed to be the cloth wrapped around the head of Jesus Christ after he died, as mentioned in the *Gospel of John* (20: 6-7).

The Sudarium is severely soiled and crumpled, with dark flecks that are symmetrically arranged but form no image, unlike the markings on the Shroud of Turin. However, some of those who accept the Shroud as authentic claim that many of the stains on the Sudarium match those on the head portion of the Shroud. Believers contend that both cloths covered the same man. The Image of Edessa is also known as the Mandylion. Two images claim to be the Mandylion: the Holy Face of Genoa at the Church of Saint Bartholomew of the Armenians in Genoa; and the Holy Face of San Silvestro, kept in the Church of San Silvestro in Capite in Rome up to 1870, and now in the Matilda Chapel of the Vatican Palace.

The Veil of Veronica, which according to legend was used to wipe the sweat from Jesus's brow as he carried the cross, is also said to bear the likeness of the face of Christ. Today, several images claim to be the Veil of Veronica. There is an image kept in Saint Peter's Basilica in Rome which is purported to be the same Veronica as was revered in the Middle Ages. The Hofburg Palace in Vienna has a copy of the Veronica, identified by the signature of the secretary of Pope Paul V, during whose reign a series of six meticulous copies of the veil were made in 1617.

The Legend of the Cross

One of the most notable of all blood relics is the True Cross that was used for the crucifixion of Jesus of Nazareth. The pieces of the cross are found in many churches as the holy relics that are venerated as the actual wood that was stained by the blood of Jesus Christ. The legends concerning the True Cross involve Adam and Eve's third son Seth and the way he re-entered the Garden of Eden to attain seeds from the fruit of the Tree of Life. These seeds eventually grew into a tree that became the wood used to fashion the True Cross.

The Book of the Penitence of Adam is an account of how Cain and Abel slew each other and how Adam's inheritance therefore passed to his third son, Seth. Seth was permitted to reach the gate of Earthly Paradise without being attacked by the guardian angel with his flaming sword, and beheld the Trees of Life and Knowledge, which had joined to form a single tree. The guardian angel presented him with three seeds from this tree, which he was instructed to place in Adam's mouth when he died. From these grew the burning bush that God used to talk to Moses, who made his magic wand from part of it. This wand was placed in the Ark of the Covenant and was planted by King David on Mount Zion, where it grew into a triple tree which was cut down by Solomon to construct the pillars of Jachin and Boaz at the entrance to the Temple in Jerusalem. Another portion was inserted into the threshold of the great gate and permitted no unclean thing to enter the sanctuary. It was, however, removed by some wicked priests, weighted down by stones, and thrown into the Temple reservoir, where it was hidden and guarded by an angel. During Christ's lifetime, the reservoir was drained and the piece of wood found and used as a bridge across the brook of Kedron, over which Jesus passed after his arrest on the Mount of Olives. It was then made into the cross on which he was crucified.

The legend that the cross was ultimately made from the Tree of Knowledge and the Tree of Life was common in the Middle Ages and has similarities to the Holy Grail legend. It is also found in the twelfth century *Quete del Saint Graal,* attributed to Walter Map.

The Cross and the Crucifixion, from *The Golden Legend*

Adam, feeling the end of his life was near, entreated his son Seth to make a pilgrimage to the Garden of Eden and secure from the angel on guard at the entrance the Oil of Mercy which God had promised mankind. Seth did not know the way; but his father told him it was in an eastward direction, and the path would be easy to follow, for when Adam and Eve were banished from the Garden of the Lord, upon the path which their feet had trod the grass had never grown.

Seth, following the directions of his father, discovered the Garden of Eden without difficulty. The angel who guarded the gate permitted him to enter, and in the midst of the garden Seth beheld a great tree, the branches of which reached up to heaven.

The tree was in the form of a cross and stood on the brink of a precipice that led downward into the depths of hell. Among the roots of the tree, he saw the body of his brother Cain, held prisoner by the entwining limbs.

The angel refused to give Seth the Oil of Mercy but presented him instead with three seeds from the Tree of Life. With these Seth returned to his father, who was so overjoyed that he did not desire to live longer. Three days later he died, and the three seeds were placed in his mouth, as the angel had instructed. The seeds became a sapling with three trunks in one, which absorbed into itself the blood of Adam, so that the life of Adam was in the tree. Noah dug up this tree by the roots and took it with him into the Ark. After the waters subsided, he buried the skull of Adam under Mount Calvary, and planted the tree on the summit of Mount Lebanon.

Moses beheld a visionary being in the midst of this tree (the burning bush) and from it cut the magical rod with which he was able to bring water out of a stone. But because he failed to call upon the Lord the second time he struck the rock, he was not permitted to carry the sacred staff into the Promised Land, so he planted it in the hills of Moab. After much searching, King David discovered the tree. His son, Solomon, tried to use it for a pillar in his Temple, but his carpenters could not cut it so that it would fit; it was always either too long or too short. At last, frustrated, they cast it aside and used it for a bridge to connect Jerusalem with the surrounding hills. When the Queen of Sheba came to visit King Solomon, she was expected to walk across this bridge. Instead, when she beheld the tree, she refused to put her foot upon it, but, after kneeling and praying, removed her sandals and forded the stream. This so impressed King Solomon that he ordered the log to be overlaid with gold and placed above the door of his Temple. There it remained until his covetous grandson stole the gold and buried the tree so that the crime would not be discovered.

From the ground where the tree was buried there immediately bubbled forth a spring of water, which became known as Bethesda. To it, the sick from all Syria came to be healed. The angel of the pool became the guardian of the tree, and it remained undisturbed for many years. Eventually, the log floated to the surface and was used as a bridge again, this time between Calvary and Jerusalem; and over it Jesus passed to be crucified. There was no wood on Calvary, so the tree was cut into two parts to serve as the cross upon which the Son of Man was crucified. The cross was set up at the very spot where the skull of Adam had been buried. Later, when the cross was discovered by the Empress Helena, the wood was found to be of four different varieties contained in one tree, and thereafter the cross continued to heal all the sick who were permitted to touch it.

Pagan Solar Deities and Crucifixion

Dozens of "saviors" have died for the sins of humanity by the hands of man, and through their deaths have interceded in heaven for the souls of their executioners whether by crucifixion, torture, beheading or many other cruel methods of death. The martyrdom of the God-Man and the redemption of the world through his blood has been an essential tenet of many great religions. Nearly all these stories can be traced to sun worship, for the glorious orb of day is the solar savior who dies annually for every creature within his universe, but year after year rises again victorious from the tomb of winter. The doctrine of the crucifixion is based upon the secret traditions of the ancient wisdom; it is a constant reminder that the divine nature of humanity is perpetually crucified upon the cross of the world. Some of the pagan Mysteries included in the ceremony of initiation a ritual crucifixion of the candidate upon a cross, or the laying of his body upon a cruciform altar later to be buried and then raised from the dead.

The list of the deathless mortals who suffered for man that he might receive the boon of eternal life is an imposing one. Among those connected historically or allegorically with a crucifixion are Prometheus, Adonis, Apollo, Arys, Bacchus, Buddha, Christna,

Horus, Indra, Ixion, Mithras, Odin, Osiris, Pythagoras, Quetzalcoatl, Semiramis, and Jupiter. According to the fragmentary accounts that exist, all these heroes gave their lives to the service of humanity and, with one or two exceptions, died as martyrs for the cause of human progress. Most of them were crucified upon a cross or tree. The first friend of man, the immortal Prometheus, was crucified on the pinnacle of Mount Caucasus, and a vulture ate his liver to torment him throughout eternity as it grew back the next day. Prometheus disobeyed the edict of Zeus by bringing fire and immortality to man; so, for humanity, he suffered until the coming of Hercules released him from his ages of torment.

Solar deities often bring the redemption of humanity with the personal sacrifice of their life. The cross of crucifixion is also seen as the World Tree that encompasses all of creation. The Norse Father God Odin pierced his own side and hung himself upon the World Tree Yggdrasil in service to humanity. These types of sacrifice often include the idea that a solar deity must incarnate in a human body so that the sacrifice of that divine life brings the possibility that humanity can then reunite with the divine and regain paradise. The solar deity takes on the cruelest of deaths and often is depicted wearing a crown of some sort to denote that the deity is being mocked as a god who can suffer the death of a human being.

Crown of Thorns

The relics of the passion of Jesus Christ presented at Notre-Dame de Paris include a piece of the True Cross which had been kept in Rome by Saint Helena, the mother of Emperor Constantine, who also had a nail from the crucifixion and the Crown of Thorns. Despite numerous studies and historical and scientific research efforts, the Crown of Thorns' authenticity cannot be certified. It has been the object of more than sixteen centuries of fervent Christian prayer and devotion. Saint John tells that in the night between Maundy Thursday and Good Friday, Roman soldiers mocked Christ and his sovereignty by placing a thorny crown on his head (*Gospel of John* 19:12).

The crown housed in the Paris cathedral is a circle of canes bundled together and held by gold threads. The thorns were attached to this braided circle. The thorns were divided up over the centuries by the Byzantine emperors and the Kings of France. There are seventy of these thorns that are all quite similar.

The accounts of fourth century pilgrims to Jerusalem allude to the Crown of Thorns and the instruments of the Passion of Christ. In 409, Saint Paulinus of Nola mentions it as being one of the relics kept in the basilica on Mount Zion in Jerusalem. In 570, Anthony the Martyr found it exhibited for veneration in the Basilica of Zion. Around 575, Cassiodorus, in his *Exposition on the 75th Psalm*, exclaimed, "Jerusalem has the Column, here, there is the Crown of Thorns!" In 870, once again in Jerusalem, Bernard the Monk noted it as well. Between the seventh and the tenth centuries, the relics were moved progressively to the Byzantine emperors' chapel in Constantinople, mainly to keep them safe from pillaging. In 1238, Byzantium was governed by the Latin Emperor Baldwin II of Constantinople who, due to great financial difficulty, decided to pawn the relics to a Venetian bank to get credit. Saint Louis, the king of France, took over the debt and paid back the Venetians. On August tenth, 1239, the king, followed by a grand procession, welcomed twenty-nine relics in Villeneuve-l'Archeveque. On August 19, 1239, the procession arrived in Paris; the king took off his royal garments and, wearing only a simple tunic and with bare feet, took the Crown of Thorns to Notre-Dame de Paris before placing the relics in the palace chapel. He built a reliquary worthy of housing these relics, the Sainte-Chapelle.

Bodily Relics

Christian teachings generally state that Christ ascended into heaven corporeally. Therefore, the only parts of his body available for veneration (by relics) are parts he had lost prior to the Ascension. At various points in history, a number of churches in Europe have claimed to possess the Holy Prepuce, Jesus's foreskin from the circumcision, sometimes at the same time. A section of the Holy Umbilical Cord believed to remain from the birth of Christ is currently in the Archbasilica of Saint John Lateran.

Saint Paul's Monastery on Mount Athos claims to have relics of the Gifts of the Magi, while Dubrovnik's Cathedral in Croatia, lays claim to the swaddling clothes the baby Jesus wore during the presentation at the Temple. The knife that was claimed to have been used by Jesus during the Last Supper was also a matter of veneration in the Middle Ages, according to the twelfth century *Guide for Pilgrims to Santiago de Compostela*. According to French traveler Jules-Leonard Belin, the knife used by Jesus to slice bread was permanently exhibited in the Logetta of Saint Mark's Campanile in Venice.

Holy Chalice (Holy Grail)

The holy chalice is the chalice or vessel which Jesus used at the Last Supper to serve the wine, as described in the *Gospel of Matthew* (26:27–28) which states: "Drink from it, all of you. This is my blood of the covenant, which is poured out for many for the forgiveness of sins."

A number of holy chalices have been reported and also given rise to legends of the Holy Grail, which are not part of Catholic tradition. Of the existing chalices, only the holy chalice of the Cathedral of Valencia is recognized as an "historical relic" by the Vatican, although not as the actual chalice used at the Last Supper. Although both Pope John Paul II and Pope Benedict XVI have venerated the chalice at the Cathedral of Valencia, neither has formally pronounced it as authentic.

A large number of other relics of Jesus continue to be displayed throughout the world. A good number of these relics involve the journey of Saint Helena, the mother of Constantine the

Great, to Syria Palaestina in the fourth century to gather relics. The authenticity of many of these relics is in question.

Very little reliance can be placed upon the authenticity of the thirty or more holy nails that are still venerated in such treasuries as that of Santa Croce in Rome, or those of Venice, Aachen, Escurial, Nuremberg, Prague, and so on. Probably the majority began by professing to be facsimiles which had touched the original or contained filings from some other nail whose claim was more ancient.

Similarly, a large number of churches claim to have relics of the Crown of Thorns which was placed upon the head of Jesus by the soldiers prior to the Crucifixion. The Scala Sancta, the stairs from Pontius Pilate's praetorium, ascended by Jesus during his trial were also reportedly brought to Rome by Saint Helena of Constantinople in the fourth century. The Basilica of the Holy Blood in Bruges, Belgium, claims a specimen of Christ's blood in a phial along with a cloth with His blood on it which was brought to the city by Thierry of Alsace after the twelfth century.

Other claimed relics, based on the Crucifixion of Christ include:

- The Holy Coat is the seamless garment of Christ (*John 19:23*) for which the soldiers cast lots at the Crucifixion. It is claimed by the cathedral of Trier, Germany, and by the parish church of Argenteuil, France. The Argenteuil tradition claims that the garment venerated in that city as the Holy Coat was brought there by Charlemagne.

- The Calvary of Crucifixion is a small group of rocks called Golgotha that is found in the Church of the Holy Sepulchre in Jerusalem. Inside the church is a pile of rocks about twenty-three feet by ten feet, which is believed to be what is now visible of Calvary.

- The Iron Crown of Lombardy and Bridle of Constantine are said to be made from nails used during the Crucifixion.

- The Holy Lance was the spear of Longinus used to pierce Jesus's side when he was on the cross.
- The Holy Sponge is in Santa Croce in Gerusalemme.
- The Column of the Flagellation of Jesus is kept in the Basilica of Saint Praxedes in Rome.

Probably the most common relics of the holy blood are the many "grails" that claim to be the vessel used at the Last Supper. What this vessel represents has come to be a complex set of traditions both Christian and pagan. No two versions of the grail tell the same story. Much of what is known about grail lore comes from many different versions of the story and therefore, the authenticity of any vessel claiming to be the grail must be carefully examined.

The Holy Grail has been described as a chalice, dish, plate, bowl, platter, stone, or cup around which light shines and nourishment flows. A grail, wondrous but not explicitly "holy," first appears in European writings in *Perceval le Gallois*, an unfinished romance by Chretien de Troyes. It was seen as a processional salver (bowl or platter) used to serve food at a feast, which was also accompanied by a spearhead that bleeds into one of the salvers. Chretien's grail romance story attracted many authors who continued and elaborated his writings. There were many translations and interpreters of his stories in the later twelfth and early thirteenth centuries, including Wolfram von Eschenbach, who describes the grail as a precious stone that fell from the sky. These new grail legends, stories, and practices became interwoven with prior pagan myths, legends, and beliefs of a wondrous chalice or caldron, often accompanied by a magic spear.

The connection of the grail with Joseph of Arimathea and the Bowl of Solomon (emerald cup of King Tyre) which was claimed to have been used both at the Last Supper and Crucifixion of Jesus, dates from Robert de Boron's story *Joseph d'Arimathie* (late twelfth century). In the story, Joseph, while imprisoned, receives the Last Supper chalice from an apparition of Jesus and then subsequently sends it with his followers to Glastonbury in Great Britain where he had frequently traveled as a tin trader. Building upon this theme, later writers recounted how Joseph used the chalice/holy grail to "catch" Christ's blood while cleaning his body after the Crucifixion. Eventually, Joseph founded a line of guardians of the Holy Grail to keep it safe in Britain. The heroes of the Arthurian Round Table were direct descendants of Joseph and Longinus, the protectors of the spear and chalice. The legends that ensued from the works of Robert de Boron combined the Christian Holy Blood Mysteries with Celtic myths about cauldrons endowed with special powers to feed the righteous and resurrect the dead.

The word grail, in its earliest spelling, comes from the Old French word *graal* or *greal*, and meant "a cup or bowl of earth, wood, or metal." The most commonly accepted root of the word derives from the Latin word gradalis, which refers to a two-handed shallow cup. The Latin gradus means by degree or by stages, which usually is applied to a dish of food brought to the table in different stages during a meal. The grail is associated with a graded procession (path or way) to attain the nourishment needed to gain wisdom and spiritual insight connected to becoming the Grail King or Grail Queen. Each seeker of the grail on the quest must first understand what the grail is, and then gain the wisdom of "whom the grail serves." These are stages—gradalis—on the quest for the grail.

In *Parzival*, Wolfram von Eschenbach, citing the authority of a certain Kyot of Provencal, claimed the grail was a stone (called Lapis Exillis) that fell from heaven. He writes that the grail was kept safe at the castle of Munsalvaesche, entrusted to Titurel, the first Grail King. Some have identified the grail castle of Titurel with Montserrat in Catalonia, Spain. Other stories claim that the Holy Grail is buried beneath Rosslyn Chapel or hidden inside of the Apprentice Pillar, or that it lies deep in the spring of Chalice Well near Glastonbury Tor.

The earliest record of a chalice from the Last Supper is the account of Arculf, a seventh century Anglo-Saxon pilgrim, who described it in *De Locis Sanctis* as located in a reliquary in a chapel near Jerusalem, between the Basilica of Golgotha and the Martyrium. He described it as a two-handled silver chalice. Arculf reached through an opening of the lid of the reliquary to touch the chalice. He said that the people of the city flocked to it with great veneration. Arculf also saw the Holy Lance of Longinus in the porch of the Basilica of Constantine. These historical references are the only mention of the holy chalice of the Last Supper being situated in the Holy Land.

One of the oldest chalices revered by the Roman Catholic Church is an agate cup in the Cathedral of Valencia. It is preserved in a chapel consecrated to it, where it still attracts the faithful on pilgrimage. It is a hemispherical cup made of dark red agate that is mounted by means of a knobbed stem and two curved handles onto a base made from an inverted cup of chalcedony.

The cup was produced in a Palestinian or Egyptian workshop between the fourth century BC and the first century AD. The first explicit inventory reference to the present Chalice of Valencia dates from 1134, an inventory of the treasury of the monastery of San Juan de la Pena drawn up by Don Carreras Ramirez, Canon of Zaragoza, in 1134. The chalice is described as the vessel in which "Christ Our Lord consecrated his blood."

The Antioch Chalice

The Antioch Chalice was apparently made at Antioch in the early sixth century and is of double-cup construction, with an outer shell of cast-metal open work enclosing a plain silver inner cup. When it was first recovered in Antioch it was touted as the Holy Chalice.

The silver-gilt object originally identified as an early Christian chalice is now in the collection of the Metropolitan Museum of Art in New York City.

Chalice of Dona Urraca

The Chalice of Dona Urraca is a jewel-encrusted onyx chalice which is alleged to be the Holy Grail, the cup from which Jesus drank and served Holy Communion at the Last Supper. It belonged to Urraca of Zamora, daughter of Ferdinand I of Leon. The chalice is kept at the Basilica of San Isidoro in Leon, Spain, where historians say it has been since the eleventh century.

The origins of the chalice are not known, so the provenance begins when the chalice was transported to Cairo by Muslim travelers and was later given to an emir on the Spanish coast who had assisted victims of a famine in Egypt. From there, the chalice came into the possession of King Ferdinand I of Leon, father of Urraca of Zamora, as a peace offering by an Andalusian ruler. Dating suggests the chalice was made between 200 BC and 100 AD.

Urraca of Zamora (1033–1101) was a Leonese infantada, one of the five children of Ferdinand I the Great, who received the city of Zamora as her inheritance and exercised palatine authority in it. Her story was romanticized in *The Chronicle of the Cid*.

In her later years, Urraca gradually gave up her governing duties, retiring to a monastery in Leon, where she died in 1101. She is interred in the Chapel of the Kings at the Basilica of San Isidoro of Leon, along with her siblings Elvira and Garcia. Her chalice remains on display for pilgrims to worship.

The Mystery of the Passover Cup

Cup symbolism in the Jewish Old Testament is much like the stories of the grail wherein a chalice is incorporated into a ritual involving wine and bread. In the Christian *New Testament*, the only biblical mention of a cup is in connection with Passover when Jesus celebrated this feast with His disciples. He raised a cup at least twice during the meal to make important statements about Himself that can be found in *Luke* 22:17–20:

And he took the cup, and gave thanks, and said, "Take this, and divide it among
yourselves: For I say unto you, I will not drink of the fruit of the vine, until the kingdom of God shall come."
And he took bread, and gave thanks, and brake it, and gave it unto them, saying, "This is my body which is given for you: do this in remembrance of me."
Likewise also, the cup after supper, saying, "This cup is the new testament in my blood, which is shed for you."

Throughout the Hebrew scriptures, the cup is often used as a symbol of God's judgment. For example, the cup of fury, the cup of judgment, the cup of trembling, and the cup of horror and desolation appear throughout the *Old Testament*. Yet we also find the Psalmist crying out, "I will take up the cup of salvation, and call upon the name of the Lord" (*Psalm* 116:13). So, the symbol of the cup for the Hebrew people carries with it pictures of both wrath and redemption, of judgment and blessing. None of these references mentions the Passover. Yet, the themes of judgment and salvation are woven together beautifully in the Passover story. God poured out His judgment on the Egyptians but spared the Israelites who obeyed Him by placing the blood of a lamb on the doorposts of their homes. Each year, Jewish families retell these events through the Seder, the ceremonial meal that commemorates Passover.

How the cup became a Jewish Passover symbol remains a mystery. We do know that by the time Jesus observed the Passover, drinking a cup during the meal was an official part of the observance. An ancient rabbinic source, the *Mishnah*, instructs those celebrating to drink from the cup four times during the Passover Seder (*Pesahim* 10:1). That tradition remains to this day.

Each time the cup is filled, it has a different name, and opinions vary as to what certain cups symbolize. Most agree that the first cup is the Kiddush, which means sanctification. With this cup, we begin the Passover Seder. The second cup is called the cup of plagues. The third cup is referred to as either the cup of redemption or the cup of blessing. The fourth cup is often called *hallel*, which means praise, though some traditions call it the cup of acceptance, while still others use it as the cup of Elijah. The latter combine the second cup (plagues) with *hallel*—because Jews praise God for the plagues He used to bring them out of Egypt. Jewish tradition says little else about the cups—though we're told they should be filled with red wine to remind us of the blood of the Passover lamb.

The *New Testament* names one of the cups—the cup taken after supper, which is traditionally the third cup. Jesus calls this cup "the new covenant in My blood, which is shed for you" (*Luke* 22:20). The Apostle Paul calls it, "the cup of blessing which we bless," as well as "the cup of the Lord" (*1 Corinthians* 10:16-21).

Both Jesus and Paul draw on something from Jewish tradition to provide insights not previously understood. By calling the cup "the new covenant in my blood," Jesus makes a direct reference to the promise of *Jeremiah* 31. God had declared that He would make a new covenant because the previous covenant had become "broken" (*Jeremiah* 31:32). To violate a covenant agreement with God would surely incur His wrath and judgment—a terrible cup. But instead, God promised a new covenant of grace and salvation.

Jesus declared that this new covenant would be poured from the cup of salvation in His blood. The cup of redemption stood for more than the Hebrews' escape from Egypt; it stood for the plan and purpose of God for all the ages. Judgment and salvation, wrath and redemption are brought together in the mystery of one cup, explained by the Messiah in the upper room. Jesus was not speaking of the cup in a purely symbolic manner. He was describing events that would soon occur in His own life.

Later that evening in the garden of Gethsemane, Jesus cried out to the Lord in anguished prayer, "Father, if it is Your will, take this cup away from Me; nevertheless, not My will but Yours, be done" (*Luke* 22:42). In His humanity, Jesus could wish that this cup of judgment—the one that everyone except Him deserved for breaking God's covenant—would pass over Him. Yet, as the obedient Son of God, Jesus knew that the cup of blessing could only be poured out for the salvation of many if He would first drink the cup of God's judgment on all humanity.

Despite the agony of separation from the Father, Jesus was willing to drink this cup, to bear this judgment, to suffer this horror and death that we might be free and forgiven. In calling this new covenant the cup of blessing, as it was known in the Jewish Passover, the Apostle Paul points out the powerful connection between Passover and the ritual of the Last Supper. This cup embodies the problem of judgment as well as the promise of redemption and can be seen as a direct corollary to the Holy Grail.

The Holy Nails

According to tradition, when Saint Helena found the True Cross of Christ, she also found the nails of the Crucifixion, some say three and others say four. From the thirteenth century onwards in Italian iconography, we see the feet of Christ pierced by a single nail, while in other parts of Europe, the idea of four nails lasted much longer. Gregory of Tours (sixth century) tells us that Empress Helena, in the crossing from Jerusalem to Rome, to calm a dangerous storm threw one of the nails into the sea. According to Socrates Scholasticus and Sozomeno (fifth century), Helena had one of these nails embedded in the bridal bite of Constantine's horse and another in his helmet (or crown) for protection.

The Holy Nail of Milan, also called Sacro Morso, is a kind of bridle that has at one end a ring attached to another larger ring. It is formed by two other elements: a curved iron in the shape of a U with two rings at the ends and a sort of coiled wire. It is suspended at forty-two meters above the main altar of the Milan Cathedral, enclosed in a large cross.

Tradition attributes the arrival of this relic to the fourth century as a gift from Emperor Theodosius to Saint Ambrose, then bishop of Milan. Milan, at that time, was the administrative capital of the Western Roman Empire. It is difficult to determine whether the relic present in the Cathedral and venerated as the Holy Nail is the same that Saint Ambrose spoke of in his speech at the funeral of Emperor Theodosius in 395.

The Nail of Carpentras

In Carpentras, near Avignon, the Nail of Carpentras is revered in the treasury of Saint Siffrein Cathedral. This relic was brought from Carpentras to Constantinople by Pope Virgil (537–555) as a gift to the Emperor Justinian. The relic remained in Constantinople until the end of the Fourth Crusade, in 1204, when it was brought to Rome.

When Clement V, in 1309, moved the papal seat to Avignon, he took the Holy Nail with him. The relic was immediately taken to Carpentras to be protected from all subsequent riots and schisms. Nicholas V (1447–1455), the first Roman Pope elected after reconciliation, declared it authentic.

Carpentras' Nail is completely different from that of Milan. It is a bridle like that used by the Romans. The inside is seventeen centimeters long and is made up of two hooked pieces. The nail is the symbol of the city and is present in all the coats of arms. In 1720, Provence was hit by a plague epidemic that miraculously did not affect Carpentras. This miracle was attributed to the fact that the city was protected by the sacred bridal bite stored there.

Iron Crown of Lombardy

The Iron Crown of Lombardy is both a reliquary and one of the oldest royal insignias of Christendom. It was made in the Early Middle Ages, consisting of a circlet of gold and jewels fitted around a central silver band, which tradition holds to be made of iron beaten out of a nail of the True Cross. The crown became one of the symbols of the Kingdom of the Lombards and later of the medieval Kingdom of Italy. It is kept in the Cathedral of Monza, outside Milan. Thirty-four coronations with the Iron Crown were counted by the historian Bartolomeo Zucchi from the ninth to the seventeenth century (beginning with Charlemagne).

The Iron Crown was believed to contain a centimeter-wide band of iron within it, said to be beaten out of a nail used at the crucifixion of Jesus. According to tradition, Saint Helena, mother of Constantine the Great, had the crown forged for her son around a beaten nail from the True Cross which she had discovered. Pope Gregory the Great passed this crown to Theodelinda, princess of the Lombards, as a diplomatic gift. Theodelinda donated the crown to the church at Monza in 628.

In some accounts, the crown was used in Charlemagne's coronation as King of the Lombards. Contemporary accounts of the initiations of the earlier kings of the Lombards stress the importance of the king holding the Holy Lance while wearing the Iron Crown.

The crown was in use for the coronation of the kings of Italy since at least the eleventh century. Old research dates the crown to the eighth or early ninth century, but according to a recent study, the crown in its current state is the result of two different works made between the fourth and ninth century. This seems to validate the legends about the origin of the crown that date it back to the Lombard era and the coronation of their kings.

Chapter 11

The Search for the True Holy Lance

The spear of the Archangel Michael has many pre-Christian corollaries found throughout myths, legends, and cultural beliefs from around the world. We intend to demonstrate in this chapter that the idea of the "heavenly spear" is a tradition that is widely known and was folded into the holy blood mysteries of the early Christians and their reverence for relics. The importance of the spear that "pierced the side of Christ" is little understood, and elements of the story appear throughout Christian legends that have been mixed with pre-Christian Holy Grail lore. It becomes quite confusing when one tries to sort out what elements arose from what traditions. An amalgamation of these traditions is found when we study the nature of the spear and the chalice that were intimately connected to the holy blood relics of Jesus of Nazareth.

There are many claims throughout European Christian churches to being the authentic keeper of the "original" chalice that Jesus used at the Last Supper. It is quite confusing and difficult to ascertain the truth about which of these chalices might be the original. Historical records meld into a mush of indistinct claims that make it even harder to figure out if there is an original chalice of Jesus.

Another of the important holy blood relics is the spear of Gaius Cassius Longinus, the Roman Centurion who pierced the side of Christ with his Roman *hasta* (thrusting spear). This spear has become as crucial a component of the quest for the grail as the Holy Grail chalice itself. The Irish and Celtic myths concerning the grail usually have a spear that is part of the story, and the Procession of the Grail includes a spear dripping blood into a grail (bowl or platter). So too, without the spear of the centurion Longinus, the Crucifixion could not have been completed. Longinus's spear was guided by the Archangel Michael, according to many traditions, to carefully strike the heart that would bleed for the world.

Just as there has been a long tradition of seeking the Holy Grail, so too, many have sought the Holy Spear of Longinus that was directed by the love and mercy of Archangel Michael. The search for the spear, often called the "Spear of Destiny," has been as impassioned as the quest for the grail. The spear and the chalice go together just like Longinus (spear) and Joseph of Arimathea (chalice) worked together for the rest of their lives establishing the grail mysteries of King Arthur at Glastonbury.

We intend in this chapter to take all of the diverse versions of the Spear of Longinus and put them into a timeline to see the patterns of this holy blood relic as it traveled throughout history. We will also trace stories of "heavenly spears" from many myths and religious beliefs to demonstrate the common thread that weaves throughout. We are most especially concerned with trying to find whatever provenance (chain of custody) of the Spear of Longinus that might exist, even if the information is derived from legends, Church histories, local tales, and other existing sources. We have yet to find a simple, consistent provenance of the Spear of Longinus, but we can find circumstantial evidence about those who guarded this holy spear.

Just as the Maidens of the Wells of Europe were the keepers of the springs and provided a "golden bowl" (grail) to travelers to dip water from the well, so too the Maidens of the Holy Lance of Love (Spear of Longinus) guarded and protected the Spear of

Longinus (and other holy blood relics of Jesus) in a long line of what we call Grail Queens; indeed, many of them were literally queens. This "order" of Maidens of the Wells, Grail Maidens, and Grail Queens served the grail and continued the tradition of the Grail Procession which provided food and drink for questers who found the Grail Castle. In most traditions, the bleeding tip of the spear dripping into the chalice was seen as integral to the complete story of the Holy Grail. Of course, it is well known that it was not the spear nor the chalice that were the key to the mystery—it was the holy blood they both had touched that made them sacred.

Tracing the Spear of Longinus through history is difficult at best. Much of what is known about the spear is speculative, contradictory, and often spurious. The traditions point out multiple spears that existed at the same time and often they were not similar and after closer examination were found to be "frauds." There are also multiple well-known copies of these spears that still exist. Different stories tell that the spear was owned by Longinus, Maurice, Constantine, and many others. Some spears have staffs while others are just the spearhead. Numerous spearheads have been broken over time. The Spear of Antioch was found in 1099 AD after supposedly being buried for centuries. Thus, no one knows for sure if and where the true spear of Longinus resides. Speculation about these ideas have inspired many books and movies, and yet the answers remain hidden.

We will follow, in our version of the story, the history of all of the spears that we can find in Christian tradition as we focus our search for the history and provenance of the Spear of Longinus. In the end, you the reader will have to decide which stories seem the most reasonable to you if you wish to construct a true and rightful history of the Spear of Longinus, the Holy Lance of Love.

We are told about the Spear of Longinus (Lance of Love) in the *Gospel of John* 19:31–37 in the following words:

> The Jewish leaders didn't want the victims hanging there the next day, which was the Sabbath,

> So, the soldiers came and broke the legs of the two men crucified with Jesus.
>
> But when they came to Jesus, they saw that he was dead already, so they didn't break his legs.
>
> One of the soldiers, however, pierced his side with a spear, and blood and water flowed out.
>
> This report is from an eyewitness giving an accurate account; it is presented so that you also can believe.
>
> These things happened in fulfillment of the Scriptures that say, "Not one of his bones will be broken," and "They will look on him whom they pierced."

The quotation above demonstrates that the early Christian community at Jerusalem understood the fact that Jesus's bones had not been broken as being further proof that he really was who he said he was—the Messiah predicted by the *Old Testament* prophets.

Victims of crucifixion could suffer in agony on the cross for several days. The dying process could be shortened by breaking the victim's legs so that the victim could no longer push up with their feet for gasps of air. The thieves on both sides of Jesus had their legs broken, but when the Roman soldiers reached Jesus, one of them—reportedly a centurion named Gaius Cassius Longinus—saw he was already dead and proved it to his fellows by using his spear to pierce Christ's side. Blood and water poured out, so there was no need to break his bones.

The Jews carried before them their "spear of authority" called the Spear of Phinehas, which was described in detail in the *Old Testament*. The legends about the Jewish Spear of Phinehas and its history are wrapped in mythology, symbols, and imaginative stories.

Phinehas was the grandson of Aaron, guardian of the Ark of the Covenant, who provided continuity all the way back to the Garden of Eden through ownership of the spear. It was said that a heavenly "flaming spear" guarded the Tree of Life. This spear was given to Seth who passed it down through the guardians of the Hebrew Holy of Holies. The Spear of Phinehas was also believed to be the same spear that Saul, in his madness, hurled at King David. Later, according to some versions of the story, the Spear of Phinehas was used by Longinus to pierce the side of Jesus Christ hanging on the "new Tree of Life," releasing the blood (and water) which filled the chalice held by Joseph of Arimathea. This tradition is a combination of the Hebrew and Christian traditions that have been woven together to garner authority and prestige for one or the other side of the story.

The simpler reality is that both stories are true, as we will demonstrate later in this chapter by giving a different version of the events that fit numerous traditions.

The Spear of Longinus itself became a highly revered religious relic to the Christians and therefore the likelihood that the Spear of Longinus and the Spear of Phinehas are the same is very slim. Even though the Spear of Phinehas was never heard about in Jewish history after that point, it seems to vanish after the Crucifixion.

Another tradition says that the Spear of Longinus was unearthed by Helena, the Mother of Constantine, at the same time and place as the Holy Nails and the True Cross that were used in the Crucifixion. Some stories tell that Constantine carried the Spear of Longinus into battle and used one of the holy nails as a bridle bit for his horse and put the other nail in his helmet.

Still another version of the "lore of the spear" has the Spear of Longinus being found by Raymond, the leader of the First Crusade, in Saint Peter's Church at Antioch and was used to lead the crusaders to victory in Jerusalem. This Spear of Longinus, the Holy Lance of Antioch, was supposedly lost after the battle of Ascalon but was actually spirited away one year later by Elvira of Castile to France, and then later to Spain to be guarded by the Queens of the Grail.

Another claimant to being the authentic Spear of Longinus is the Lance of Maurice, a Roman Catholic Church creation from the eighth century that was given to the Kings of France by the Pope and has been handed down ever since and now resides in the Hapsburg reliquary in Vienna. This lance is the most well-known of the spearheads alleging to be the Spear of Longinus, but it is a manufactured relic that may have one of the Holy Nails incorporated into it. At least two copies of this spearhead are currently in European treasuries.

Some people claim that the first Christians (Chaldeans) possessed the Spear of Longinus. They called it the Echmiadzin Spear and it is still displayed to this day in their central cathedral in Armenia. The style and age of this spearhead are not correct to be a good candidate to be the actual Spear of Longinus, but many still believe it is authentic.

There are other spearheads that claim to be the authentic Spear of Longinus that are easy to rule out simply because of their design, let alone the scientific dating of these spearheads. So far, only one spearhead meets the generally accepted characteristics of the Spear of Longinus: a first century Roman hasta spear, possibly made in Palestine, possibly hardened with meteorite, revered and protected for centuries, and possessing special powers to heal or give the owner victory in battle. The spears we present below are claimants to the title of the true Spear of Longinus. It has been demonstrated that these spearheads shown below are not likely the true spear that pierced the side of Christ.

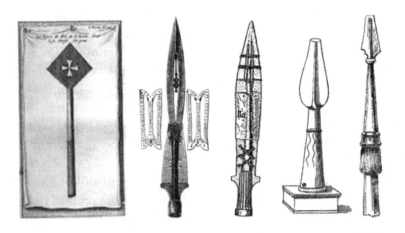

Various Spearheads Alleged to be the "True" Spear of Longinus

The true provenance of the Spear of Longinus became hidden in history and many stories abound about who had it and where it was kept. One spear that was alleged to be the Spear of Longinus was taken from the hands of Saint Maurice, commander of the Theban Legion, as he was dying by the hands of Emperor Maximian in 302 AD in Valais, Switzerland. Maurice had been given this spearhead by his father, who was also a Roman centurion. It is this spearhead that was given to the Kings of France in 717 AD, as a gift from the pope. The "Lance of Saint Maurice" has been dated to that very year.

Accompanying the Lance of Maurice in the Schatzkammer is a beautiful "holy grail" that dates back to the third century. With most spearheads claimed to be the Spear of Longinus you will usually find a stone chalice or bowl that is also claimed to be the authentic chalice used by Jesus: the Holy Grail.

The Spear of Longinus is also known as the Lance of Saint Maurice, the Spear of Phinehas, the Holy Lance of Love, the Holy Lance of Antioch, and the Spear of Destiny, among other names. Whether it was a weapon forged by ancient Hebrews and passed down over the centuries and kept protected in the Holy of Holies in the Temple in Jerusalem, or whether it was a Roman centurion's hasta that was handed down from father to son as a "victory spear," the power and mystery of this holy blood relic stirs the imagination and is the cause of great wonder and much speculation.

According to the *Gospel of John* (19:31–37), as Jesus hung on the cross, a Roman centurion pierced his side with a spear. Blood and water spurted forth from the wound. The mixture splattered in Longinus's eyes, restoring his vision, which had been failing. It was then that he exclaimed, "Indeed, this was the Son of God!" as recorded in *Mark* 15:39. Great miracles happened that day that made the "blind" Longinus able to see both physically and spiritually.

The circumstances surrounding Jesus's Crucifixion had such a profound effect on Longinus that he later sought out the Apostles so he could learn from them as a convert to the teachings of Jesus Christ. In one version of his legendary life, he moved to Caesarea in Cappadocia and became a monk, where he was eventually condemned to death and tortured many times for being a Christian. The spear itself became a holy blood relic protected by the Apostles and kept by the Three Marys, along with the other blood relics that had been given to the Mother of Jesus.

Over the centuries, an object claiming to be Longinus's spearhead has passed through the hands of some of Europe's most influential leaders. This relic of the Passion of Jesus Christ has been written about for nearly two thousand years. A legend arose that "whosoever possesses this Holy Spear and understands the powers it serves, holds in their hands the destiny of the world for good or evil."

Much of what follows is an attempt to track the Spear of Longinus through legend, myth, religious belief, and the stories that accompany the holy blood relics of the Passion of Jesus of Nazareth. Few of the stories are provable and are based upon traditions that have been handed down for centuries. Putting all the versions together in a timeline can help develop a broad perspective as we examine the many possible paths of the grail, whether cup or spear.

Legendary Pathways of the Heavenly Spear

Among those who are alleged to have possessed the Spear or Sword of Tubal-Cain/Phinehas at one time or another in the Hebrew lineage are:

Tubal-Cain, the son of Cain, (3000 BC) was told by God to forge a spear and a sword from a meteorite and hide them for use by a later generation "when they would be needed." When the sword and spear were held by the same person, they were invincible. This was the beginning of the Hebrew legend that ultimately became the Spear of Phinehas which was kept in the Holy of Holies of the Temple in Jerusalem during the Crucifixion of Jesus and was brought out to the Mount of Calvary at the time of the death of Jesus on the cross.

Phinehas was a priest during the Exodus journey who was the grandson of Aaron and son of Eleazar, the High Priests (*Exodus* 6:25). He distinguished himself as a youth at Shittim with his zeal against the Heresy of Peor. He was displeased with the immorality with which the Moabites and Midianites had successfully tempted the Israelites (*Numbers* 25:1-9) to intermarry and to worship Baal-peor, so he personally executed an Israelite man and a Midianite woman while they were together in the man's tent, running the Spear of Tubal Cain through the man and the woman and bringing to an end the plague sent by God to punish the Israelites for sexually intermingling with the Midianites. This "Spear of Phinehas" had been separated from the sword that Tubal Cain had forged at the same time. It was foretold that the spear and sword must never be separated, or else evil would possess both. Thus, evil followed both the spear and sword as they were used for wickedness and war. They were coveted for their power and often were used as a rally banner during battles. The Spear of Phinehas was kept in the Holy of Holies along with the Ark of the Covenant to protect it and to be used as a symbol of authority and strength when needed.

Ehud, the Son of Gera, defeated the King of Moab with Tubal-Cain's sword in *Judges* 12:30. Again, separating the sword and spear led to evil, battles, death, and continued wars. The prophecy was broken because kings wanted to conquer their enemies and needed the power of these two "heavenly" weapons that were turned to the dark tasks of evil, death, and war.

Ahab was the seventh king of Israel and the husband of Jezebel of Sidon who was given the sword of Tubal-Cain. The Old Testament presents Ahab as a wicked king who followed the ways of his wife Jezebel, killing his subject Naboth and leading the nation of Israel into idolatry. Of King Ahab, it is recorded that he "did more evil in the eyes of the Lord than any of those before him" (*1 Kings* 16:30). Thus, the tradition of doom that follows separating the spear and sword continued with Ahab, whose evil became legendary.

Jehu functioned as a commander in the army of Ahab before he himself became king (*2 Kings* 9:5–25) in the northern kingdom of Israel. Jehu was the son of Jehoshaphat, whose job it was to obliterate the house of Ahab along with the worship of Baal that pervaded Israel at the time. "Jehu will put to death any who escape the sword of Hazael, and Elisha will put to death any who escape the sword of Jehu (Tubal-Cain)" (*1 Kings* 19:15–17). Jehu slaughtered all the priests of Baal and destroyed the temple and its sacred stone, thus eradicating Baal worship in Israel (*2 Kings* 10:23–28).

Joshua was told by the Lord in *Joshua* 8:18–26, "stretch out the spear [of Tubal-Cain/Phinehas] that is in thy hand toward Ai, for I will give it into thine hand. And Joshua stretched out the spear that he had in his hand toward the city. For Joshua drew not his hand back, wherewith he stretched out the spear, until he had utterly destroyed all the inhabitants of Ai." Thus, the power of the spear seems to have magical forces that can sway the course of a battle for the one who possesses the Spear of Phinehas/Tubal-Cain.

King Saul and David both were said to have possessed the Spear of Phinehas as we read in *1 Samuel* 26:

> So David and Abishai came to the people by night: and, behold, Saul lay sleeping within the trench, and his spear [of Tubal-Cain/Phinehas] stuck in the ground at his bolster.
> David said, "The Lord forbid that I should stretch forth mine hand against the Lord's anointed: but, I pray thee, take thou now the spear that is at his bolster, and the cruse of water, and let us go."
> So, David took the spear and the cruse of water from Saul's bolster; and they got them away, and no man saw it, nor knew it, neither awaked: for they were all asleep; because a deep sleep

from the Lord was fallen upon them. Then David went over to the other side and stood on the top of a hill afar off; a great space being between them: and David cried to the people, "now see where the king's spear is, and the cruse of water that was at his bolster."

Then said Saul, "I have sinned: return, my son David: for I will no more do thee harm, because my soul was precious in thine eyes this day: behold, I have played the fool, and have erred exceedingly. And David answered and said, Behold the king's spear!"

Roman Victory Spears—Centurion Hasta

The traditions of Roman centurions handing down a Roman hasta from father to son is quite common with soldiers who converted to Christianity. Longinus was said to have received his centurion's hasta from his father, who had received it as a reward for his faithful service to Rome as a "victory spear." The centurion Roman hasta was a thrusting spear with a staff about as long as the soldier was tall, much shorter than the common soldier's staff. Centurions usually were mounted on horses and thus could not carry a long staff. The "nova magnum" aspect of a Roman hasta denoted that the bronze spearhead had been tempered with the substances found in meteorites, which was commonly used to strengthen spearheads forged in first century Palestine. These rare metals, minerals, and substances in the meteorite were able to temper the bronze into a metal as hard as steel. This extreme hardness made the spearhead much more valuable and useful, and the mysterious meteorite substance added to the mystery of the spearhead being "divine," or sent from "heaven," from whence meteorites come. Because these spearheads were extremely hardened and lasted a long period of time, they were passed down from soldier to soldier as a most valuable treasure.

The tradition of giving and receiving ritual spears and swords in the Roman army was a high honor that went right up to the generals and the Caesars. These spears and swords were considered sacred and were passed down from warrior to warrior, often from father to son. Some spears and swords possessed by Caesars were said to have come from the god Mars, Mercury or other great heroes like Theseus and Peleus. These "divine" weapons were treated with the greatest honor while much pomp and ceremony surrounded their public display. The hasta of the centurion was not so much a weapon as it was a sign of authority and respect for the office and the "divine" power of Rome. These traditions were amalgamated into the legends of Saint Longinus, as well as the fact that Longinus was a living example of these Roman traditions of respect for a "divine" spear handed down to him from his father, who was also a Roman centurion.

Among those who are alleged to have possessed a "divine" spear" at one time or another in the Roman lineage are:

Pompey had a famous victory spear that was considered sacred. The ancient Roman tradition used by the Caesars was that the ruler should fashion his own spear after a great victory and consecrate it in the temple dedicated to Mars. It was also common that those who were distinguished in war were rewarded by their superiors with a spear as an honor, a "victory spear." Pompey's victory spear was held on display in the Temple of Mars and was taken down when used in battle. Pompey's victory spear was passed down from Caesar to Caesar as a coveted prize. The belief in the power of the victory spear to bring success in battle was attributed to the intervention of the god Mars who "possessed" the victory spear while the spear was held aloft by the owner. Thus, the victory spear became the rallying point for battles, and great reverence and awe accompanied the worship of these sacred weapons.

Gaius Cassius Longinus, the Roman Centurion who pierced the side of Jesus, received his Roman centurion hasta spear from his father, who received it from his father. It was said that Julius Caesar gave an honorary spear to the grandfather of Gaius Cassius Longinus for his bravery and courage in the Gallic Wars. This spear was said to have been handed down to his son who then handed it down to Longinus, his grandson, who was the centurion at the Crucifixion. This victory spear then became known as the Spear of Longinus.

Herod the Great (King of Judea, ruled 37–4 BC) was said to have possessed the Spear of Longinus after the crucifixion and passed it down to others who brought it to Rome, where it was displayed in the Temple of Mars. There is an alternative story that says that an alleged Spear of Longinus ended up in Rome that was found by Helena in Jerusalem. Yet another alleged Spear of Longinus was found by the Templars and displayed in Jerusalem in the Church of the Holy Sepulchre for hundreds of years off and on. The alleged Spear of Longinus was seen by and reported on by many pilgrims to Jerusalem.

Queen Boadicea, in approximately 60 AD, took the spear from Longinus and Joseph of Arimathea in Glastonbury, England, and locked them and their companions in Thetford Castle, Suffolk, as she conducted many successful battles holding the Spear of Longinus as the rally banner. When she was finished conquering the Romans in London, she returned the spear to Longinus and released the captives from Thetford Castle. Longinus and Joseph returned to Glastonbury with the spear and the chalice and continued their work to spread the teachings of Jesus.

Maurice, a Roman centurion, received a victory spear from his father, who is said to have received it from high-ranking Romans—presumably the Romans who passed the Spear of Longinus down from Herod to Rome. Maurice was said to have held onto this "possible" Spear of Longinus until his death in 302 AD. Maurice died a martyr to keep the Spear of Longinus from the Emperor Maximianus, who Maurice did not want to have the power that came with the spear. He, and the entire Roman Theben Legion were martyred in this cause as they refused to surrender the Spear of Longinus to Maxinianus. It is this Spear of Longinus—the Lance of Saint Maurice—that was supposedly in the hands of the pope when he gave it to the Frankish kings in

717 AD. This Lance of Saint Maurice was created by the Vatican and has been tested and proven not to have come from the first century. Ostensibly, the Vatican justified their provenance of the Spear of Longinus as coming through the hands of the Roman Caesars, to Saint Maurice, to the Roman Catholic Church.

Maximianus Herculius left Rome for Gaul in 307 AD, where he married his daughter Fausta to Constantine in a bid for his aid. The Lance of Saint Maurice, which Maximianus received after the slaughter the Theban Legion, was given to Constantine as part of Fausta's dowry. Again, this is one version of how Constantine came into the possession of the Spear of Longinus. Other accounts have his mother Helena bringing it first to Rome and then later to Constantinople. Numerous accounts of travelers witnessed the alleged Spear of Longinus both in Rome and Constantinople. Accounts describe Constantine using the Spear of Longinus in processions in the Hagia Sophia and in battles.

Constantine (288–337) was the first Christian emperor who used the spear to gain many victories. It was his mother, Helena, who discovered the True Cross and Holy Nails as well as the Spear of Longinus in Jerusalem and brought them back to Rome and then subsequently Constantinople. Helena had a Holy Nail added to the spearhead and another to the helmet that Constantine wore into battle. The third holy nail of Constantine was fashioned into the bridle bite of his horse. History records that Constantine carried the Spear of Longinus into victory at the battle of Milvian Bridge, and while surveying the layout of his new city, Constantinople. Eusebius of Caesarea, who became a spiritual advisor to Constantine, witnessed the Spear of Longinus during the height of Constantine's power in the fourth century:

> "It was a long spear, overlaid with gold. On the top was fixed a wreath of gold and precious stones, and within this the symbol of the savior's name, two letters indicating the name of Christ by means of its initial characters—those letters the emperor was in the habit of wearing on his helmet at a later period. From the

spear was also suspended a cloth, a royal piece, covered with a profuse embroidery of most brilliant precious stones and which, being also richly interlaced with gold, presented an indescribable degree of beauty to the beholder. The emperor constantly made use of this sign of salvation as a safeguard against every adverse and hostile power and commanded that it should be carried at the head of all his armies."

Constantine was in possession of the Spear of Longinus in Constantinople for many years but eventually needed money and pawned the head of the spear to a Sultan for a time. Constantine redeemed it later and sent it to Saint Louis IX of France, who made a beautiful reliquary for it and displayed it prominently.

Julian the Apostate (322–363), the nephew of Constantine, sought to restore the empire to paganism and was assassinated with the spear by Saint Mercury. This story can be seen as a metaphor for the Spear of Longinus being a spiritual weapon of great power that was necessary to slay the emperor who abolished the Roman belief in Christianity. Only a spiritual weapon as strong as the Spear of Longinus could conquer the person who ended Christian supremacy throughout the Roman Empire. The Spear of Longinus is sometimes used as a symbol instead of a physical reality, as it was in the case of Julian.

Theodosius the Great, Emperor of the East (379), was well aware of the Spear of Longinus and its long history in Constantinople and Rome. He returned the Roman Empire to Christianity after Julian had outlawed it. In 381, at the Council of Constantinople, Theodosius had the Spear of Longinus visible at his side, and later he carried the spear into battle in the Alps in 394.

Emperor Titus received the treasures of Jerusalem in Rome in 71 AD, and they subsequently fell into the hands of Alaric in 410, when Rome was sacked by the Visigoths. In this version of the provenance, instead of the Roman Spear of Longinus coming into the hands of Caesars or Maurice the centurion, the spear stayed in Rome in the Temple of Mars until the conquerors sacked Rome and carried off the greatest of the victory spears that had belonged to Helena. This great prize of war was held in the highest esteem by Alaric.

Alaric the Visigoth became king after Theodosius in 395 AD. Alaric sacked Rome in 410 and reportedly sat upon the throne of the emperor with the Spear of Longinus proudly displayed in his hands. Alaric was said to have both taken the Spear of Longinus back to France and subsequently England, or to have passed it down to the next Roman ruler.

Emperor Justinian I and Empress Theodora (482–565) regarded the spear as their most valued possession with Justinian saying that the Spear of Longinus spoke to him and told him to suppress paganism. The spear was said to have been displayed both at the Hagia Sophia in Constantinople and the Golden Basilica in Antioch during the reign of Justinian and Theodora.

Christian History and Sightings of the Spear of Longinus

As we have seen with the history of the various spears claiming to be the Spear of Longinus in the timeline above, there are many stories and little proof to construct a clear provenance of the spear that pierced the side of Christ. Church histories lead us in many directions, and we cannot count on the stories of the Romans because they have been conflated with Roman victory spears. The desperate desire of kings to have the power of the "Spear of Destiny" drove them to fight over the spear and make numerous copies of the spear as doubles to throw off the attempts to steal it. Some rulers were so obsessed with the spear that they kept it with them always and believed that if they let go of the spear, even for a moment, they might lose their power and even die. This type of obsession is clearly the result of selfish desire and not the divine mercy and love that the spear was noted to possess. The Spear of Longinus healed the world by letting

Christ's blood enter into the earth and sanctify the future of the planet. Personal desire and greed have no place with the true Spear of Longinus.

Throughout church history, we have many claims of people who said they encountered the spear in a variety of places. These claims are found in historical works, ecclesiastical writings, works of art, local legends, church histories, and oral traditions. These witnesses may be describing one of the many copies of the Spear of Longinus, or perhaps they are describing the real Spear of Longinus. At this point on the trail of the provenance of the Spear of Longinus, history becomes mythology and holy blood relics become very popular as replicas grew in number.

We will now add a list of encounters with spears claiming to be the authentic Spear of Longinus to our timeline. These events are presented here to give a full picture of what a researcher of the Spear of Longinus will encounter. Discernment and discretions are needed to sort out what is true and what are hopeful claims.

Among those who are alleged to have encountered or possessed the Spear of Longinus at one time or another are:

Attila the Hun was said to have stopped his invasion before the gates of Rome in 434 AD, when Pope Leo I bought him off with a vast treasure trove that included the Spear of Longinus. It is said that Attila rejected the spear, saying that it was of no use to him because he didn't believe in Jesus.

Saint Antoninus of Piancenza in 570 AD, while describing the holy places of Jerusalem, tells us that he saw in the basilica of Mount Sion "the crown of thorns with which Our Lord was crowned and the spear with which He was struck in the side."

M. de Mely in his book *Exuviae* (III, 32), mentions the Spear of Longinus at the church of the Holy Sepulchre in the so-called Breviarus. And again, in a miniature of the famous Syriac manuscript in the Laurentian Library at Florence (586) the opening of Christ's side is given a prominence which is highly significant.

The name "Longinus" is written in Greek characters above the head of the soldier who is thrusting his spear into the side of Jesus. This shows that the legend of the spear is as old as the sixth century.

Cassiodorus in 621 AD and Gregory of Tours in 712 AD venerated a spear in Jerusalem believed to be identical with that which pierced the savior's body.

Nicetas brought an alleged spear of Longinus to Constantinople from Persia. In 615 AD, Jerusalem was captured by a lieutenant of the Persian King Chosroes, and the sacred relics of the Passion of Christ fell into the hands of the pagans. According to the *Chronicon Paschale*, the point of the spear was broken off and given in the same year to Nicetas, who took it to Constantinople and deposited it in the church of Saint Sophia.

Arculpus in 670 AD, saw the second and larger portion of the Spear of Longinus in Jerusalem and venerated it in the church of the Holy Sepulchre.

Saint Willibald came to Jerusalem in 715 AD and did not find the Spear of Longinus on display. He believed that the larger relic, as well as the point, had been conveyed to Constantinople. The spear's presence in Constantinople seems to be clearly attested by many pilgrims, and, though it was deposited in various churches in succession, it seems possible to trace the spearhead and distinguish it from the companion relic of the point of the spearhead.

Charles Martel (Frankish ruler and grandfather of Charlemagne, 688–741 AD) used the Spear of Longinus to stem the Arab invasion at the battle of Poitiers in 732.

Charlemagne the Great (Carolingian King of France, Emperor of the West, 771–814 AD) carried the Spear of Longinus through 47 victorious battles and conquered Spain as far south as the Ebro. Charlemagne replaced the Merovingian Empire, who used a Tribal Spear as their symbol, with his own Carolingian Dynasty that used the Holy Spear of Longinus as their symbol. Charlemagne was said to have carried the Spear of Longinus with him everywhere.

Heinrich I inherited the Spear of Longinus through the lineage of the German kings. In the early 900s, the Spear of Longinus came into the possession of the Saxon Dynasty of Germany, passing eventually to Heinrich I (Duke of Saxony, Saxon King of Germany, ruled 919-936). The Spear of Longinus was present at Heinrich's victorious battle against the Magyars.

Rudolf II, King of Burgundy, was given the spear in 921-922 AD by Count Samson of Northern Italy in return for driving the armies of Berengar out of his lands. Rudolf then exchanged the spear with Henry I of Germany in return for the city of Basel and the southwest corner of the German Reich.

Heinrich I (Henry I) sent the Spear to the English king Athelstan, who annihilated the armies of the Norsemen and their allies at the battle of Brunanburh in 937 AD. Athelstan sealed his alliance with Germany by giving his sister, Edith, in marriage to Henry's son and successor Otto I, who reigned from 936 to 973. The Spear of Longinus went with her as part of her dowry, and from that time on it has remained a treasure of the Germanic people.

Otto the Great, Saxon King of Germany and Holy Roman Emperor, ruled from 936-973 AD, was the son of Heinrich I and the heir to the Spear of Longinus. Pope John XII used the spear to christen him Holy Roman Emperor in 936. Otto went on to carry the spear into victory over the Mongols in the Battle of Leck, and in 955, when he crushed the invading Hungarians who were besieging Augsburg. It was placed on a podium in the cathedral of Madgeburg in 968.

Otto II (Saxon King of Germany, Holy Roman Emperor, ruled 973-983 AD) inherited the spear from his father. The Spear of

Longinus was used by the Holy Roman Emperors from Otto I on and was a part of their imperial insignia and regalia, which eventually found its way to Vienna, Austria.

Otto III in 996 AD (Saxon King of Germany, Holy Roman Emperor, ruled 983–1002), had the spear borne in front of him when he journeyed to Rome to be crowned Holy Roman Emperor. From then on, the Spear of Longinus played a decreasing role in military history, although it was always carefully preserved from the hands of invaders.

Henry II, "the Saint" (Saxon King of Germany, Holy Roman Emperor, ruled 1002–1024 AD), received the Spear of Longinus from Otto III and cherished it as a holy relic rather than a banner of war.

Henry IV (German Holy Roman Emperor) **and Empress Ann**, his mother, were known to possess the spear in 1070 AD. In 1084, Henry IV added the silver band that bears the inscription "Nail of Our Lord" to the spear. The spear was used in his 1084 coronation in Rome. Henry gave the Spear of Longinus to his daughter Agnes, who married Frederick I (Barbarossa) as the spear passed into the Hohenstaufen family.

Pope Innocent III doubted Henry IV's spear's authenticity, as *Burchard's Diary* demonstrates, because of the rival spears known to be preserved at Nuremberg, Paris, and other places. Due to the discovery of the "Holy Lance of Antioch" by the revelation of Saint Andrew in 1098, during the First Crusade, the doubts grew greater. This new Holy Lance of Antioch was buried for many years and only discovered in a church in Antioch through a revelation. The Holy Lance of Antioch was then used by Raymond IV, the leader of the First Crusade, as a rally banner to lead the crusaders to conquer Jerusalem. Subsequently, after the battle of Ascalon, the Holy Lance of Antioch was supposedly lost.

Raynaldi, the Bollandists, and many other authorities believed that the spear found in 1098 afterwards fell into the hands of the

Turks and was the spear sent by Bajazet to Pope Innocent. From M. de Mely's investigations, it is speculated that it is identical to the relic now jealously preserved at Eschmiadzin in Armenia. This was never in any proper sense a spear (centurion hasta), but rather the head of a standard, and it was venerated independently in Armenia by Chaldean Christians. The Spearhead of Eschmiadzin is generally not believed to be the same as the Holy Lance of Antioch, which was a first-century Roman centurion hasta.

Frederick Barbarossa (House of Hohenstaufen, Holy Roman Emperor ruled 1152–1190 AD), displayed the spear in 1177 in Venice while acknowledging the papacy of Alexander III. Barbarossa died from drowning within minutes after accidentally dropping the Spear of Longinus into a stream while he was bringing the Spear of Longinus to the Third Crusade. It is because of stories like this that the legend of the "Spear of Destiny" was believed by so many rulers.

Henry VI (King of Germany, Holy Roman Emperor, ruled 1190–1197) possessed the Spear of Longinus but used it seldom.

Otto IV (Holy Roman Emperor, ruled 1198–1218) believed that the Spear of Longinus was magical, as well as powerful, claiming that it could heal the sick.

Frederick II (King of Germany, Holy Roman Emperor, ruled 1218–1250) possessed the Spear of Longinus and claimed that it helped him conquer Jerusalem, Italy, and Sicily.

Krakow, Poland has a purported Spear of Longinus since at least the 1200s. German records indicate that the spear was a copy made from the German spear possessed by Henry II, with a small sliver of the original spearhead embedded in the copy. Another similar copy was given to the Hungarian king at the same time.

Saint Louis received the point of the spear set in an icon from Baldwin sometime after 1244 AD. Saint Louis enshrined the point of the Spear of Longinus with the Crown of Thorns in the church of Sainte Chapelle. During the French Revolution, these relics were removed to the Bibliotheque Nationale. Although the Crown has been preserved, the other parts of the icon, including the point of the spear, disappeared.

King Charles IV of Bohemia had a golden sleeve put over the silver sleeve and inscribed it with the phrase, "Lance and Nail of the Lord" in 1350 AD, after supposedly retrieving the Spear of Longinus from a Cistercian monastery in the Tyrol Mountains.

Sir John Mandeville declared in 1357 that he had seen the blade of the Spear of Longinus both at Paris and at Constantinople, and that the latter was a much larger relic than the former.

Sigismund was made Holy Roman Emperor in 1411 AD. In 1424, he announced: "It is the Will of God that the Imperial Crown, Orb, Scepter, Crosses, Sword, and Lance of the Holy Roman Empire must never leave the soil of the Fatherland." This treasury of relics, known collectively as the Reichkleinodien or Imperial Regalia, was moved from his capital in Prague to his birthplace, Nuremberg.

Sultan Bajazet was in possession of the "Constantinople Spear" (Spear of Longinus) in 1492 AD, as described in *Pastor's History of the Popes*. Sultan Bajazet sent it to Innocent VIII to conciliate his favor towards the sultan's brother Zizim, who was then the Pope's prisoner. This relic is in Rome where it is preserved under the dome of Saint Peter's Cathedral.

The Imperial Regalia, including the Spear of Longinus, spent the years from 1424–1796 AD in Nurnberg where the spear was publicly displayed each Easter until 1523.

Sultan Mohammed II possessed the larger part of the broken Spear of Longinus that had remained in Constantinople until the fall of the city in 1453 AD. His son, Bajazet, gave it to the Grand Master of the Templar Knights in exchange for certain favors.

The Grand Master, in turn, gave it to the pope. It was received with rejoicing in Rome in 1492 and placed in Saint Peter's.

Nuremburg, Vienna, Ofen, and Temesvort held the Spear of Longinus during the Napoleonic Wars (1796). The Spear of Longinus's second sojourn in Nurnberg was from 1938–46, owing much to the desire of Hitler and his circle to possess it.

Benedict XIV, in his book *De Beatitudes* (IV, ii, 31), states that he obtained from Paris an exact drawing of the point of the lance, and that in comparing it with the larger relic in Saint Peter's, he was satisfied that the two had originally formed one blade. In 1904, M. Mely published an accurate design of the Roman relic of the lance head for the first time, and the fact that it has lost its point is conspicuous.

Nuremberg Fortress held the Spear of Longinus when the army of Napoleon Bonaparte approached Nuremberg in the spring of 1796. Many were terrified that Napoleon would seize the Spear of Longinus (Spear of Destiny) and rule the world with it. The city councilors decided to remove the Imperial Regalia to Vienna for safe keeping. The collection of relics was entrusted to the Imperial Regalia Elector, Baron von Hugel, who promised to return the objects as soon as peace had been restored and the safety of the collection assured. The Holy Roman Empire was officially dissolved in 1806. Baron von Hugel took advantage of the confusion over who was the legal owner of the Imperial Regalia and sold the entire collection, including the Spear of Maurice (Spear of Longinus? Holy Lance of Antioch?), to the Habsburgs. Baron von Hugel's crime did not come to light until after Napoleon's defeat at Waterloo. When the city councilors of Nuremberg asked for their treasures back, the Austrian authorities' response was a sharp rejection.

Kaiser Wilhelm II, in the early twentieth century, had the Spear of Longinus in his possession for a brief time. It eventually ending up in the Hofsburg Treasure House in Vienna where it is on display to this day.

Baron von Hugel had the Imperial Regalia in his possession and he promised to return the objects as soon as peace had been restored and the safety of the collection assured. However, the Holy Roman Empire was disbanded in 1806 and the Reichskleinodien remained in the keeping of the Hapsburgs after Baron von Hugel sold it to the Hapsburg family. When the city councilors of Nuremberg asked for the Reichskleinodien back, they were refused. As part of the Imperial Regalia, it was kept in the Imperial Treasury and was known as the "Lance of Saint Maurice." During the Anschluss, when Austria was annexed to Germany, the Imperial Regalia was returned to Nuremberg and afterwards hidden. The Imperial Regalia was found by invading American troops and returned to Austria by American General George Patton after World War II.

Baron von Hugel was born Johann Aloys Josef Freiherr (Baron) von Hugel on November 14, 1754 in Koblenz (then the Electorate of Trier). He made a rapid career in the State Service of Trier, rising from a low-ranking Justice Official up to a Government Chancellor. In March of 1794, he was accepted and given a high rank at the Austrian Imperial (Holy Roman Empire) service. In 1802, he was appointed Austrian minister responsible for the Holy Roman Imperial affairs. In the same year, he was sent to Munich, then appointed envoy at the Court of Elector and Imperial Archchancellor Karl von Dalberg. In 1804, at the age of 51, he served as the Austrian Imperial Envoy at the Reichstag (Imperial Assembly) of Regensburg and received the Grand Cross of Saint Stephen in 1803. In 1806, he came to Vienna, where he served until 1810, until he was transferred as Envoy to Dalberg. He then served as Austrian Envoy in Hesse—Darmstadt and Nassau, then (from 1813)—as Civil Governor of Frankfurt. After Prince Metternich became the Austrian Chancellor (1821), von Hugel handed in his resignation. He died in 1826 in Regensburg.

Dr. Robert Feather, an English metallurgist and technical engineering writer, tested the Spear of Maurice, found in the

Imperial Regalia for a documentary in January 2003. He was given unprecedented permission not only to examine the spear in a laboratory environment but also to remove the bands of gold and silver that hold it together. In the opinion of Dr. Feather and other academic experts, the likeliest date of the spearhead is the eighth century AD—only slightly earlier than the museum's own estimate.

The Incongruent Provenance of the Spear of Longinus

As we have seen with the timeline of the provenance of the Spear of Longinus, it is next to impossible to ascertain whether the four or five known "Spears of Longinus" are real or just copies of the true holy blood relic that Longinus used on Calvary. Scientific dating of the known claimants to being the actual Spear of Longinus has not found a spearhead from the first century (or before) that fits the description. In fact, there are very few authentic first century Roman centurion hastas left anywhere, even in museums. To find a well-preserved spearhead that fits the description of the Spear of Longinus is nearly unheard of and certainly would arouse attention from the many people searching for the alleged "Spear of Destiny" (Spear of Longinus) because of the legends of its great power.

Thus, there is little satisfaction chasing the provenance of the Spear of Longinus because it leads down many roads to many claimants but not to a spearhead that meets the description necessary to be the genuine Spear of Longinus. The greatly revered church relics that claim to be the authentic spear are no less amazing and worthy of respect and devotion as a representative of the authentic powers of the Spear of Longinus. Temporal powers wanted the true spear but were willing to put their faith in what they had, even if it was a known copy. The belief in second-degree relics is seen by many to embody the "look-alike" with the same magical powers of the original.

But there is still the case of the Holy Lance of Antioch that was found in the Church of Saint Peter at Antioch in 1098 AD by Raymond IV, the leader of the First Crusade. This spear/lance was reported lost and never recovered again. Of course, the likelihood of such a relic being "lost" is highly doubtful. Therefore, there might be one candidate that fits the description of the Spear of Longinus in history that could have gone underground (literally) and been hidden and preserved. That spear is the Holy Lance of Antioch.

The Lance of Antioch

Another story about a holy blood spear that might be the Spear of Longinus was about a spear found in Antioch, where it was allegedly unearthed by a Crusader named Peter Bartholomew in 1098 AD while the Crusaders were under siege from the Seljuk Turks. Peter Bartholomew reported that he had a vision in which Saint Andrew told him that the Holy Lance was buried in Saint Peter's Church in Antioch. At the time, some were skeptical, but others were convinced. After much digging in the church, Peter Bartholomew took over digging and, in a few moments, discovered the lance and gave it to Raymond. For some of the crusaders, this was a marvelous discovery. This new revelation and holy discovery resulted in the Christian army being able to rout the Muslims a few days later. With the Holy Lance of Antioch in Raymond's hands as he led the battle the crusaders decisively defeated the Muslims and captured all of Antioch.

The details of the wondrous discovery of the Holy Lance of Antioch go as follows. On June 10, 1098, a monk by the name of Peter Bartholomew, the servant of a member of Count Raymond's army, came before Raymond and Bishop Adhemar. He told of having received several visions over the preceding months from Saint Andrew in which the saint told him that the Holy Lance—the spear that pierced Christ's side as he hung on the Cross—lay buried in Saint Peter's Church in Antioch. Raymond was convinced, but Adhemar was skeptical, so they did not act upon the information.

News of the vision spread, with everyone having his own opinion. That very evening, another priest told of a vision he had had. Since he swore it was true, and because his reputation was good, Adhemar believed him.

On June 14, a meteor was seen to fall into the Muslim camp: a very good omen. On the next day, a group that included Raymond of Toulouse (the leader of the Crusade), the historian Raymond of Aguilers, and Peter Bartholomew went to the cathedral and began to dig. The digging went on for hours, with various people taking turns. Count Raymond gave up and left. Then Peter Bartholomew jumped into the hole to take a hand. He very soon cried out that he had found the lance. Raymond of Aguilers says he himself touched the iron while it was still embedded in the ground. The lance was taken to Raymond of Toulouse. News that the holy Spear of Longinus had indeed been found raced through the camp. Such a miracle was surely a portend of victory, and plans were made on the spot to sally out to meet the Turks.

The next day, the Christians gathered their forces, set a day for the attack, and prepared. The Holy Lance of Antioch was affixed to a standard and was carried before the Christians as a sort of banner at the head of the army. When the Muslim leader Kerbogha saw the crusaders in full array, he tried to send out for a truce, but the crusaders advanced anyway. Emirs began deserting Kerbogha on the field of battle. When Dukak of Damascus left, the entire army collapsed. The battle ruined Kerbogha and saved the crusaders who then captured all of Antioch and proceeded toward Jerusalem with the Holy Lance of Antioch before them.

The City of Antioch

At the time of Jesus Christ's death, Antioch bustled with commerce, diplomacy, and news of religious movements throughout the Roman world. Although relatively little is known about the Apostolic Church of Jerusalem, it is believed that the disciples of Jesus saved and maintained certain holy blood relics of his

Passion. In the decades following the Crucifixion, Jewish authorities expelled, arrested, and executed the leaders of the new Church and, at some time during this period of persecution, martyrdom, and war, these relics were surely transported out of Judea for their protection and preservation. There can be little argument that, for the better part of the period that encompassed the persecution of the Jerusalem Church, Antioch provided the most logical and likely repository for the relics of the Passion of Jesus.

Nicolaus of Antioch served as one of the first seven deacons of the Jerusalem Church and, upon the execution of Saint Stephen, a number of Christians fled to Antioch, where they preached to the Jews. In approximately 40 AD, under the leadership of Barnabas and Paul, Christian missionaries shifted their attention to the Gentiles. Within a year, Antioch was hosting the world's first Gentile Christian community whose members were being referred to as "Christians."

By the middle of the first century, two distinct and official Christian churches existed side by side: the mother church of Jewish Christians in Jerusalem and the mother church of Gentile Christians in Antioch. While some believe that Barnabas and Paul may have conveyed the relics of Christ's Passion to Antioch, it is also possible that they arrived there during the Roman war against the Jews, when many Christians fled from Judea to Antioch and Asia Minor.

Some suggests that it was Peter who brought the Shroud, together with certain other holy blood relics of the Passion, to Antioch. Ordained chief of the Apostles by Jesus himself, Peter might certainly have been entrusted with the most sacred possessions of the new church after Mary was assumed into heaven. Peter was the first to enter the empty tomb where the Shroud was discovered, and he seems to be identified as a custodian in two of the earliest reports concerning Christ's burial cloth.

In the fourth century, Saint Nino, who had visited Jerusalem, recounted that the Shroud had been preserved by Pilate's wife, given to Saint Luke, and hidden until it was found and kept by

Peter. Not only did Peter live in Antioch and debate there with Paul over the circumcision of gentiles, he also used the city as the base for his missionary activities between 47 and 54 AD, but also, according to ancient tradition, he established the Church of Antioch and served as its first bishop.

Antioch has laid claim to Passion relics other than the Shroud, and it is logical to conclude that all such preserved relics would probably have been transported together to the same safe haven.

In 1910, local Arabs unearthed, at the traditional site of Antioch's ancient church, a silver chalice comprised of an unfinished inner cup and a finished outer holder, akin to a reliquary, exquisitely decorated with ten human figures in two groups of five. Only in the middle of the first century did two groups of five men each govern the respective churches of Jerusalem and Antioch and only at such time would a Christian religious object have displayed such a depiction. Dated to the first century and considered genuine by many archeological and scientific authorities, the Great Chalice of Antioch has been called "a most sacred cup, in all probability the one which once served the Lord and his disciples at the Last Supper, the most precious object in Christian history, legend, and tradition."

Finding the Chalice of Antioch and the Holy Lance of Antioch buried in the grounds of Saint Peter's Church is too much of a coincidence not to imagine that this chalice and spear were the authentic holy blood relics that were protected by the Mother of Jesus until her Assumption into heaven eleven years after the Crucifixion. The Three Marys were traditionally believed to have lived at Ephesus until the Assumption. It is highly likely that the holy blood relics were transferred to Antioch by Peter after the Assumption of Mary at Ephesus. Thus, the Holy Lance of Antioch seems to be the only ancient Roman centurion hasta that history tells us about. Also, the location that the spear was found, and its circumstances and subsequent "power to conquer" make the Holy Lance of Antioch a good candidate for being the "most authentic" spear that historical research can unearth claiming to be the original Spear of Longinus.

It is highly likely, and simply logical, that Raymond gave the Holy Lance of Antioch to his wife, Elvira of Castile, when she returned to Europe with their young son Alfonso Jordon. After the Battle of Ascalon, Raymond was not made the King of Jerusalem and thus there would have been a great debate about who should possess the Holy Lance of Antioch. Raymond, no doubt, wished to hold onto this wondrous "Spear of Destiny" that he had used in five successful battles in a row. He had conquered and freed Jerusalem with the Holy Lance of Antioch in his hands. Surely, Raymond would not have given up the spear easily.

Raymond, like all crusaders, had made a pact with the pope to give all relics found in the Holy Land to the Vatican upon his return to Europe or upon his death. But there was one exception to that agreement, and that was that a wife or daughter of a king who had taken the vows of the "Infantado" or "Infantada" could hold the relics found in the Holy Land by their husband, father, or brother and basically become the guardian of them in their castles throughout Europe. Essentially, the vows of the Infantado (not married) or Infantada (married) made the women agents of the pope who were "attending" the relics and guarding—or even hiding—the relics from the infidels in Spain and the Muslim invaders of Europe and the Holy Land. These females became the holy blood relic guardians and essentially became the model for the many stories about the Grail Maidens who guarded and served the grail.

The Infantada stream of Grail Maidens (also grail Queens) returned from the Holy Land with many relics that were spirited away to fortresses in Spain and castles throughout Europe owned by Infantada Queens—Queens of the Grail.

It seems only logical that Elvira of Castile, Raymond's wife (Infantada), brought the Holy Lance of Antioch and other relics back to her castle in Toulouse and then on to her family's castles in Spain after she returned from Jerusalem with her young son Alfonso Jordon. Elvira was a powerful queen from one of the most important families in Spain. She would have many places to guard or hide the holy blood relics throughout France and

Spain. She traveled extensively after returning from the Holy Land and appears to have passed the Holy Lance of Antioch to her family in Leon. From there, it was hidden in a sepulchre of a mighty Grail Queen until it was removed hundreds of years later by a queen of the Habsburg family and placed in the Imperial Regalia.

This proposed provenance of the Spear of Longinus, the Holy Lance of Antioch, is the most reasonable explanation of how the spear returned to Europe and was protected and preserved by the Infantada of the holy blood relics—the Queens of the Grail. The Holy Lance of Antioch is reported to be quite humble and has avoided detection for centuries. We also have evidence that the spearhead suspected to be the Holy Lance of Antioch was placed on a staff around 717 AD, about the same time that the Spear of Saint Maurice was being manufactured by the Vatican. You will hear more about the Holy Lance of Antioch and its whereabouts in future chapters.

To fill in some of the details of the provenance of the Holy Lance of Antioch (presumed to be the Spear of Longinus), we will first need to hear more about Raymond of Toulouse and his family from what we know from history.

Alfonso Jordan

Alfonso Jordan (1103–1148 AD) was the son of Raymond IV of Toulouse by his third wife, Elvira of Castile, and was born in the castle of Mont-Pelerin at Tripoli, in today's Lebanon. As a child, he was known as the Count of Tripoli from 1105 until 1109, and thereafter Count of Toulouse (as Alfonso I) until his death. Alfonso was born while his father was on the First Crusade, attempting to create the County of Tripoli on the Palestinian coast. He was surnamed Jordan after being baptized in the Jordan River.

Alfonso's father died when he was two years old, and he remained under the guardianship of his cousin, Guillaume Jourdain, count of Cerdagne (d. 1109), until he was five years old.

He was then taken to Europe by his mother, Elvira of Castile, and his brother Bertrand gave him the county of Rouergue. In his tenth year, upon Bertrand's death (1112), he succeeded to the county of Toulouse and marquisate of Provence. Toulouse was taken from him by William IX, count of Poitiers, in 1114, who claimed it by right of his wife Philippa of Toulouse, daughter of William IV of Toulouse. He recovered a part of this kingdom in 1119 but continued to fight for his possessions (including relics) until about 1123. When at last he was successful, he was excommunicated by Pope Callixtus II for having expelled the monks of Saint-Gilles, who had aided his enemies.

Alfonso next fought for the sovereignty of Provence against Raymond Berenger III; not until September 1125 did the war end in an amicable agreement. Under it, he became absolute master of the regions lying between the Pyrenees and the Alps, Auvergne and the sea. His ascendancy was an unmixed good to the country; during a period of fourteen years, art and industry flourished.

Was part of the success of Alfonso due to his mother possessing the Spear of Antioch, which he might have used in the many battles he won?

Elvira of Castile also flourished in France and eventually went to Spain with Alfonso. Again, Alfonso seemed undefeatable in his campaigns but was excommunicated twice for defending people the pope wanted eradicated as heretics. Alfonso seemed to take up the side of those who had come from the Holy Land and the Far East, especially religions that deified the feminine nature of the divine.

In 1144, Alfonso again incurred the displeasure of the Church by siding with the rebels of Montpellier against their lord. A second time he was excommunicated, but in 1146 he took a vow to go on a crusade to the Holy Land at the meeting of Vezelay called by Louis VII. In 1147, he embarked for the East in the Second Crusade. In 1148, Alphonse had finally arrived at Acre in the Holy Land. Among his companions he had made enemies and he was destined to take no share in the crusade he had joined.

He was poisoned at Caesarea, either by Eleanor of Aquitaine, the wife of Louis, or Melisende, the mother of Baldwin III (king of Jerusalem) suggesting the poisoning.

The relics of Alfonso were at issue early on when he came to power. There were continuing battles over the relics of Raymond of Toulouse that had been passed down through the Counts of Toulouse. The Holy Lance of Antioch did not seem to be among these relics. It was more traditional that the wife of Raymond would hold the most precious relics for either her husband or her son as an Infantada. Thus, the provenance of the Holy Lance of Antioch fades into obscurity through Elvira of Castile and the female Infantada tradition that guarded and protected the holy blood relics.

The most authentic claim to be the true Spear of Longinus is the Holy Lance of Antioch. It is the best candidate from what we are told about the lance in the histories written by eye-witnesses, and it fits the general story that we know about the Apostles and what they might have done with holy blood relics. Other spears that claim to be the Spear of Longinus are not old enough and were "made" during the eighth century, when the desire for relics was at its height. When Raymond of Toulouse was successful at conquering Jerusalem, relics began to flow back to the pope in Rome. Unfortunately for the pope, the Holy Lance of Antioch was not one of those relics.

The Vatican's Lance of Saint Maurice

A lance claiming to be that which produced the wound in Christ's side is now preserved among the imperial insignia at Vienna and is known as the lance of Saint Maurice. This lance was used as early as 1273 AD in the coronation ceremonies of the Emperor of the West, and from an earlier date as an emblem of investiture. It came to Nuremberg in 1424, and it is also probably the lance known as that of the Emperor Constantine, which enshrined a nail or some portion of a nail of the Crucifixion.

Before their destruction, the Templars had established the largest banking system in Europe, and they owned thousands of castles and tracts of land. Along with this great material wealth, the Templars had also amassed spiritual wealth, seeking to acquire all religious artifacts associated with the life and death of Jesus Christ. It is well known that kings and popes used the Templar strongholds to store holy relics and other valuables. Thus, the Templars became almost synonymous with holy blood relics and represented the "Solider of God" turned into the guardian of holy blood relics. Many holy blood relics were in the possession of the Templars at one time or another, and it is possible that the true Spear of Longinus was protected and hidden in their treasury for some time.

One of the earliest documented stories of the Lance of Saint Maurice is credited to Attila the Hun, who acquired it as he cut his path of destruction through Europe. When his army was weakened from famine and pestilence in Italy, he galloped his horse to the gates of Rome and hurled the lance at the feet of the officers who had been sent out to surrender the city. "Take back your Holy Lance," he said, "it is of no use to me, since I do not know Him that made it holy."

Stories of the power of the Lance of Saint Maurice (Spear of Destiny) have persisted for centuries. The Lance of Saint Maurice, after being used by the Holy Roman Emperors, was put on display in the Hapsburg Palace in Austria and remains there to this day. It is rumored that when the Nazis had possession of the Lance of Saint Maurice (Spear of Destiny), they made a copy of it and switched it with the one in the Imperial Regalia. This legend cannot be confirmed and remains a question to be answered by witnessing the "effects" of the spear on the one who possesses it, for good or ill.

The Spear of Echmiadzin

Another claimant to be the Spear of Longinus (Spear of Destiny) is found in Armenia. This spear is found in Geghard, a medieval monastery in the Kotayk province of Armenia. Geghard is partially carved out of the rock of the adjacent mountain, which is surrounded by cliffs. While the main chapel was built in 1215 AD, the monastery complex was founded in the fourth century by Gregory the Illuminator. The name commonly used for the monastery today, Geghard, meaning "Monastery of the Spear," originates from the spear which had pierced Jesus at the Crucifixion. This spear was allegedly brought to Armenia by the Apostle Jude, called here Thaddeus, and stored amongst many other relics. Now it is displayed in the Echmiadzin treasury.

Geghard-avank monastery was famous because of the relics that it housed. The most celebrated of these was the spear, but other relics of the Apostles Andrew and John were donated in the twelfth century. This made the "Monastery of the Spear" a popular place of pilgrimage for Armenian Christians over many centuries.

No works of applied art have survived in Geghard, except for the legendary spear. The shaft has a diamond-shaped plate attached to its end, and a Greek cross with flared ends is cut through the plate. A special reliquary was made for this spearhead in 1687, and it is now kept in the museum of Echmiadzin monastery.

The likelihood that the Spear of Echmiadzin is the authentic Spear of Longinus is ruled out due to its age and its shape, which clearly demonstrate that it could not have been used as a centurion's hasta, nor as the Jewish Spear of Phinehas.

Krakow's Holy Lance

The most precious treasure and relic stored in Krakow is at the same time one of the most important symbols in Polish history. It is the head of the Lance of Saint Maurice: a medieval ceremonial weapon considered the oldest insignia of power in Poland. A copy of the Lance of Saint Maurice (Spear of Destiny), symbolizing the power of the empire, was a gift from the German

Emperor Otto III, who offered it to King Boleslaus the Brave at the Congress of Gniezno in 1000 AD. Precisely a quarter of a century later, Boleslaus was crowned the first king of Poland. For centuries, the spear was stored in the Cathedral Treasury, and only taken out for the most important ceremonies.

The Krakow Lance is now held in Krakow cathedral. The Krakow "Spear of Destiny" is slightly different than the Viennese Lance of Saint Maurice and is known to be a replica, though no less valued by believers.

The Hapsburgs' Imperial Regalia

Today there exist several historic spears claiming to be the Spear of Longinus, but the best known is the one in the Hofburg Museum in Vienna, Austria. This spear/lance is said to be the spear of the Roman soldier Gaius Cassius Longinus and is allegedly traced back through history to Constantine the Great, the Roman Emperor who first adopted Christianity in the early fourth century. This spear/lance is made of iron, and the long, tapering point is supported by a wide base with metal flanges. Within a central aperture in the blade, a hammer-headed nail (thought to be from the Holy Cross) has been secured by a cuff threaded with metal wire. According to legend, the spear passed from the possession of Longinus into Roman hands and then on to Saint Maurice and down through the Holy Roman Emperors.

According to some authors, the spear was possessed by a series of successful military leaders including Theodosius, Alaric, Charles Martel, Charlemagne, and Frederick Barbarossa. A legend grew around the spear that whoever possessed it would be able to conquer the world. Napoleon attempted to obtain the spear after the battle of Austerlitz, but it had been smuggled out of the city prior to the start of the battle. According to the legend, Charlemagne carried the spear through forty-seven successful battles, but died when he accidentally dropped it. Barbarossa met the same fate only a few minutes after it slipped out of his hands while he was crossing a river. The spear finally wound up in the possession of the House of the Hapsburgs and by 1912 was part of the treasury collection stored in the Hofburg Museum.

This spear/lance was examined by scientists and dated to the eighth century and it is not a centurion's hasta. The likelihood that the Lance of Saint Maurice in Vienna is the authentic Spear of Longinus is slim to none.

Pre-Christian Sacred Spears

The pre-Christian myths, legends and beliefs in a divine or heavenly spear abound. From the principal "stirring force" of the ocean of creation, to Odin's spear, Gungnir, that never misses, the archetype of the spear from heaven has inspired cultures throughout the world and down through history. One could even imagine that the World Spear is the axis of the Earth, or the trunk of the World Tree or even the human spinal cord. Everywhere in mythology, the spear is described as the tool of power of the highest sky-god, solar hero, or king. Zeus has his lightning bolts (spears) that he throws down from Mount Olympus and the Tibetan deities often have a dorge, or diamond-hard lightning bolt that can destroy demons when thrown with wisdom. Athena has Nike, the goddess of Victory, in her left hand, but in her right hand is Athena's spear. Wisdom sits on her shoulder as an owl, and she is outfitted for battle. Athena's spear is invincible, and Nike always assures victory.

The spear of power, or holy spear, must be wielded with strength and might but also wisdom and mercy. The heavenly spear descends with fire and power, like a falling star as a message from the gods. No doubt, the ancients revered meteors as living proof of gods on high who send down fiery spears from heaven to earth, filled with gifts from the gods: fire, iron, gold, crystal, and many other wondrous metals and minerals found in meteorites. The fiery tail of a falling star no doubt drew the attention of the wisest of the clan. Fire reigning down from heaven sounds much like Prometheus, who brought fire down to humanity as a gift stolen from the gods.

We have compiled a list of various heavenly spears that have been considered holy, sacred, and magical throughout history from a variety of cultures. It is easy to surmise that the archetype of the spear, which often is combined with a sword, is one of the most powerful tools for good or ill, depending on who possesses it. The heavenly spear was commonly seen as the weapon of the supreme god of the sky who used it to vanquish evil.

Holy Spears from Around the World

Brahmadanda

The rod of Brahma (also known as Meru-danda) is called the Brahmadanda. It is capable of nullifying the effects of any divine weapon, no matter how destructive. If hurled, the impact of this weapon is lethal to even the celestials.

Trishula

The trishula is a trident, commonly used as the principal symbol in Hinduism and Buddhism. In India and Thailand, the term also often refers to a short-handled weapon that may be mounted on a staff. In Malaysia and Indonesia, trisula usually refers specifically to a long-handled trident. The trishula is wielded by the god Shiva and is said to have been used to sever the original head of Ganesha. Durga also holds a trishula, as one of her many weapons. The three points have various meanings and significance and have many stories behind them. They are said to represent various trinities: creation, maintenance, and destruction; past, present, and future; the three gunas. When looked upon as a weapon of Shiva, the trishula is said to destroy the three worlds: the physical world, the world of the forefathers, and the world of the mind. The three worlds are supposed to be destroyed by Shiva into a single non-dual plane of existence that is bliss alone.

Subrahmanya

Subrahmanya is famed for his beauty and valor, and for his courting of Valli. His spear is seen as worthy of worship, and it was the most useful weapon in Subrahmanya's battle against the evil asuras. There is also a philosophical importance to the spear because it represents gnana—learning. The long shaft of the spear represents many years of learning. The broad portion of the spear represents the many tomes read to acquire knowledge. The pointed tip represents analysis and synthesis of what has been read.

Although, according to some accounts, the spear was given by Siva to Subrahmanya, there are temples that celebrate the handing over of the spear to Subrahmanya by the Goddess Parvati. Subrahmanya's spear is treated with reverence, and in many temples, the spear is worshipped with as much fervor as the Lord. The spear is seen as the embodiment of Subrahmanya himself. It is described as being as beautiful as the eyes of Valli, Subrahmanya's consort. Daily worship of the spear will rid the believer of sins and will help conquer desires and the fear of death. The symbolic significance of the spear is to be borne in mind while worshipping Subrahmanya, and worship of his spear will also liberate devotees from the cycle of rebirths.

Amenonuhoko

Amenonuhoko (heavenly jeweled spear) is the name given to the spear in Shintoism that is used to raise the primordial land mass from the sea. It is often represented as a naginata (spear). According to the Kojiki, Shinto's genesis gods Izanagi and Izanami were responsible for creating the first land. To help them do this, they were given a spear decorated with jewels—named Ame-no (heavenly) nu-hoko (jeweled spear)—by older heavenly gods. The two deities then went to the floating bridge between heaven and earth and churned the sea below with the naginata. When drops of salty water fell from the tip, they formed into the first island. Izanagi and Izanami then descended from the bridge of heaven and made their home on the island.

Yima's Golden Dagger

In the second chapter of the *Vendidad of the Avesta*, the omniscient Creator Ahura Mazda asks Yima to rule over and nourish the earth, to see that the living things prosper. Yima accepts the request and Ahura Mazda presents him with a golden seal and a long dagger inlaid with gold. Yima, shining with light, faced southwards and pressed the golden seal against the earth and boring into it with the poniard (long dagger), saying "O Spenta Armaiti, kindly open asunder and stretch thyself afar, to bear flocks and herds and men." The earth swells and Yima rules for six hundred years as life and prosperity arise from the plowing of the ground with the Golden Dagger.

The Spear of Mithras

In Mithraic myth, Mithras caught and subdued a bull, slaughtering it by thrusting a spear in its right side. The sacrifice of a bull and the baptism in its blood of a suitably prepared and mature Mithraic initiate assured the initiate a place in the outer reaches of the universe. The priest offered prayers during the ritual, concluding it by thrusting a consecrated spear into the flank of the bull. Steaming blood showered through the perforated boarding under which the initiate presented his face to the dripping blood in ecstasy. The baptized initiate emerged in glory, like a newborn babe into a new world, freed from sin and bestowed with the promise of immortality. Cleansed, the initiate later banqueted on the carcass drinking the blood and eating the body of the bull. Overcoming the bull symbolized control of one's inner beast and a purification of one's animal instincts to gain access to Heaven. These blood baptisms continued well into the latter half of the fourth century.

Odin's Spear Gungnir

Gungnir is the spear of the god Odin in Norse mythology. The spear is described as being so well-balanced that it could strike any target. Odin's spear is made from the wood of the world tree, Yggdrasil, and engraved with the runic letters from which Odin's power derives. According to the *Poetic Edda*, the spear was fashioned by the dwarves. Loki, Odin's son, discovers the spear whilst visiting the dwarves and flatters the dwarves and asks for the spear, which they give him. In the *Poetic Edda's* poem *Voluspa*, the Aesir-Vanir War is described as officially starting when Odin throws a spear over the heads of an assembly of Vanir gods.

The Spear of Lugh

Lugh is an important god of Irish mythology and a member of the Tuatha De Danann, the faery-like original rulers of Ireland. Lugh is portrayed as a youthful warrior hero, king, and savior. He is associated with skill, crafts, and the arts, as well as with oaths, truth, and the laws that are part of rightful kingship. Sometimes he is interpreted as a storm, sky, or sun god. Lugh is known by the epithet Lamfada (of the long arm) for his skill with a spear, for he wields an unstoppable fiery spear and a sword named Fragarach (the answerer). Lugh's spear was said to be impossible to overcome.

Lugh obtained the Spear of Assal as a fine imposed on the children of Tuirill Piccreo. Lugh demanded the spear named Areadbhair (slaughterer) which belonged to Pisear, the king of Persia. The tip of Areadbhair had to be kept immersed in a pot of water to keep it from igniting. Lugh had no need to wield the spear himself, for it was alive and thirsted for blood so much that only by steeping its head in a sleeping-draught of pounded fresh poppy seeds could it be kept at rest. When battle was near, it was drawn out; then it roared and struggled against its thongs, and fire flashed from it as it tore through the ranks of the enemy, never tiring of slaying. Lugh used an incantation to always make it hit its mark and another incantation to cause the spear to return to him.

The Spear of Phinehas

In the *Old Testament* book *Numbers* 25:7–13, it is written:

> When Phinehas son of Eleazar, the son of Aaron the priest, saw this, he left the assembly and took a spear in his hand and followed the Israelite into the tent. He drove the spear into both of them, right through the Israelite man and into the woman's stomach. Then the plague against the Israelites was stopped; but those who died in the plague numbered 24,000. The Lord said to Moses, "Phinehas son of Eleazar, the son of Aaron the priest, has turned my anger away from the Israelites. Since he was as zealous for my honor among them as I am, I did not put an end to them in my zeal. Therefore, tell him I am making my covenant of peace with him. He and his descendants will have a covenant of a lasting priesthood, because he was zealous for the honor of his God and made atonement for the Israelites."

The Nisibene Hymns (5–7) by Ephraim Syrus tells us: "The lance of Phinehas again has caused me to fear, for by the slaughter he wrought with it he hindered the pestilence. The lance guarded the Tree of Life, it made me glad and made me sad; it hindered Adam from life, and it hindered death from the people. But the lance that pierced Jesus, by it I have suffered; He is pierced, and I groan. There came out from Him water and blood; Adam washed and lived and returned to Paradise."

Greek Spears

Homer tells us that Chiron was the wisest and most just of all the centaurs. (*Homer* Il. xi. 831.) He was the instructor of Achilles, whose father Peleus was a friend and student of Chiron who received, at his wedding with Thetis, the spear which was subsequently used by Achilles. Centaurs were distinguished for their knowledge of medicine and Chiron himself had been instructed by Apollo and Artemis, and was renowned for his skill in hunting, medicine, music, gymnastics, and the art of prophecy. All the most distinguished heroes of Grecian story are, like Achilles, described as the pupils of Chiron in these arts. Among his pupils were many heroes: Asclepius, Aristaeus, Ajax, Aeneas, Actaeon, Caeneus, Theseus, Achilles, Jason, Peleus, Telamon, Heracles, Oileus, Phoenix, and—in some stories—Dionysus.

During the beginning of the Trojan war, Achilles had been isolated in the mountains with Chiron and therefore had not been called upon to do battle. When he heard of the coming war, he immediately set out for Troy. Chiron presented the boy with a magic spear that would fight true—for only him. A relic claimed to be Achilles' bronze-headed spear was for centuries preserved in the Temple of Athena on the acropolis and was shown in the time of Pausanias in the second century AD.

Spear of Achilles

The Spear of Achilles was made from an ash tree from Mount Pelion. The spear was given to Achilles either by his father, Peleus, or by his tutor, the centaur Chiron. Achilles killed Hector with this spear during the Trojan War. Achilles was credited as being a master of weaponry, particularly with swords and spears, and was a son of the nymph Thetis and Peleus, a king of the Myrmidons. When Achilles was born, Thetis tried to make him immortal by dipping him into the river Styx. The Olympian god Hephaestus made Achilles a complete set of armor, a shield, and a wondrous spear upon his mother's request.

Many Heavenly Spears and the Spear of Longinus

Almost all ancient religious teachings, myths, and animistic beliefs have some type of spear or sword with magical properties at the heart of their Mysteries. Our focus on the Spear of Longinus, that pierced the heart of Jesus Christ, points at the central Mysteries of both Christianity and pre-Christian beliefs, including the grail mysteries. The ancient secrets and symbols of the heavenly spear falling from the sky-gods start with animistic beliefs in meteorites as "gods come to earth" and evolve into the many stories of spears used during the creation in heaven, including the Spear of the Archangel Michael. We have traced the path of numerous spears through many cultures to demonstrate that truth reappears ubiquitously and simultaneously in all cultures because the ancients could "see" the truth and simply described it a bit differently in each culture.

When the holy blood relics of the Christians were venerated, it was no accident that the holy cup and the holy spearhead were similar to the Holy Grail and spearhead referred to in European Holy Grail traditions. It is no accident that it was the Christian women who cherished, preserved, and protected the holy blood relics of Jesus and it was Grail Maidens and the Infantada who guarded, protected, and served the grail. The Mother of Jesus was, no doubt, faithful in re-enacting the Last Supper, just as Jesus had asked his followers to do. Of course, the very cup that was used at the Last Supper and to catch the blood of Jesus on the cross, would be considered sacred and the most appropriate vessel to be used during the re-enactments of the Last Supper with the Mother of Jesus and those gathered around her at Ephesus. The wine would be magically transformed into the blood of Jesus in this cup. The bread would be cut with the spearhead of Longinus and then would be transformed into the body of Jesus through this early Holy Eucharist. The cup and spearhead were the tools to accomplish the injunction Jesus gave his followers: "Do this in memory of me."

In the Russian Orthodox Church, a small replica of the Spear of Longinus is still used in the Holy Eucharist ceremony to this day. A holy cup and a sacred spearhead were used in Christian rituals of the Last Supper, while a similar cup and spearhead were also used in the Grail Maiden's Procession of the Holy Grail. The Grail Maidens carried a cup (sometime bowl, chalice, or platter) and a spearhead that dripped blood from the point into the cup. This procession was performed three times a day in the Grail Castle before the Grail King and Grail Queen. This ritual is similar in many ways to the Holy Eucharist rituals of the Russian, Greek, and Roman churches. The Last Supper ritual was developed immediately after the death and resurrection of Jesus Christ and did not consciously copy existing pre-Christian rituals but were similar in spiritual principles of truth.

The personal relics that had touched the blood of Jesus would have been held in the highest regard and would have been guarded by Longinus, Joseph of Arimathea, Peter, and the other apostles while these relics were in Mary's care. What happened to the holy blood relics of Jesus after the Assumption of the Mother of Jesus is not known and becomes the subject of speculation and personal belief.

We have tried to present a comprehensive picture of the Spear of Longinus and the way the Christian ideas are similar to the truths of earlier traditions that added much to existing Celtic, Irish, English, French, and Spanish traditions of the Holy Grail, the Maidens of the Wells, the Courts of Love, chivalry, and the legends of King Arthur and his Knights of the Round Table.

Following the development of the lore of the "cup and spear" throughout ancient history and into modern times demonstrates that the wisdom of the Holy Grail continues to evolve and that pre-Christian spiritual beliefs were a prefiguring of what happened with Jesus Christ in Palestine and afterwards with his followers of "The Way."

Chapter 12

Rudolf Steiner's Grail Quest

"The Holy Lance as an imaginative picture within Parsifal's vision is also an historical and physical object. The centurion Longinus, who pierced the side of Christ on the Cross gave rise to a legend which comes from Zobingen near Ellwangen. The Syrian Ephraim in the 39th Hymn of his so-called 'Nisibinian Hymns' brings this lance into connection with the lance of Phinehas. He says the lance originally guarded the Tree of Life. Adam, who had fallen, returned to Paradise through it."

Dr. Walter Johannes Stein,
The Ninth Century and the Holy Grail (1928)

One of the deepest Christian interpretations of the Holy Grail is given by the Austrian philosopher and scientist Dr. Rudolf Steiner (1861–1925), who coined the phrase "science of the grail" to describe his particular "spiritual science," which formed into an international organization called Anthroposophy. Steiner wrote twenty-four books and gave over five thousand lectures on the Christian spiritual traditions of the Western esoteric path. His writings comprise a comprehensive worldview (cosmology) that is magnificent in its breadth and depth. When it comes to studying the Holy Grail, Steiner is an essential element that should not be ignored, no matter how difficult his presentation is to penetrate and comprehend. Steiner is not for the casual student, but no spiritual subject is complete until you have considered his insight on the topic. Then, if you are familiar with his language and style, you will develop an overview that all other facts can fit into. Without a cosmology of the spirit like Steiner's Anthroposophy, the Holy Grail will simply remain incomprehensible and unattainable.

There was a unique friend of Rudolf Steiner's, who he considered his colleague and peer and whose name was Walter Johannes Stein. Stein had developed some clairvoyant abilities and used them to study the Holy Grail in a most profound way. It was this study that led Stein to discover the work of Rudolf Steiner and seek him out personally as a source of confirming his own personal spiritual research. Steiner loved Stein so much that he allowed Stein to attend lectures of the Anthroposophical Society without being a member. This special exception was unheard of and was only given to Stein. Once, when the strict "guardian" at the entrance would not let Stein in because he did not have a membership card, Steiner said he would not give the lecture until Stein was admitted. Steiner was known to completely change the lecture he had planned to give because Stein had shown up unexpectedly. Steiner eventually chose Stein as one of the original teachers the in the first Waldorf School that Steiner founded and led.

Walter Johannes Stein had three "major" students who carried his work on the Holy Grail forward after his death. Stein wrote numerous books on the Holy Grail himself, his principal work being *The Ninth Century*. Stein's students were Werner Glas, Rene Querido, and Trevor Ravenscroft. All three students wrote books on the Holy Grail subject but one of them became a huge sensation with his book *The Spear of Destiny*, which claims that Hitler's great desire was to possess the "Spear of Destiny," which legend suggests is the ultimate tool of power and world domination. This idea is only partially true but made such a great story that the book was very popular and created an international sensation in the Anthroposophical Society as many new members who were "crazed" with the Ravenscroft furor poured in.

Werner Glas and Rene Querido wrote short books on the grail that were read by few and had little impact, but both men led Waldorf teacher training institutes in America and trained hundreds of Waldorf teachers. The rich history and research of Glas and Querido came through in all that they taught their Waldorf teacher trainers. The Waldorf Institute of Mercy College in Detroit and the Rudolf Steiner College in Fair Oaks, California, were centered on teaching Waldorf education, but they also were "Holy Grail Colleges" of a sort. Steiner's Anthroposophy, the philosophy behind Waldorf education, is full of "Grail Science" that is applied to child development and pedagogical ideas that help nurture the student with spiritual content that is presented in a non-religious, non-sectarian but truly Christian fashion. Steiner's schools are inherently Christian-oriented but not Christian-based. They are, in fact, schools of the Holy Grail. Ravenscroft himself was not a teacher, like Stein, Glas, and Querido were. They were leaders in the world-wide Waldorf school movement and together, trained thousands of Waldorf teachers over the years.

I was fortunate in that I was able to have endless conversations with Werner Glas and Rene Querido because I was Werner's protégée for over a dozen years; I studied and taught at Rene Querido's teacher training institutes in California and New York. I attempted to carry on the tradition of grail studies that drove Walter Stein to Rudolf Steiner to begin with. I also became a Waldorf teacher and teacher trainer for over three decades. Therefore, I have had the good fortune of being able to concentrate my grail studies through my vocation and have those studies reinforced through wonderful teachers. It is out of this Anthroposophical involvement and training that I am presenting this book, and I also wish to set the record straight about the true path of the Spear of Destiny and the stories told by Trevor Ravenscroft, which need correction. I do not wish to disparage Ravenscroft, but much of what he writes is incorrect and did not arise from his teacher Walter Stein or from Rudolf Steiner's Anthroposophy.

I was told the life of Trevor Ravenscroft by both Werner and Rene. It seems that Ravenscroft was severely damaged during the war and was what was called "shell-shocked" at that time. Adolf Hitler himself describes his war experiences and clearly describes that he, too, was shell-shocked and never recovered from the hallucinations that arose from the condition. In a way, Ravenscroft suffered the same type of hallucinations, delusions, and "magical thinking." He never intended to write a "true history of the grail" as Stein, Glas, and Querido did. Ravenscroft was a mystery writer who fell on hard economic times and decided to take the deep, historical truths of the Holy Grail and conflate them into an historical novel about Hitler's desire for the tool of power, the "Spear of Destiny." The combining of Anthroposophy and a thriller novel created a compelling story, even though it lacked historical validity or spiritual confirmation.

The phenomena of the book *The Spear of Destiny*, and Ravenscroft's other two books, started a new spiritual thriller genre in writing that has moved to the big screen with Dan Brown's movies. These poorly researched books skim the surface for sensationalism and a good plot line that is in contradistinction to the facts and the often "boring realities" of spiritual development. Gluing legends, myths, and beliefs into a fast-paced, thrilling novel or movie is what a modern materialistic reader wants—not the slow plodding of historical research and facts that do not "connect the dots" into a grand resemblance of truth. Dan Brown, like J. K. Rowling, needed to do more research before he tried to represent huge historical movements as a two-hour mystery that gets solved by a Hollywood actor through contrivance and silly nonsense. Ravenscroft, unfortunately, has led the modern movement to create partially true presentations of profound, archetypal truths that are watered down into glib, unremarkable pieces of spiritual materialism.

Werner Glas had me work with Marcia Lucas to rewrite Georg Lucas's first two failed screenplays for Star Wars. Later, this collaboration led to helping write all the Indiana Jones movies with Kathleen Kennedy. Through this experience, I learned quite clearly that the general public, and particularly the entertainment industry, is not interested in the truth of the story—just dynamic sensationalism that draws a large audience. The secrets of the grail that I shared with Kennedy, Lucas, and Spielberg were wasted on childish endeavors to profit from ancient truths that still hide as "open secrets," even after the movie is over or the book is read. We need the effort of the quest for the grail to build the spiritual stamina necessary to penetrate these open secrets of the Holy Grail. Great spiritual secrets can, in many instances, be displayed on the silver screen or in books and yet still be little understood. Once these great truths and wisdom-teachings are given out through a passive experience of watching them stream by in a movie, the effort to "quest for the grail" is supplanted by a caricature that deflates its meaning, substance, and true nature. The "holy grail" becomes a cartoon, and the beholder is made to replace education with entertainment that is often forgotten quickly and based in error.

When one reads a good book about the Holy Grail, it is incumbent upon the reader to study further and see if what the author has said is true. The Holy Grail cannot be simply offered to the seeker on the quest. The grail knight must go through a desolate wasteland and endure great suffering and become "awakened" to gain the grail and become the Grail King or Grail Queen. Being entertained about the core spiritual practice that creates ascension and transcendental communion and the subsequent spiritual nourishment that arise from the experience, cannot be placed in a book or a movie. The Holy Grail is a direct experience that has been written about since the beginning of history. Millions have had the direct experience of finding their own grail and being fed, nourished, and supported by its magical grace. Christians and non-Christians all experience a common spiritual communion when they contact the beings of the spiritual world. They describe these experiences in similar details, no matter what tradition. Turning the quest for the spiritual part of our self, the Holy Grail, into entertainment defiles the path and belittles it into insignificance and triviality.

These indications about trivializing the Holy Grail led to the creation of a Disney Land entertainment center where every sign, symbol, and cartoonization of the Holy grail is displayed in bright colors and loud sounds, but the Holy Grail itself is absent. Spiritual materialism leads to trivialization of the most sacred traditions from myths, legends, and beliefs based upon direct experience of the spiritual reality of the Grail and the hierarchy that serves it. Do not be fooled by shallow versions of who you actually "are" when you unite with your higher self and complete the quest for the Holy Grail.

Rudolf Steiner was the first to publicly suggest that the grail quest was actually a personal initiation experience coded into the narrative. His pupil Walter Stein took up Steiner's intuitions about the grail as a symbol. But Stein also argued that "grail experiences" arose in the Carolingian court in the ninth century and then reappears in the twelfth. He identified the grail protagonists with historic personages circulating around the Carolingian court in the mid to late ninth century. According to Stein, the grail material, especially in Wolfram's *Parzival* could be interpreted as real (although esoteric) history. Rudolf Steiner's grail interpretation has provided a very rich vein of wisdom that Stein built upon with his own personal research.

A different narrative from Stein's book, *The Ninth Century*, has been told by Walter Stein's student Trevor Ravenscroft in his books *The Spear of Destiny*, *The Cup of Destiny*, and *The Mark of the Beast*.

These books revolve around the legend of the spear that pierced the side of Christ on the cross, as described in the *Gospel of John*, wielded by a Roman centurion named Gaius Cassius Longinus. The spear was called the Lance of Longinus, or the Holy Spear, or because it was used at the most critical moments in humanity's history, the "Spear of Destiny."

Ravenscroft traces this spear through history and shows it to have been in the possession of some of the most influential people in history. He informs us that the spear was already an ancient talisman of power, and its owners included Joshua, Saul, Phinehas, and Herod the Great before its fateful use at the Crucifixion of Jesus. According to Ravenscroft, subsequent owners included Constantine the Great, Theodosius I, Alaric, Theodoric, Justinian I, Charles Martel, Charlemagne, and Otto the Great, among others. Ravenscroft also tells us of Adolf Hitler's alleged obsession with the spear after he first sighted the sacred relic in 1909.

Ravenscroft claims that the grail is the "knowledge" to use the Spear of Destiny in some supernatural way. He conjectures that there are two ways to achieve this spiritual knowledge: either using "black arts" involving drugs and sex-magic, or by a much harder route of "learning the ABCs of white magic." These are the very terms Wolfram von Eschenbach used in the introduction to his romance *Parzival*. Once this knowledge is obtained, the innate power of the spear can be used for good or evil; the use is determined by the method by which the user gained the knowledge of the Holy Grail. If he used "black arts," then he will wield the spear for evil; if not, then he is free to choose the path toward the good.

Much of the correct information about the grail that Ravenscroft has presented in his books is taken from Walter Stein and Rudolf Steiner, but the parts that are not taken from these reliable sources are complete confabulation and nonsense. It takes great discernment and discretion to separate out what parts came from Steiner and what parts are simply nonsense created by Ravenscroft to connect the dots of his mystery thriller. The reader should beware that wishing and magical thinking does not create good scholarship, nor does it lead the seeker toward the Grail Castle.

Even though reading and understanding Rudolf Steiner is difficult, he is still one of the best resources to plumb the depths of spiritual research into the Holy Grail. Steiner has told us more about the spiritual nature of the grail in relationship to human spiritual development than any other writer. There is little speculation in Steiner's presentation because he can clairvoyantly see the actual current effects of the Holy Grail upon the different "bodies" of the human being. Steiner gives us wisdom that we can validate through our own spiritual research. He also has given historical research that has led to physical confirmation of facts that were not known before. In other words, Steiner proves and demonstrates that what he is saying is true and verifiable. This is the bases for what he calls the "Science of the Grail"—a step-by-step process for spiritual advancement that is also called the Quest for the Holy Grail, or "The Way" by early Christians. The Science of the Grail is a Christian path that elucidates pre-Christian beliefs into a rich narrative of legend, tradition, and direct spiritual experience of the grail.

The grail path is the path of spiritual development that teaches the grail knight how to tame the dragon of the lower self and conquer evil to gain eternal life. From grail knight to grail guardian to grail keeper, we can see that the path that spiritual development replicates—the quest for the Holy Grail. Steiner' philosophy of life, called Anthroposophy, is a set of cosmological teachings that lay out the path of spiritual development to the higher self—the path to the Grail Castle. Through practicing the spiritual exercises of Grail Science, the seeker learns to understand the grail and commits to seeking it everywhere. The questing soul must learn the magic of the grail that helps develop the Seeker of the Grail into the Grail Queen or Grail King. The path to the Holy Grail is the same path that a student of Rudolf Steiner's may take through studying his teachings and developing his virtuous nature.

Chapter 13

The Holy Grail is Your Higher Spirit — Seek It!

No true conclusion to a study on the Holy Grail can ever be reached, for it is an ever-rising path into spirit-land that must be climbed one step at a time and, when attained, the victorious one must turn and help all those who are also climbing to the summit. The Grail Queen or Grail King is committed to serving all of the Grail Seekers and Grail Keepers. The quest is never finished; the newly budding flowers of our spirit bring forth love, mercy, and grace that can be shared freely like an over-flowing chalice of light that beams warmth, light, and life to all who behold it.

We can only outline the topology of the grail quest, for it is different for each seeking soul. There are common signposts along the way that those who have followed the pilgrim's path can share with those who come after them. The Camino de Santiago, the Reconquista, or the Crusades to the Holy Land called the pilgrim soul to an experience of the spirit that was worth dying for if necessary. This type of soul-commitment drives the grail knight to quest ever anew, no matter what the consequences. The grail knight's goal was eternal life, even at the cost of physical death.

You may be disappointed that there are no definitive conclusions in this study of the Holy Grail and the holy blood relics. We have tried to demonstrate that the many traditions concerning grail lore all point to a common story, no matter what time in history they are drawn from. The Grail Mysteries did not start with the holy blood relics of Jesus of Nazareth but, in fact, culminate with them. The Passion of Jesus of Nazareth, "The Way of Suffering," was the perfect archetypal example of what all humanity must go through to understand this "veil of tears" that we live in to gain eternal life. We must suffer through to understanding and wisdom gleaned from the commitment to the path, the quest, "The Way." This "Way" of Christ that promises to bring to us "the way, the truth, and the life" is the essence of the Holy Grail Mysteries.

Christ's holy blood relics became symbols and representations of the Holy Grail that was sensed and predicted by pre-Christian Mystery wisdom found in the Mystery Schools of the ancients. These teachings accurately predict the descent of the Solar Logos (second person in the Holy Trinity) into a human body once and only once, so that the divine could enter the stream of human spiritual consciousness and provide the nourishment and transformation needed to advance human spiritual evolution. Those who understand and live these mysteries are given the wisdom to embody their own eternal spirit—their higher self, the angel they are becoming.

We can point the way and teach the meaning of the signposts while presenting a topological map of the ascent up the "mountain of the grail" to try to help others in the process of ascension, but it is the personal responsibility of each seeker to find their unique path up the mountain. We all arrive at the summit, but often from different directions. Thus, the importance of one or another aspect of the Mystery of the Holy Grail may take on more importance for one or another seeker. One seeker may need a ritual that reminds them of the grail experience as it is found in the Catholic Holy Eucharist, while another may need to find objects from history that help convince them of the efficacy of their Grail path, and yet another aspirant may need to believe that Jesus and Mary Magdalene had offspring who became the founders of the different Grail Streams. Some seekers need more signs and physical proof to demonstrate the current power of the grail. The Grail Seeker uses whatever doorway or path is necessary to take the next step on the quest toward the spirit.

The question of whether the grail is "physical" and "real" is not even a consideration for some because they believe it was physical but now has transformed and is preserved in the etheric (living) realm that surrounds the Earth. The alchemist on the grail path may be quite satisfied to know that carbon is the Philosopher's Stone—the Holy Grail—that can be found in all organic, living substances. The historian may decide that the Chalice of Valencia or the Chalice of Leon may be the actual vessel used by Jesus Christ during the Last Supper and is, in fact, quite "physical" and "real," or that the Spear of Maurice or the Spear of Antioch may be the true "Spear of Destiny." Yet another seeker may be satisfied to believe through faith that Jesus had children and therefore his holy blood continues to this day. Whether in a spiritual, etheric, astral, or physical form, the seeker's personal grail becomes a tool with which to approach and enter the spiritual world. The quest for the Holy Grail is an inner, personal path that leads to one's own higher self and the tools and the path used are seldom the same for any two aspirants.

The path to the grail can take many forms, from ancient animistic worship of grails that fall from the sky, to the matriarchal Mysteries of blood and birth, to the modern worship of Jesus Christ through the new Holy Blood Mysteries of the Eucharist. Every path leads to the re-embodying of our paradisiacal higher self, which waits for the seeker to claim as their own. Some may need physical "proof" to believe, while others need nothing physical to remind them of their spiritual home. Churches have preserved and even manufactured holy relics to help the believer on the path. Weekly reminders of the blood sacrifice of Jesus Christ through the Holy Eucharist that permanently supplanted human and animal blood sacrifices are conducted to "do this in memory of me" as a spiritual tool to help in the process of ascension. Each Grail Seeker must decide for themselves what it takes to convince them that they are eternal beings seeking to re-enter their heavenly home.

The modern "holy grail" can be considered anything that is the penultimate expression of what will help advance the seeker on the path. It could be a special piece of music, literature, art, architecture, or a thousand other doorways to your higher self. Two seekers may be looking at a "holy grail," but only one sees it. Even then, will the seeker take the step to commit to seek and understand the Holy Grail? In other words, it is not the physical Holy Grail that is sought after, but the process of spiritual evolution that is the true attainment of the grail quest.

Once the grail is the object of desire, other desires arise to distract the seeker from the difficult path of ascending the mountain of spirit. Having or holding the grail may or may not aid in the quest. The Grail King Anfortas had the grail but was wounded by his lower self and could not ascend on the path until a new Grail King who could accomplish the ritual of the Grail Procession with a pure heart was found. Having a physical "holy grail" may not actually help the seeker at all. Without a Grail Castle to enact the Grail Procession, the grail is not fully realized.

There is a counter-pole to the Grail Castle called the Castle of Marvels, which is a trap for the seeker who has not tamed their selfish desires. As soon as the seeker commits to the path, tames lower desires, and develops the higher morality to desire to help others, the Grail Castle or the Castle of Marvel appears. Which castle appears depends on whether the grail knight is pure of heart or not. Taming the astral body, the dragon of desire, is a pre-requisite before attempting to do battle with evil knights, conquer Castle Marvel, or vanquish the evil black magician Klingsor who arises to confront anyone who believes they are ready to sit on the throne of the Grail King or Grail Queen. Klingsor is the "guardian of the threshold" who mirrors back to the seeker images of their personal sins and shortcomings. This is necessary because the seeker's personal evil is not allowed into the pure Grail Castle—the spiritual world.

The path to the grail starts in the seeker's heart as a desire to find truth, beauty, and goodness in the world and in the personal self. Without purification and renunciation, the seeker will not "see" the grail and be invited to join the quest. Our personal sins and evil hide the vision of the grail from us, and it can be degraded into a silly legend that is meaningless. But the pure souls who are unencumbered by immorality, pride, and selfishness can see the grail before the eyes of their spirit; it calls them forward in the process of conquering the dragon of selfishness. Is it any wonder then that the Grail Seeker is given a fiery spear or flaming sword to conquer the dragon of the lower self?

One of the best meditations on the true nature of the Holy Grail that can be found in the human body is the Comte de Saint Germain's poem, *Philosophical Sonnet*. This alchemical poem presents an analogy showing that the grail can be found in the human body and its processes. The bread and wine are described as tools that can show "The Way" to the grail. It is a poem about the Grail Quest demonstrating that the Grail Seeker needs go no further than their own heart to unravel the Holy Grail Mysteries and activate the processes of ascension. Study of this poem will bring results on the path and show "The Way, the Truth, and the Life" that are found through seeking and finding the higher self as the Holy Grail.

Philosophical Sonnet, by the Comte de Saint Germain (1712-1784)

Curious scrutator of all nature,
I have known of the great whole, the principle and the end,
I have seen gold thick in the depths of the double mercury;

I have seized its substance and surprised its changing.
I explain by that art, the soul with the womb of a Mother,
Make its home, take it away, and as a kernel
Placed against a grain of wheat, under the humid pollen;
The one plant and the other vine-stock, are the bread and wine,
Nothing was, God willing, nothing became something,
I doubted it, I sought that on which the universe rests,
Nothing preserves the equilibrium and serves to sustain,
Then with the weight of praise and of blame,
I weighed the eternal, it called my soul,
I died, I adored, I knew nothing more.

Whether as an analogy, living imagination, or literal truth, the seeker needs the tools of the spirit mentioned in the poem above to aid and support the process of ascension to the eternal. We can become the overflowing chalice of light and love that is so often depicted in spiritual beliefs throughout the world and associated with the grail. We can become the Holy Grail we are seeking. We can become the new blood sacrifice that reveals the mysteries of love and compassion for others. The Holy Grail then becomes a living fountain of grace and mercy that can be found in our own heart, mind, and actions. We can become the Queen or King of the Holy Grail Castle and protect the sacredness of our higher self and the higher-selves of anyone who can enter the Grail Castle. Once we become the Grail Queen or Grail King, the higher I (spiritual self) of the human being begins to grow into an angel. This is the message of Jesus Christ and his teachings, and He has come to help in that process and protect the higher I (I am) of every human being from the battles raging to steal that I AM—that Holy Grail—and destroy the path to the Grail Castle.

It is the task of the modern grail knight on "The Way" to the Grail Castle to take their own spiritual growth and development under control and plan the path that will lead to the goal—the original paradisiacal home, often called the Grail Castle, Heaven, Eden, or New Jerusalem. We must find our original higher self that has been preserved in the living (etheric) realm surrounding the earth and let it flow into the grail of our heart as rain from heaven, or water from New Jerusalem's rivers of life. When we pick the fruit from the Tree of Knowledge and find the path of the grail, we then can proceed to the Tree of Life and eat the fruit that makes us "like unto gods." This task was also given to Adam, the patriarchs, Soldiers of God, Grail Knights, Grail Seekers, Grail Keepers, and all true aspirants of the spirit. We are tasked with finding paradise and redeeming the "Fall from Grace" just as the Archangel Michael, through the Mystery of Golgotha, has redeemed the War in Heaven and conquered Lucifer and Satan through the spiritual blood sacrifice of Jesus Christ, the solar logos.

We are a moon that waxes and wanes with the advancement of our spiritual development—our Quest for the Holy Grail. Someday, when we have created a grand enough grail in our heart, we will become able to hold the full glory and gifts of the sun as we grow brighter in service to others. Eventually, we will become a planet that has transformed into a sun, and each individual will be like a selfless sun that gives warmth, light, and life to everything and everyone. We will become that shining *tzohar* that Abraham wore around his neck or the Stone of An that gave light and nourishment to Noah's Ark. Someday, we will become a Holy Grail in whatever fashion we imagine, and we will share this Holy Grail outwardly with the world to nourish all beings. We will become co-creator gods that take our part in restoring life and beauty to the entire world. Then, we will be a true Queen or King of the Holy Grail Castle that we have always been meant to be. Even then, the driving question will still remain: "What is the Holy Grail and who does it serve?" When that question is answered in full by the seeker, the seeker becomes the very thing that was being sought.

Are you ready to commit to the quest and find the Holy Grail of your higher self?

Bibliography

Albinus. *The Book of Jasher*. AMORC, 1934.

Baigent, Michael, Richard Leigh, and Henry Lincoln. *The Holy Blood and the Holy Grail*, Corgi, 1983.

Baigent, Michael and Richard Leigh. *The Messianic Legacy*. Jonathan Cape, London, 1989.

Baigent, Michael and Richard Leigh. *The Temple and the Lodge*. Jonathan Cape, London, 1989.

Barnwell, John. *The Arcana of the Grail Angel*. Verticordia Press, Bloomfield Hills, 1999.

Begg, Ean & Deike. *In Search of the Holy Grail and the Precious Blood*. Thorsons, 1995.

Black Koltuv, Barbara, Ph.D. *Solomon and Sheba*. Nicolas-Hays, Maine, 1993.

Brook, E. W. *Acts of Saint George in series Analecta Gorgiana 8*, Gorgias Press, 1925.

Brown, Arthur and Charles Lewis. *Bleeding Lance*. Modern Language Association of America, 1910.

Buechner, Howard A. and Wilhelm Bernhart. *Adolf Hitler and The Secrets of The Holy Lance*. Thunderbird Press, 1988.

Buechner, Howard A. and Wilhelm Bernhart. *Hitler's Ashes—Seeds of a New Reich*. Thunderbird Press, 1989.

Budge, Wallis E. A. *The Book of the Mysteries of the Heaven and Earth*. Ibis Press, Maine, 2004.

Bulgakov, Sergei. *Sophia—The Wisdom of God*. Lindisfarne Press, 1993.

Bulgakov, Sergei. *The Holy Grail & the Eucharist*. Lindisfarne, 1997.

Burgoyne, Michael H. *A Chronological Index to the Muslim Monuments of Jerusalem*. In *The Architecture of Islamic Jerusalem*. Jerusalem: The British School of Archaeology in Jerusalem, 1976.

Cahill, Suzanne E. *Transcendence & Divine Passion—The Queen Mother of the West in Medieval China*. Stanford University Press, 1993.

Caldecott, Moyra. *Myths of the Sacred Tree*. Destiny Books, Vermont, 1993.

Childress, David Hatcher. *Pirates and the Lost Templar Fleet: The Secret Naval War Between the Knights Templar and the Vatican*. Adventures Unlimited Press, 2003.

Cioran, Samuel D. *Vladimir Solovev and the Knighthood of the Divine Sophia*. Wilfrid Laurier University Press, Ontario, 1977.

Crowley, Cornelius Joseph. *The Legend of the Wanderings of the Spear of Longinus*. Heartland Book, 1972.

Cruz, Joan Carroll. *Saintly Men of Modern Times*. Our Sunday Visitor Publishing, ISBN 978-1-931709-77-4, 2003.

Debu, Michael. *Mary and Sophia*. Floris Books, 2013.

Dillenberger, John. *Mages and Relics: Theological Perceptions and Visual Images in Sixteenth-century Europe*. Oxford University Press US, ISBN 978-0-19-512172-8, 1999.

Eschenbach, Wolfram von. *Parzival*. Penguin Books, 1980.

Francke, Sylvia. *The Tree of Life and the Holy Grail—Ancient and Modern Spiritual Paths and the Mystery of Rennes-le-Chateau*. Temple Lodge, 2007.

Gabidzashvili, Enriko. *Saint George: In Ancient Georgian Literature*. Armazi—89: Tbilisi, Georgia, 1991.

Gabriel, Douglas, *Eternal Curriculum for Wisdom Children*, Our Spirit, 2017.

Gabriel, Douglas J., *The Spirit of Childhood—The Waldorf Curriculum*, Trinosophia Press, 1995.

Gabriel, Douglas, *The Eternal Ethers—A Theory of Everything*, Our Spirit, 2017.

Gabriel, *Goddess Meditations from Isis to Sophia*, Trinosophia Press, 1994.

Gabriel, Tyla N. D. and Douglas, *The Gospel of Sophia—Sophia Christos Initiation*, Volume 3, Our Spirit, 2016.

Gabriel, Tyla N. D., *The Gospel of Sophia—A Modern Path of Initiation*, Volume 2, Our Spirit, 2016.

Gabriel, Tyla N. D., *The Gospel of Sophia—The Biographies of the Divine Feminine Trinity*, Volume 1, Our Spirit, 2014.

Ginzberg, Louis. *Legends of the Jews From Joseph to the Exodus*. Jewish Publication Society of America, Philadelphia, 1977. Volume II.

Glas, Werner. *Intuition, Intellect and the Racial Question*. Rudolf Steiner Books, New York, 1964.

Godwin, Malcolm. *The Holy Grail—Its Origins, Secrets, and Meanings Revealed*. BCA London, 1994.

Good, Jonathan. *The Cult of Saint George in Medieval England*. Woodbridge, Suffolk: The Boydell Press, 2009.

Goodspeed, Edgar J. *The Apocrypha*. Vintage Books, New York, 1959.

Griffin, Justin. *The Holy Grail: The Legend, the History, the Evidence*. McFarland, ISBN 978-0-7864-0999-0, 2001.

Guthrie, Kenneth Sylvan. *The Second Book of Acts*. New Light Center, Santa Rosa, 1978.

Hallam, Elizabeth. *Chronicles of the Crusades*. Weidenfeld and Nicolson, New York, 1989.

Houlden, James Leslie. *Jesus in History, Thought, and Culture*. Santa Barbara: ABC-Clio Inc., ISBN 978-1-57607-856-3, 2003.

Jowett, George. *The Drama of the Disciples*. Covenant Publishing, 1972.

Querido, Rene. The Mystery of the Holy Grail: A Modern Path of Initiation. Rudolf Steiner Publications, 1991.

Kirchweger, Franz. *The Holy Lance in Vienna. Insignia—Relic—Spear of Destiny*. Vienna: Kunsthistorisches Museum, 2005.

Knoche, Grace F. *The Mystery Schools*. Theosophical University Press, California, 1999.

Lacy, Norris J. *Lancelot-Grail: The Old French Arthurian Vulgate and Post-Vulgate in Translation*. Volume 1–5. New York: Garland, 1992.

Lacy, Norris J. *Grail: The New Arthurian Encyclopedia*. Garland Reference Library of the Humanities 931. New York: Garland Pub, 1991, 212–213.

Lievegoed, Bernard. *Mystery Streams and Europe and the New Mysteries.* Anthroposophic Press, New York, 1982.

Lincoln, Henry. *The Holy Place.* Jonathan Cape, 1991.

Loomis, C. Grant. *White Magic, An Introduction to the Folklore of Christian Legend.* Cambridge: Medieval Society of America, 1948.

Loomis, Roger Sherman. *The Grail: From Celtic Myth to Christian Symbol.* Princeton University Press, 1991.

MacCulloch, J. A. *The Religion of the Ancient Celts.* Constable and Constable, London, 1991.

Maclellan, Alec. *The Secret of the Spear: The Mystery of the Spear of Longinus.* Souvenir Press, 2004.

Mahoney, Dhira B. *The Grail: A Casebook. Arthurian Characters and Themes,* vol. 5. New York: Garland, 2000.

Malory, Thomas and Helen Cooper. *Le Morte D'Arthur: The Winchester Manuscript.* Oxford, Oxford University Press, 1998.

Matthews, Caitlin. *Sophia—Goddess of Wisdom.* Aquarian Press, London, 1992.

Matthews, John. *The Grail: Quest for the Eternal.* The Illustrated library of sacred imagination. New York: Crossroad, 1981.

Maclellan, Alec. *The Secret of the Spear.* Souvenir Press, 2004.

Menachery, George. *Saint Thomas Christian Encyclopaedia of India.* Vol. II Trichur—73.

Michell, John. *New Light on the Ancient Mystery of Glastonbury.* Somerset, 1990.

Morizot, P. *The Templars.* Anthroposophic Press, 1960.

Morris, Colin. *Policy and Vision: The Case of the Holy Lance Found at Antioch.* John Gillingham & J. C. Holt.

Natsheh, Yusuf. *Architectural Survey, in Ottoman Jerusalem: The Living City 1517-1917.* London: Altajir World of Islam Trust, 2000.

Nickell, Joe. *Relics of the Christ.* Lexington: University Press of Kentucky, ISBN 0-8131-2425-5, 2007.

Nutt, Alfred Trubner. *Studies on the Legend of the Holy Grail; With Especial Reference to the Hypothesis of Its Celtic Origin.* New York: Cooper Square Publishers, 1965.

Oakley, I. C. *Masonry and Medieval Mysticism*. Theosophical Publishing House, London, 1900.

Peterson, Holger. *Signs of Change. Transformations of Christian Traditions and their Representation in the Arts, 1000–2000*. Amsterdam/New York: Rodopi, 2004.

Pfeiffer, E. E. *The Task of the Archangel Michael*. Mercury Press, New York, 1946.

Prestwich, J. O. *War and Government in the Middle Ages*. Boydell, 1984.

Prokofieff, Sergei O. *The Spiritual Origins of Eastern Europe and the Future Mysteries of the Holy Grail*. Temple Lodge, London, 1993.

Prokofieff, Sergei, O. *The Heavenly Sophia and the Being Anthroposophia*. Temple Lodge, London, 1996.

Querido, Rene. *The Golden Age of Chartres*. Floris Books, Edinburgh, 1987.

Ragon, Jean-Marie. *The Mass and its Mysteries Compared to the Ancient Mysteries*. 2011.

Rahn, Otto. *Crusade Against the Grail*. Inner Traditions, Vermont, 1933.

Ravenscroft, Trevor and Tim Wallace-Murphy. *The Mark of the Beast: The Continuing Story of the Spear of Destiny*. Weiser Books, 1997. ISBN 0-87728-870-4.

Ravenscroft, Trevor. *The Cup of Destiny*. Rider and Co., London, 1981.

Ravenscroft, Trevor. *The Spear of Destiny*. Neville, Spearman, London, 1972.

Robinson, James. *The Nag Hammadi Library*. Harper, 1990.

Roboz, Steven. *The Holy Grail from Works of Rudolf Steiner*. Steiner Book Center, Vancouver, 1984.

Ruffin, Bernard. *The Shroud of Turin: The Most Up-to-date Analysis of All the Facts Regarding the Church's Controversial Relic*. Huntington: ISBN 978-0-87973-617-0, 1999.

Schier, Volker and Corine Schleif. *Seeing and Singing, Touching and Tasting the Holy Lance. The Power and Politics of Embodied Religious Experiences in Nuremberg, 1424–1524*.

Schier, Volker and Corine Schleif. *The Holy Lance as Late Twentieth-century Subcultural Icon*. Subcultural Icons, Walnut Creek: Left Coast Press, 2009.

Schmidt-Brabant, Manfred & Sease, Virginia. *The Archetypal Feminine in the Mystery Stream of Humanity.* Temple Lodge, London, 1999.

Sease, Virginia. *Paths of the Christian Mysteries—From Compostela to the New World.* Temple Lodge, 2003.

Seldon, Richard. *The Mystery of Arthur at Tintagel.* Rudolf Steiner Press, 1990.

Sheffy, Lester Fields. *Use of the Holy Lance in the First Crusade.* L. F. Sheffy, 1915.

Sinclair, Andrew. *The Sword and the Grail.* Century, London, 1993.

Smith, Jerry and George Piccard. *Secrets of the Holy Lance.* Adventures Unlimited Press, 2005.

Stein, Walter J. *The Death of Merlin.* Floris Books, Edinburgh, 1989.

Stein, Walter Johannes. *The Ninth Century World History in the Light of the Holy Grail.* Temple Lodge Press, 1991.

Stein, Walter Johannes. *King Arthur Lohengrin Merlin.* Kolisko Archive Publication Burnemouth, England, 1936.

Steiner, Rudolf. *Christ and the Spiritual World and the Search for the Holy Grail.* Rudolf Steiner Press, 1963.

Steiner, Rudolf. *Cosmic Christianity and the Impulse of Michael.* Rudolf Steiner Press, 1953.

Steiner, Rudolf. *The Archangel Michael.* Anthroposophic Press, New York, 1994.

Steiner, Rudolf. *The Christian Mystery.* Anthroposophic Press, New York, 1998.

Steiner, Rudolf. *The Etherization of the Blood.* Rudolf Steiner Press, 1971.

Steiner, Rudolf. *The Knights Templar, the Mystery of the Warrior Monk.* Rudolf Steiner Press, 2007.

Steiner, Rudolf. *The Mission of the Archangel Michael.* Anthroposophic Press, New York, 1961.

Steiner, Rudolf. *The Temple Legend.* Rudolf Steiner Press, 1985.

Steiner, Rudolf. *The Tree of Life and The Tree of Knowledge.* Mercury Press, New York, 2006.

Straiton, Valentia E. *The Celestial Ship of the North.* Kessinger Publishing, Montana.

Taylor, Thomas. *The Eleusinian & Bacchic Mysteries*. Wizards Bookshelf, San Diego, 1997.

Tennyson, Alfred Lord. *The Holy Grail. Idylls of the King*. London: Penguin Books, 1996.

Troyes, Chretien de. *The Story of the Grail Arthurian Romances*. London: Penguin Books, 1991.

Voragine, Jacobus de. *The Golden Legend*. Arno, 1941.

Wallace-Murphy, Tim and Marilyn Hopkins. *Rosslyn Guardian of the Secret of the Holy Grail*. New York, 1998.

Welburn, Andrew. *Rudolf Steiner -The Holy Grail*. (selections) Sophia Books, 2001.

Whatley, E. Gordon, Anne B. Thompson, and Robert K. Upchurch. *St. George and the Dragon in the South English Legendary* (East Midland Revision, c. 1400) Originally published in *Saints' Lives in Middle English Collections,* Kalamazoo, Michigan: Medieval Institute Publications, 2004.

Wilson, Ian. *Holy Faces, Secret Places*. London: Doubleday, 1991.

Wyatt, Isabel. *From Round Table to Grail Castle*. Lanthorn Press, Sussex, 1979.

Made in the USA
Monee, IL
12 April 2024

56841612R00144